D1347111

Alastair Sim

Alastair Sim

THE STAR OF SCROOGE AND THE BELLES OF ST TRINIAN'S

MARK SIMPSON

This book is dedicated to the memory of

Christopher Quinton (1962–2005)

First published 2008
This edition published 2009

The History Press
The Mill, Brimscombe Port
Stroud, Gloucestershire, GL5 2QG
www.thehistorypress.co.uk

© Mark Simpson, 2008, 2009

The right of Mark Simpson to be identified as the Author
of this work has been asserted in accordance with the
Copyrights, Designs and Patents Act 1988.

All rights reserved. No part of this book may be reprinted
or reproduced or utilised in any form or by any electronic,
mechanical or other means, now known or hereafter invented,
including photocopying and recording, or in any information
storage or retrieval system, without the permission in writing
from the Publishers.

British Library Cataloguing in Publication Data.
A catalogue record for this book is available from the British Library.

ISBN 978 0 7524 5372 9

Printed and bound in Great Britain

Contents

	Preface	7
1	From Birth to the Fulton Lectureship (1900–1925)	13
2	Naomi (1926–1929)	29
3	The Professional Stage Actor (1930–1934)	37
4	'Quota Quickies' and the Early Film Years (1935–1939)	47
5	Cottage To Let (1940–1941)	61
6	Alastair Sim and James Bridie (1942–1945)	69
7	Green For Danger (1946–1949)	79
8	The Happiest Days of your Life (1950–1953)	99
9	Miss Fritton and The Belles of St Trinian's (1954–1957)	121
10	Sim v Heinz: the Faltering Years (1958–1965)	145
11	The Chichester Festival Years (1966–1974)	169
12	Escape to the Dark: the Last Years (1975–1976)	187
	Filmography (including cast and credits)	193
	Play Chronology	219
	Endnotes	222
	Bibliography	241
	Acknowledgements	246
	Index	249

Preface

Alastair Sim – One of the most reserved, most enigmatic actors in British pictures.[1]

Kenneth Tynan, the famous theatre critic, once described an Alastair Sim performance as that of a 'tentative pantomime dame standing in for Tommy Cooper.'[2] The playwright Ronald Mavor described him as 'a great artist, and a great clown'[3], but the film director David Lean thought him a mere 'grotesque'.[4] Such diverse opinions suggest a contradiction and indeed no better word exists to describe Alastair; a principled man who held 'high ethical standards, morally, socially [and] politically'[5] and was much admired by his peer group, but who was also 'stuck with prejudice'[6] and extremely vulnerable to ridicule.

For a man whose screen persona was often that of an affable eccentric, little is known about his private life. He loathed the trappings associated with showbusiness, was keen to avoid publicity at all costs and would give no consideration to an autobiography. Alastair gave few interviews: 'Down at Nettlefold studios they call Alastair Sim the 'uninterviewable'[7] and *Picturegoer* in 1950 issued the following warning: 'His dislike of self-analysis is a formidable obstacle to would-be biographers.'[8] This has evidently been the case to date for little of any substance has ever been written about him. Let us put that right.

Alastair Sim was a fascinating man who successfully combined the skills of actor, director and producer at a time when such multi-talented individuals were few and far between. Early film success came in the

1930s but it wasn't until the 1950s that the producer/director partnership of Frank Launder and Sidney Gilliat began to make clever
use of his idiosyncratic mannerisms in a brand of humour that was
quintessentially British. Films such as *The Happiest Days of your Life*
(1950), *Laughter in Paradise* (1951) and *The Belles of St Trinian's* (1954)
are testament to this fact. Alastair's screen character would typically
find itself in a delightfully topsy-turvy scenario, whether as a headmaster defending his boys from the invasion of a girls' school, or a
respectable man of society trying to get arrested in order to meet
the demands of a vindictive relative's will. As the plot unfolded, his
lugubrious face – a face seemingly designed for the sole purpose of
comedy – would maintain an expression of utter bewilderment as
fate continually dealt him one cruel blow after another; his voice, a
lilting, beguiling, Scottish dialect, would argue pitifully for reason in
this, the most unreasonable of worlds.

War-hardened cinema audiences, looking for light escapism, fell
in love with this eccentric British underdog who bore no malice
towards his fellow man no matter what indignity was thrust upon
him. The character was so in tune with the times, finding a natural empathy with those who had suffered during the Blitz but who
were now looking expectantly towards a bright and happy future.
Even though this dates the films of this period they still resonate
with concerns of modern times. Authority today still has the ability
to exercise its power from behind a large desk, still favours pomposity and self-importance, and still has the tenacity and temperament
of a bad-tempered patriarch. All of which, crucially, make it vulnerable to the vagaries of fate.

His screen acting career came to a temporary halt in the late 1950s
when whimsical light-hearted comedy was blatantly exposed as
superficial nonsense next to the harsh realism of the kitchen-sink
dramas. The affable eccentric became redundant, or rather a character to be mocked and despised; a senile degenerate rather than a
mildly likeable buffoon. Times had moved on, leaving the cosseted
England of the early 1950s as a fading memory.

Ridicule was heaped upon embarrassment as Alastair's screen
decline was accompanied by an unsuccessful attempt to sue Heinz
over a baked beans commercial. What was he thinking? Alastair, previously the saviour of movies, winner of awards, the high idealist

amongst men, became the butt of jokes. Once-adoring critics now acquainted us with a different story: his personality had dominated films and overshadowed the contributions of fellow actors; he was a difficult and demanding director; his acting style was too repetitive and clichéd. One could deny it all of course, but unfortunately there was some truth in these criticisms, and therefore they hurt all the more. Almost a decade passed by during which little was accomplished. Then a glorious return ensued as Alastair achieved considerable success on stage at Chichester in the late 1960s and '70s.

The reader may be familiar with the account of Alastair's life so far, but there is so much more to discover about him.

Whereas film in its celluloid format acquires eternal life, performances on stage are ephemeral; articles are written and photographs taken, but the memories of those who bought their tickets and sat in the stalls are fleeting. Therefore of particular interest to the uninitiated will be Alastair's stage career. Would anybody believe that Alastair's original intention was to succeed as a serious actor, preferably in verse drama? Only after the threat of being typecast as a villain (along, it has to be said, with some sensible advice) did he finally don the mantle of a clown. Even so, the clowning took a form that was quick, easy and lacking in subtlety, and so soon became known as 'manic comedy' on both stage and screen. The laughs flowed easily but often from poor quality productions that begged for a change in direction. Luckily fate intervened to put him back on the right course.

In 1938 Alastair met the Scottish playwright James Bridie. Here was a man after his own heart, dedicated to an examination of the essential qualities of the Scottish man. Bridie presented his ideas in intelligent plays, the dialogue of which appeared natural and appealing – at least to those north of the border. Alastair formed an immediate friendship with Bridie and together they shared huge critical and popular success in the London West End with *Mr Gillie*, *Mr Bolfry* and *Dr Angelus*. But how many people have heard of these plays today?

Perhaps most intriguing of all is Alastair's reticence. He was once reported as saying, 'All the public need to know about me, is what they see.'[9] But is this the statement of an intensely private man thrown into the media spotlight, or that of a nervous, defensive man with something to hide? Alastair was twenty-six when he first became acquainted with his future wife, Naomi, who was just twelve at the time. They became friends, and over time, this friendship developed into an 'understanding'.[10] Naomi's rhetorical question, 'I wonder what [Alastair's] friends can have made of our relationship?'[11] poses some serious questions.

It has been suggested that Naomi was of that rare breed – a soul partner to Alastair. She took responsibility for their home and cared for their daughter, Merlith, while also undertaking the role of trusted critic. She acted as a temporary surrogate mother to a succession of aspiring young actors and actresses whom Alastair would invite to stay over at their family home. Sometimes these were damaged people seeking refuge and at other times youngsters with a raw talent for the stage that Alastair felt he could help nurture. George Cole was the first and best known of these actors. And yet, even this act of altruism was viewed with suspicion from some quarters, even implying that the relationship was not an entirely healthy one. However, his friends regarded such accusations as nonsense. Alastair was someone who 'wore his heart on his sleeve'[12], and in so doing, made himself vulnerable to all sorts of allegations.

One must always seek balance and it is worth referring to George Cole who once said of Alastair, 'he was a deeply caring person about everything.'[13] Everything? Alastair had once confided in a friend that 'marriage is very important'[14] but he did not preclude 'a bit of bedding on the side.'[15] It was a hypocritical statement in some respects and indeed even his friends sometimes frowned on Alastair's steadfast adherence to gauche values.

And what of those questioning his motives behind his drag performance as Miss Fritton, the headmistress in *The Belles of St Trinian's* (1954). Was he 'a little bit the other way?' as was suggested by some – or simply following in the long-established and common British tradition of theatrical cross-dressing?

In this biography, Alastair's thoughts emerge through his rare interviews, his speeches, and correspondence – many letters of which have only recently been made available to the general public. To this I have added the recollections of actors, actresses, stagehands, writers, directors and producers who worked with Alastair and from those who were invited into the closely guarded citadel that was the family home – 'Forrigan'. For example, Geoffrey Jowitt and Larry Barnes recall their time as teenage actors with Alastair in his first two seasons of *Peter Pan* (1941–42 and 1942–43). Sidney Gilliat, the writer and director of some of the great British films of the 1940s and '50s, in a private letter made available for this book, offers a compelling account, full of insight, of the Launder and Gilliat association with Alastair Sim. Judy Campbell describes his calming and yet mischievous personality on the set of *Green For Danger* (1946). James Bridie, the Scottish playwright, writes of his deep friendship and respect for Alastair. Avril Angers, co-star in *The Green Man* (1956), recollects her surprise at Alastair's naivety towards the showbusiness media. Ian Carmichael discusses Alastair's refusal to sign autographs and his reluctance to use props in *School for Scoundrels* (1959). Peter Copley, who appeared with Alastair in *A Clean Kill* (1959) and *The Bargain* (1961), provides us with a wonderful insight into Alastair as a director. The producer and director John Howard Davies, Alastair's friend and neighbour, provides a first-hand insight into Alastair's views on politics and religion, and Sir Ian McKellen (director of *The Clandestine Marriage* (1975)) reveals Alastair's concerns regarding his own mortality.

In addition to these personal reflections, I have added numerous reviews of Alastair's performances from a variety of publications. Some of the early reviews have been sourced from the Theatre Museum Archives, others from hours spent over microfiches in libraries. What follows chronicles the life and career of Alastair Sim in a series of chapters that break down neatly into key periods of his life. Films play an important part in this narrative structure, identifying a screen career that was more varied than most people might at first imagine. Complementing this are the various laws, events in history and social trends that together created the perfect environment for the British eccentric to flourish on stage and screen.

Alastair Sim died of cancer in 1976, aged seventy-five, but his legacy is the warmth and sense of humility that his screen character often displayed, along with a comic timing and genius that placed him in a category of his own. I hope this preface has whetted your appetite and suggested that there is much more to find out about Alastair than simply being a successful British comedy actor of the 1950s.

Mark Simpson
March 2008

I

From Birth to the Fulton Lectureship

As I passed imperceptibly from a beautiful child to a strong and handsome lad, I wanted more than anything else in the world to be, of all things, a hypnotist. I practised on gentle dogs – with the result that even to this day I am nervous in their presence.

– Alastair Sim[1]

When James II declared Edinburgh the capital of Scotland he had a wall built around the city which sent a clear message to the English and their culture. A wall which to this day still features psychologically in the minds of some of those living north of the border and whose influence will appear, at times, in this biography. As the Scots and English learned to live as neighbours, the insular nature of this defensive structure turned against the people it was supposed to protect. A city wall is no ally in a time of prosperity and expansion. Edinburgh's commercial traders looked to the heavens for an innovative solution to their problem. If they could not expand outwards, then they would grow upwards. Consequently, during the eighteenth century, Edinburgh developed the world's first skyscrapers.

All was not well however. The architectural skill necessary to produce such high-rise buildings was still in its infancy, and so as a result of inexperience combined with poor craftsmanship, the skyline of

Edinburgh began to take on an altogether different, if not slightly wobbly, shape. The extra levels not only made the buildings structurally unsafe but also exacerbated the spread of disease. Residents from the upper storeys would throw out their waste in a *laissez-faire* manner regardless of who might be walking beneath. Noblemen taking a gentle evening stroll through the city did not take too kindly to this heavenly downpour of culinary by-products and excrement and so moved away, taking with them their business and wealth.

In time, the City Fathers of Edinburgh commissioned a young architect by the name of James Craig to redevelop the city. Craig foresaw the need for a road, or high street, to act as the main focal point, and so with this in mind, he designed the new city – around George Street. Contrary to the plans, the focus of trade quickly became established on Princes Street and from then on, this became known as the main thoroughfare in Edinburgh.

Several roads run off Princes Street including the busy Lothian Road, which records state was completed around 1791. It was at number 96–98 of this street, in the late 1800s, that Alexander Sim owned a lively and well-frequented tailor's shop. The appearance of a man during the Victorian era was as important as his vocation, and no man could succeed without being well-dressed – as the apt saying went, 'Clothes Maketh the Man'. As a consequence, the tailor's shop was one of the most important shops in the city. Alexander Sim was not alone in this business and other outfitters thrived in Edinburgh such as the more prestigious Gieve's.

Alexander Sim took his social responsibilities very seriously and during his lifetime he became a Justice of the Peace and served on the board of several committees in Edinburgh. His outlook on life was traditional and formal, as befitted a successful Victorian. Unfortunately this sometimes gave him a rather serious demeanour which some interpreted as cold and distant. As we shall see, this was quite misleading since Alexander frequently demonstrated the characteristics of an altruist. His preference was to operate quietly from behind the scenes, avoiding the limelight, so as not to draw attention to himself. When business had finished for the day, Alexander would close his shop and retire to the family rooms above his premises where he lived with his wife, Isabella, and their son and two daughters.

Isabella McIntyre had been born on the small Scottish island of Eigg. Although Eigg is blessed with a rich history and has unique geographical features, it is also a lonely place. To find companionship she made frequent trips to the neighbouring small islands – Rum, Canna and Muck – until finally, in her teens and able to speak only Gaelic, she packed her belongings and moved to the mainland.

Isabella's move was a brave one since she was naturally very shy but she did have a kind heart and a generous nature which meant that she made friends easily. One of her sayings was, 'I'm not clever – but I'm cute'[2], taken here to mean that Isabella considered herself astute with a mature and sensible attitude regarding her expectations from life. When she met and married Alexander Sim she understood immediately that her responsibilities would include the business as well as her family. Her life was always going to be busy and hard. She accepted, as the natural order of things, that when Alexander had finished for the day, her task would be to go downstairs and scrub the floors in order to make the shop presentable for the following day's customers.

On 9 October 1900 Isabella gave birth to her fourth child whom they named Alastair George Bell Sim. As a young boy Alastair developed a very close bond with his mother as he helped her of an evening to clean the shop while his father rested in the family rooms upstairs. Alexander undoubtedly worked hard during the day, managing his business and selling to customers, and Isabella was content to perform her family duties. However, a young impressionable Alastair saw it differently. He thought his father '. . . pompous, hypocritical and unable to appreciate his mother.'[3] This feeling of resentment took hold of Alastair during these formative years and his relationship with his father would always be marred by communication problems. Alexander would say 'Mark my words, that boy will end on the gallows'[4], but actions that Alexander undertook during his lifetime to help Alastair suggest that this statement was made more in jest than seriousness.

Alexander may well have been disappointed with his son's behaviour at times and possibly with good reason. For example, Alastair would at one point eschew civilisation altogether and roam the highlands of Scotland with a band of men devoted to nothing more than casual work and drinking; a period that his Victorian father would certainly have found difficult to comprehend. Nevertheless, at a critical point in Alastair's life, Alexander would play an important role in helping him to establish his drama school – something that would prove to be the catalyst for Alastair's career as an actor. Indeed, Alexander appears to have been devoted to his son, even if he was not entirely optimistic about his future, and Naomi Sim, Alastair's future wife, described Alexander as 'a very kind man'.[5]

One can see attributes in the personalities of both parents that would shape the views and behaviour of Alastair as he developed. His mother: genial, good-natured, with an appreciation of one's role in life; his father: traditional, principled and altruistic. All of these qualities would find their way into Alastair's own personality as he matured. Alastair's attitude towards his father – his inability to forgive – may have been an early example of how Alastair would sometimes become trapped by his own self-imposed principles. This characteristic in later life would lead to ridicule and criticism from his friends.

The Sims eventually gave up their cramped conditions above the family shop and moved to 73 Viewforth, in the district of Bruntsfield. This was still close enough to the commercial area of Edinburgh for Alexander to continue his tailor's business but also convenient for Alastair to attend Bruntsfield Primary School, a five-minute walk from their house. When Alastair was old enough he became a student at James Gillespie's High School which was located in Gillespie Crescent but transferred to a new site off Warrender Park Road in 1914. Alexander had close ties to Gillespie's; he was a school governor and his shop was responsible for supplying the school uniform.

Alastair remembered his father visiting the school one day and telling the teachers that they should not hold back from 'beating his son' just because he, the father, was a JP. It is an interesting choice of anecdote by Alastair since the intention is clearly to present his father in an unfavourable light. It may have been that Alexander was simply making sure that his privileged position in society did not unfairly benefit his son. In using these quotations, the 'gallows' and the 'beating', Alastair may have been trying to convey the image of a tough childhood but he certainly did not come from an impoverished, uncaring family.

In school, from an early age, Alastair enjoyed the attention he received from performing in front of his classmates. His teacher, Margaret Bell, used to recall that he loved to recite poetry 'and especially liked to intone "A horse, a horse, my kingdom for a horse".'[6] A classmate of Alastair's was Ronnie Corbett's mother who remembered Alastair as 'a slightly untidy boy at that age ... slightly extroverted ... and even at that stage in his life, he was quite good on his feet, and quite good with words.'[7] These are two very interesting observations which could be misinterpreted as evidence of Alastair's youthful desire to become an actor. In fact they are much more insightful in that they demonstrate that even at an early age Alastair had a keen interest in the spoken word. For it is verse drama that would be his initial calling, long before he even thought about appearing on stage as a professional actor. Other school friends described his love of mimicry and his fondness for the gruesome or grotesque.[8]

According to Naomi in her autobiography, *Dance and Skylark*, Alastair left school at fourteen and began an apprenticeship as a shop messenger boy in his father's business. Although it is not disputed that he worked for a period for his father, his Intermediate School Certificate[9] is dated 1916, which suggests that he stayed on at school until he was almost sixteen. Furthermore, given that when Alastair was eighteen he began studying chemistry at university, it seems more than likely that any so-called 'apprenticeship' must have been on a part-time or seasonal basis to allow him time for further academic studying.

The dysfunctional relationship between father and son meant that whatever form this 'apprenticeship' took, it was bound to be short-lived. Alastair looked for a job elsewhere and eventually found a post with Gieve's, the men's outfitters, who were based in the more important and fashionable Princes Street. He was no doubt flush with the belief that he could succeed in obtaining employment without his father's help but the reality of the situation was that Alexander had quietly negotiated the move behind the scenes.

Alastair's fresh start at Gieve's, again one presumes on a part-time or seasonal basis, was doomed to failure. Alastair, it seemed, was unable to parcel up purchases to the exacting standards of the fastidious senior staff. He was redeployed to the ties department where the final sale simply consisted of slipping the chosen tie into an envelope and handing over the package to the customer – accompanied, naturally enough, with a reassuring smile. Even this proved problematic. Alastair, as a young man, was unable to comprehend the traditional Victorian values associated with retailing. These unwritten laws acknowledged that an important part of the retail service was the neat and careful presentation of the purchased item to the customer accompanied by a deferential disposition. Another mutual parting of ways occurred.

Alastair commented of this time: 'I passed my youth uninspired by any sense of awe. Which was a very great pity. Because without that sense there can be no inspiration.'[10] However, inspiration must have struck at some point because by 1918 he had successfully applied to Edinburgh University to study to become an analytical chemist. Alastair was a man of contradictions. He undoubtedly had natural intellect but could also be lazy; he could be stubborn and defensive and yet also an egocentric dreamer. When Alastair made his Rectorial Address at Edinburgh University in 1949, he referred to his youth thus:

> I don't know whether I was a typical young man or not. I certainly thought I was exceptional in some indefinable way, apparently beyond the perception of those who knew me, and I was mostly concerned with planning and replanning my own particular success story. This took only the most nebulous of forms, but I know that my aim was to combine the minimum of work with the maximum of authority. I was just as bold as I dared to be in the company of my fellows, and just as bright as their fierce competition allowed. I was naturally much bolder and much brighter in the select company of my own imagining.[11]

Alastair's university days were short-lived. Soon after turning eighteen, he received his call-up papers to the Officers' Training Corps (OTC). Although the news in the papers often referred to 'Great Advances' there could be no doubting in anyone's mind the human carnage that was taking place on the battlefields of Europe. For most men, the OTC was a time for quiet reflection on their own sense of mortality, but Alastair's experience of army life brought out a real anger from within him. He loathed the OTC with its oppressive and rigid discipline.

This is a complex emotion which some could interpret as either the reactions of a pacifist or the naïve musings of someone who had no real grasp of the need for discipline within an army. Or perhaps, understandably, Alastair was simply terrified of the thought of dying a meaningless death on a foreign battlefield. For whatever reason, his strong reaction against the dehumanising stricture of army life helped him to develop his own beliefs in the rights of the individual to freedom and self-expression. These were high principles that he would continually evolve throughout his life leading to his association with the movement for a World Government. The playwright Ronald Mavor said of Alastair:

> The characters he played and the plays he directed celebrated the individual's right to be himself; not to be larger than life, but to be life lived up to its potential. And this didn't mean pushing people around; it meant cherishing them. He was a wise man.[12]

Alastair's posting was imminent when the armistice was signed on 11 November 1918 – he was spared first-hand experience of the war. On his release, he returned home and surprised his family by announcing that he did not intend to continue with his university education but instead wanted to become an actor. This provocation was not received well in the Sim household. Indeed, such was the opposition that Alastair immediately packed his bags and headed for the highlands. There, he joined a group of travellers, mostly men, who would roam from one place to another, undertaking whatever manual jobs they could find. This usually consisted of farm work or forestry work; the hard-earned cash was then spent in the evening at a local pub. The work didn't always have to be legal. An article published in a magazine in 1936 summed up this period of Alastair's life:

> Alastair Sim started to study chemistry, but wanted to go on stage, against his parents' wishes. So he ran away from home and until 1921 he led the life of a gipsy [*sic*]. Sometimes he was a ghilly, sometimes a gamekeeper, sometimes, alas! A poacher! But all the time he was studying poetry.[13]

It is difficult to envisage Alastair sitting on some tree stump, surrounded by his malcontent friends, gutting an animal whilst merrily reciting verse from some Shakespearean play. That said, this image is reminiscent of one of those typically eccentric characters he played so successfully on film. Indeed, it is quite possible that he benefited enormously from this experience in that it provided him with an opportunity to observe people at close quarters, and in so doing, to develop a repertoire of mannerisms that he could bestow on his film and stage characters later in life.

Nevertheless it is questionable, given what is now known about Alastair's character, just how well he fitted in with this lifestyle. For example, his drinking exploits with 'the men' must have been somewhat curtailed by the fact that he developed a deep aversion to whisky. For a period afterwards, Alastair became teetotal although later in life he developed a special liking for Hock. James Bridie, the playwright, who was to become a great friend, said of this unconventional period in Alastair's life: 'It is of no harm to an artist, especially to an artist in a popular art, to have rubbed shoulders with all kinds of men... If he ever starved in a garret, it was not for very long.'[14]

After what appears to be about a year of roaming wild, experiencing the vagaries of life, Alastair gave up his bohemian carefree existence and returned to his family home in Edinburgh – one suspects, without too many regrets. He even managed for the first time to hold down a full-time job at the Borough's Assessor's office. Candidly, he was to say later, 'However highly painted we imagine them to have been, most early lives are pretty dull, except to those who are actually living them.'[15]

Alastair's reticence concerning his early life leaves us with only a vague understanding of the motivations behind the maturing adolescent. However, what is known with certainty is the anxiety he experienced as his hair began to fall out. A young man in his twenties is naturally self-conscious of his looks and Alastair was no different from any others in this respect. He tried various lotions and new fad ideas, but all to no avail; out came his hair in handfuls. The irony of the situation, although understandably Alastair could never have appreciated it at the time, was that the famous Sim bald head – domed, with comic tufts of hair framing each ear – would play a crucial role in determining his future success. As the film magazine *Picturegoer* put it:

Sim himself makes the most of his physical appearance to convey humour, pathos, buffoonery. He is prematurely bald. Excellent; most clowns have to buy balding wigs. He has a loose, untidy lipline. Fine; all the better for registering doubt, apprehension. He walks with a gangling, an undulating glide. Splendid; just the thing to raise a laugh immediately he appears.[16]

When Alastair eventually began his acting career he immediately benefited from his appearance as a mature, serious man by progressing fairly quickly into playing the meatier roles reserved for the character or personality actor. This meant he did not have to suffer the interminable non-existence of being the juvenile lead night after night. As he said later of this troubled period of his life, 'And to think of all the time and money I used to spend in trying to save my hair.'[17]

Alastair's interest in the spoken word had never waned from his schooldays, and so on returning to the more conventional day-to-day life in Edinburgh, this verse-speaking ghilly began to enter himself into poetry reading competitions. Within a year of his return, he had won the gold medal for verse speaking at the Edinburgh Musical Festival. Mrs Tobias Matthay, Professor of Dictation and Elocution at the Royal Academy of Music, wrote of his gold-winning performance, 'I was then much struck by the truth of his interpretation'[18] and went on to say, 'he is the possessor of a sympathetic and resonant voice ... and ... one who brings a love of the best literature into his daily life.'[19]

The time spent studying poetry and reading the great works of literature had brought an even greater fascination with words, not just simply in their meaning, but also in the way that a different intonation could give a word a multitude of meanings. This in turn inspired his interest in elocution. Although this provided him with a hobby, it still left him without a profession. That is until one day in the early autumn of 1924, when, as Alastair would have us believe, inspiration struck:

As I was approaching the ripe age of twenty-five ... I came to the amazing conclusion that my true vocation was teaching. I had already been ensnared by the bright ring of words. I thought I understood a message

in them, and I wished that all should hear. You will note that I meant
well. You may also note a total absence of any sense of the ludicrous.[20]

. . . and also an absence of accuracy, because he had in fact been teaching for several years before this portentous revelation. The Edinburgh
Education Authority certified that at the Dalry Training College he
had 'taught with great success Elocution in the Continuation Classes
during Sessions 1922–23 and 1923–24.'[21] The head teacher, George
Murray, who observed Alastair at work as a teacher, described him
as 'very successful in maintaining the interest of his pupils. . .'[22] and
'thoroughly conversant with all the branches of his profession.'[23] In
particular he noted: 'All the branches of his subject were carefully
explained and illustrated, particularly the mechanism and production of the speaking voice.'[24]

A biographical note written on Alastair in the mid–1930s suggests
that sometime around 1920–21 Alastair had enrolled on a course that
allowed him to gain a teaching qualification in elocution. This is
confirmed to some extent by a letter written by Mrs Tobias Matthay,
who says that he was a student of hers sometime after she had seen
his gold medal-winning performance at the Edinburgh Musical
Festival. Given that Mrs Matthay was a Professor of Diction and
Elocution at the Royal Academy of Music in London, one presumes
it meant that Alastair spent some time studying in London. However,
it is not clear as to the exact nature of this teaching qualification,
although it was clearly sufficient to allow him to teach elocution for
the Edinburgh Education Authority.

A teaching career in Edinburgh at that time would have been a
relatively safe choice. At the turn of the century, a great deal of effort
and resources had been invested in the Scottish educational system.
In particular, the 1908 Education (Scotland) Act required all schools
to provide continuation classes. These classes predominantly took
place in the evening, were aimed primarily at teenagers and involved
the teaching of technical subjects so as to prepare youngsters for
full-time employment. In other words, a teenager could have a part-
time job during the day, but was expected, although not initially
compelled, to attend continuation classes in the evening. Even so,
something in the region of twenty-five per cent of children between
fourteen and eighteen were taking some form of continuation class

in Edinburgh in the period shortly after the introduction of this act. By 1918, these classes had been made compulsory and would have required a significant increase in teaching resources. Consequently there were plenty of posts for aspiring teachers in Edinburgh during the early decades of the twentieth century.

Dalry Training College, where Alastair taught between 1922 and 1924, was a specialist educational institution. Its origins dated back to the 1850s when it was established as a training college for teachers who were planning to teach classes in church schools. It was thought at the time that such teachers required specialist skills. Some of these teachers actually became clergymen, which is why many articles written on Alastair say that he began his career teaching budding parsons how to speak.

Student enrolments at Dalry had been on the decline for some time and by 1924 plans were already being considered to transfer the remaining students to Moray House in Canongate. Alastair however decided to move to Moray House in a different capacity – as a student himself.

In the autumn term of 1924, Alastair enrolled on a course entitled 'Educational Methods for Continuation School Teachers' at the Edinburgh Provincial Training Centre at Moray House. One presumes that this was an advancement on the qualification he had acquired several years earlier, perhaps undertaken with a view to improving his CV. This would have allowed him to apply to more prestigious institutions, which as we shall see, was indeed his plan. Alastair immediately impressed his teachers at Moray House, demonstrating a high intellect and natural talent at teaching, not surprising given that he already had two years' experience. His teacher, Daniel Calderwood, wrote of him:

> So struck was I with Mr Sim's qualifications that I ventured to invite him to join the group of experts who carried out our Demonstration Work and to teach an Elocution lesson for the benefit of his fellow-students. The experiment proved a splendid success, as, in an hour which brought to us all both delight and profit, he showed himself to be not only a charming elocutionist but also a teacher with skill of the first rank.[25]

At the completion of this course, he applied to Edinburgh University for the post of the Fulton Lectureship in Elocution. On the back of some very good references, especially one from the principal of the training centre[26], the interview panel agreed unanimously to offer him the post as from 1 October 1925. In Alastair's words:

> So I taught, I judged, I assessed – with passion and enthusiasm – and indulged to the full my fancied flair for helpful and constructive criticism. Mark you, I did no great harm. I may even have done some good.[27]

Alastair's theory on elocution is reported to have been as follows: '. . . no matter how swiftly words [are] spoken they should not lose their full syllabic content. If that content [is] maintained then you would be understood no matter how quickly you [speak].'[28]

Descriptions of Alastair from his film performances of the 1950s would at some point refer to his voice and manner of speaking and comment favourably on the precise and lilting quality of his enunciation. As we have now discovered, Alastair was an expert on elocution and his style of diction reflected the many years of study he invested in the subject; each spoken word treasured for its meaning, pronounced so as not to lose its 'full syllabic content'. No better example of this can be found than in *The Belles of St Trinian's* (1954) when Alastair addresses each of his young pupils in a speech where the sentiments of endearment are more focussed on the spoken words than the actual recipients.

One day a student came to Alastair with a problem. The student had a slight hesitancy in his speech and he wondered if Alastair could help him overcome his awkward social predicament. Alastair described his cure thus:

> First I taught him how to breathe. . . He had been breathing quite happily and without apparent effort for twenty odd years, but I put a stop to all that. Next I outlined the principles of voice production, with the help of a pig's larynx which I kept by me, pickled in alcohol, presumably to add excitement to the subject. . . I showed him exactly what his tongue and his soft palate ought to be doing when he articulated correctly, and the awful things they were liable

to do if he didn't. We stood making horrible faces at each other, and exchanging short fusilades [*sic*] of weird-sounding vocal noises. The strain became considerable and the atmosphere electric. So we removed our coats and rested. As I was remarking that it was 'am-m-mazingly m-m-mild for the time of year,' I became conscious that I had somehow acquired my pupil's impediment, while he – well, he, apparently, was unable to utter a sound. From then on he only nodded or shook his head to anything I said. At any rate he went away without a trace of a stammer – just breathing – a little irregularly . . . This was the first shock to my confidence, and it left me with the beginnings of a conscience, the beginnings of doubt. I was at last formally introduced to humility.[29]

Although Alastair had gained respectable employment as the Fulton Lecturer, he could not see himself remaining a teacher forever. His love of verse speaking and the theatre was drawing him increasingly in this direction, and yet he had no experience of acting, none of directing, and certainly not the financial backing to become a producer. These were significant problems, which would have put off even the most foolhardy, but Alastair was determined to achieve success in this field. In the end he resolved his predicament with a move of pure folly, or genius, depending on your point of view. Alastair set up his own school of drama and speech training. He reasoned his decision thus:

I was very fond of children. I still am fond of children – in a way. A sort of non-committal way. For instance, I like to wave to them – from a suitable distance. I also imagined that I understood the child mind, and that I knew what would please it. So I tried my hand at children's theatre, here, in Edinburgh.[30]

Alastair had a clear view of how his school should be:

I was determined that it should be no namby-pamby affair, this children's theatre of mine, nor too goody-goody either, or wishy-washy, or airy-fairy. . . I simply wanted to eschew aphoristic moralising. It was to be a grand, rollicking, rumbustious, and thrilling entertainment.[31]

As with all ideas thought up on the spur of the moment, some of the minor, and indeed major, practicalities had been overlooked. At that time Alastair was still living at home and so had no premises from which to run his school. Not only that, his income from his lecturing post was certainly insufficient for him to rent somewhere suitable to hold classes. His idea looked set to flounder from the very start; except his father had recently become the Secretary of the Veterans' Garden Association (VGA) whose offices were on the ground floor of 5 Manor Place. It just so happened that there were unrented rooms available in the building that could serve his purpose. The problem was one of obstinacy – Alastair apparently was not prepared to ask his father for help, even though they were still living under the same roof at 47 Pentland Terrace. Again, how much of this antipathy between father and son is true or exaggerated by Alastair is difficult to say. What is known is that if you wanted a private lesson in elocution in Edinburgh in 1925, you could look up the names of possible teachers in the Edinburgh Directory and find Alastair's, with his address and telephone number exactly the same as his father's. One would have assumed that he needed his father's permission to run his private classes from the family home and so there must have been some form of communication and goodwill between them.

It is not clear who, if anybody, intervened on Alastair's behalf, but it is known that Alexander managed to secure, on behalf of his son, the use of the second-floor rooms at the VGA offices. Even so, Alastair refused to acknowledge that his father had played any role in the matter.

Alastair's drama school was an immediate success but there still remained the problem of finding some larger rooms in which to rehearse productions. One can imagine the frustration in Alastair's stubborn mind when he became aware that there were still some vacant rooms on the first floor of 5 Manor Place that would prove ideal for his purposes. For once, the success of his school was too good an opportunity to be squandered because of matters of principle, and so Alastair reluctantly approached his father for help. Alexander responded and the rehearsal room situation was resolved.

Alastair began producing and directing plays and also arranging poetry readings. His natural skill in the spoken word, combined with his developing skills as a director, meant that he was soon able to enter his drama school into competitions held at Edinburgh University, as well as at Bath, Oxford and London. The school achieved some success at this level, often appearing in the top three places when the final results were announced. As a consequence, it flourished, but then one day:

> Everything went smoothly and gaily and according to plan, until I myself made an appearance on the stage. I think it was as the Erl King, but I may have been an ogre; I have tried to forget. I know I expected gales of laughter, possibly swelling to a cheer. Instead, there was a sudden deathly hush. Then thin, isolated wails of misery came from the body of the hall. These grew, and spread, and I was aware of a stampede of mothers leaving the hall with their unhappy offspring, between angry mutterings and reproachful backward looks.[32]

By this time, Alastair had already won several awards for verse speaking and so was accustomed to performing in front of people. It is unlikely therefore that his drama school provided the setting for his first performance in a play, but what is indisputable is that his next role, in *The Land of Heart's Desire*, would change his life forever. Alastair, nearly twenty-six, was about to meet his future wife – and she was just twelve years old.

2

Naomi

'Naomi, come and meet the man who's going to play the Priest. This is Mr Alastair Sim.' I was twelve, and very shy, and I never listened to names. By the end of the afternoon I was captivated and by the end of the second rehearsal I was fathoms deep in love. All through my childhood I had known moments of delighted expectancy which seemed to have no cause. From that day, and for the next fifty years, I had no need to look for one.

– Naomi Sim[1]

Autumn 1926 and Alastair was standing in Grant's, the bookshop, idly searching through the volumes on offer when a middle-aged, slightly rotund lady by the name of Miss Attwell entered the shop. Her speciality was teaching diction and poetry but at that moment she had an altogether different matter on her mind. She was hoping to enter the play *The Land of Heart's Desire* by W.B. Yeats into the annual competition of the Scottish Community Drama Association but had failed to find someone suitable to play the role of the priest. Her eyes fell on Alastair; a young man, just about to turn twenty-six, but his gait and prematurely balding head could easily be taken for that of a priest. Being desperately short of time, she approached Alastair and asked him for his help. Alastair graciously acceded to the request and agreed to attend a rehearsal at her flat in Lennox Street on the following Sunday.

When Sunday came, Alastair set off in plenty of time for the rehearsal but was delayed en route and arrived late. Miss Attwell was somewhat relieved when her doorbell rang and she saw her priest standing expectantly on her doorstep. She greeted Alastair and showed him through to the main room where the cast had gathered. A middle-aged man and woman were to play the part of the parents and a young man was to play the son. Miss Attwell, though not quite in the early flush of youth, was to play the part of the bride, and lastly, a young girl of twelve was to play the fairy girl.

Although Naomi Plaskitt was twelve, she in fact looked much younger than her age. She was always therefore in demand to play the role of the young girl in the melodramas put on by her school. Indeed, Miss Attwell, her English teacher at St Georges' school, had recently cast her in the role of 'Moth' in the school production of *Love's Labour's Lost*. Naomi had enjoyed the experience immensely, especially being the youngest member of the cast and the one who seemed to get the most attention. When Miss Attwell asked her to play the part of the fairy in *The Land of Heart's Desire*, she jumped at the opportunity and looked forward to further joyful recognition in the adult world.

Naomi's parents, Hugh and Norah Plaskitt, had an unhappy marriage. Their first daughter, Evenlode Nancy Plaskitt, was born one year after their marriage on 1 October 1911 but by then, Hugh had developed a drinking problem, and as he descended into alcoholism he became increasingly difficult to live with. Some time in the summer of 1913, Norah packed her bags and went to live with her sister Lizzie in Bedford. It could not have been easy for Norah because she was pregnant at the time, and in November 1913, Naomi was born.

Naomi was effectively born into a single-parent family and had little if any contact with her father, who eventually died of malaria in the African colonies in 1918. Without an income, Naomi's mother was financially dependent on her family and therefore spent time moving from one family house to another, living off the goodwill of others. Often they would stay with Norah's sisters in Edinburgh, who were known as the 'Great Aunts'. These family relatives offered security but in return wielded enormous influence over the lives of Norah and Naomi.

The strain of Norah's early life with Hugh, her subsequent need to constantly impose on others and the stress of not knowing how to provide for her family, caused Norah to suffer a breakdown. The 'Great Aunts' admitted Norah to a nursing home where, over time, she gradually recuperated. When Norah's health was sufficiently improved, she took Naomi and they rented rooms at 9 Eton Terrace, next to Lennox Street, where, in Miss Attwell's flat, the rehearsals were taking place for *The Land of Heart's Desire*.

When Alastair was first introduced to Naomi, she was quite taken aback: 'I had never seen anyone like this before. He was tall and gangly with crisp, black hair already receding, a lively face with huge eyes, and a very beautiful smile. About forty. . .'[2] Alastair, twenty-six, treated the young aspiring thespian with the respect due to a fellow cast member – something which Naomi greatly appreciated. The read-through of the play was a success and at the end of the afternoon, plans were made for the following Sunday's rehearsals.

Naomi had so enjoyed the experience that she spent the next week in a state of euphoria and couldn't wait to meet up once again with her fellow actors. At the end of the second Sunday of rehearsals, Miss Attwell invited Alastair and Naomi to stay on for tea. As Naomi recalled: 'soft lights, a bright fire, a low table drawn near to it spread with a white cloth and a magnificent tea, two comfortable armchairs and a stool for me.'[3] Naomi sat on the stool, eating cake after cake, gazing up at Alastair as he and Miss Attwell engaged in social conversation. At the end of tea, Alastair gave his thanks to Miss Attwell and then, since it was getting late, offered to walk Naomi home. By now, according to Naomi, she had fallen madly in love with him: 'He walked on the pavement while I walked on air.'[4] It is a sweet recollection by Naomi; the walk itself would have taken around one minute since Lennox Street runs into Eton Terrace, and anyway, Alastair would have taken this route to walk home.

It may have been Naomi's first experience of the emotion of love, or possibly her wishful desire for a father-figure, but by her own admission, she had developed a crush on Alastair. Norah was quick to notice the change in her daughter's behaviour and was naturally curious as to who this boy might be that had so affected her daughter for the first time. It is difficult to imagine what she may have thought when she found out from Naomi that far from being a boy, Naomi had fallen in love with a man fourteen years her senior. In any case, Norah insisted that, if come the following weekend Alastair were to walk Naomi home again, he should come in and say hello; she in turn would thank him for seeing her daughter safely home.

This was indeed what happened following the third Sunday of rehearsals; Alastair accompanied Naomi to her house whereupon he was invited in to meet Norah. Norah was a naturally shy person, as indeed to some extent was Alastair. Naomi once said, 'Alastair was always frightened of first encounters and needed a lot of persuasion, but when he finally met the person, he would be utterly charming.'[5] That first conversation between Alastair and Norah may well have begun uncomfortably, until that is, they began talking about the arts. Although Alastair had his own drama school, according to Naomi, he knew no one with whom he could talk about literature and poetry. By coincidence, Naomi's mother shared interests with Alastair and thus began a friendship that lasted for many years.

Rehearsals for *The Land of Heart's Desire* continued for a further five weeks until the day of the competition. Expectations were high, at least from Naomi's point of view, but 'when the great day came, the adjudicator was unimpressed. He praised me and slated the priest and I thought he was insane.'[6]

The day after the competition was Naomi's thirteenth birthday and Norah agreed to Naomi's wish to throw a birthday party. Naomi was besotted with Alastair at this stage. Her lovesick intention was to see how Alastair responded to an invite to her birthday party. If he said he would come, then she would go ahead with the party; if he said 'no', she would then abandon the whole idea. Naomi was ecstatic when Alastair said 'yes'. The rest of the cast were duly invited and Naomi's birthday party was spent repeating *The Land of Heart's Desire*, but with everyone taking on different roles. This caused much hilarity and the party was a great success although, 'since the priest had given me a birthday kiss when he arrived, I had difficulty getting to sleep that night.'[7]

Almost a year then passed during which time Naomi and Alastair had no contact. Occasionally, Naomi might catch a glimpse of him as Alastair went about his business in Edinburgh. In the following October, Naomi persuaded her mother to invite Alastair to their

Halloween party. Alastair accepted and they all ducked for apples: '. . . there was a great deal of laughter and when we were all exhausted, full of apples and rather damp, there was time to dry off in front of the fire and talk.'[8]

The conversation around the fire turned to Alastair's drama school. An important element of the drama school curriculum was the performance by his students of their set pieces in a competition at an annual show in Oxford. This show was known as the 'Oxford Recitations' and had been established by the future Poet Laureate John Masefield in 1923. Masefield saw the recitations as an opportunity to bring together good speakers of verse in a lightly competitive festival. The competition took place in the Examination Schools in Oxford and entries usually included a mixture of short plays, poetry, scenes from Shakespeare, monologues and choral work.

By 1928, Masefield had decided that the competitive aspect of the recitations had become too prominent and was spoiling what he had intended to be a natural celebration of verse speaking. He therefore removed all aspects of competition from the event and instead turned it into a festival. This he hosted in the little theatre on Boar's Hill, Masefield's own residence. The playwright Gordon Bottomley was asked to organise one of the evenings of this festival.

Bottomley wrote to Alastair proposing that he take on one of the three lead roles in a new kind of lyrical play that he had written. Featuring in this play was a chorus of eight women who 'speak sometimes all together, sometimes in two semichoruses (one of three "dark" voices, the other of four "light" ones) and are inseparable from the action.'[9] Bottomley further suggested that the chorus could consist of pupils from Alastair's drama school, although this was later ruled out because of a festival technicality.[10] Alastair was chosen by Bottomley for a lead role because the character was a verse speaker and by this time Alastair's reputation for verse speaking was widely known. In a letter to Alastair, Gordon Bottomley helpfully explained that his character was, 'Northern, – or rather, specifically, Scottish. . .'[11]. Over the next few years, Alastair and Bottomley developed a very good friendship and they exchanged many letters in which they wrote about their high ideals for the theatre whilst bemoaning the poor quality of the theatrical productions in the country.

Alastair invited Norah and Naomi to one of these competitive shows in Oxford. It was a great success all round, and over the next year, Alastair became a regular guest in the Plaskitt home. Here he would spend time with Norah talking about verse and the theatre and then would '... play football with me [Naomi] in the garden and clown for my benefit.'[12] On occasions, he would invite them to the theatre or take them to see a film.

Over the following year, Alastair began to show an increasing interest in Naomi's education. Indeed it was he who suggested that Naomi should leave school when she turned fourteen, but continue with her education by enrolling as a pupil at Alastair's own drama school. He also suggested that she should combine her drama classes with English and French classes at the university. Even by today's standards it must have seemed a curious suggestion, if not slightly unhealthy that Naomi should spend so much time in Alastair's presence, but Norah readily agreed. According to Naomi, she failed to take any of this very seriously.

After a year of studying, Alastair suggested to the fifteen-year-old Naomi that she might like to be his secretary, even though Naomi had no secretarial skills whatsoever. In return for her services, Alastair paid her four shillings a week. Alastair also encouraged Naomi with her studies and entered her into a verse speaking competition. When her performance failed to stir the judges, Alastair sent her a note of commiseration.

Alastair began spending more social time with Naomi, taking her with him when he visited friends. On one occasion when he took her to a verse speaking competition in Lanark, of which he was a judge, he was asked 'was she his daughter?' Alastair simply replied 'No' – and left it at that. By the next year, the relationship between Alastair and Naomi was developing into something more serious. Naomi was sixteen and quickly maturing into a young woman. Her initial infatuation was being replaced by a deeper love for Alastair. Alastair in turn had said to Naomi that they would get married as soon as she was seventeen. But this was not to be. Naomi would have to wait until she was eighteen before they were married.

★

It is impossible to pass this relationship by without reflecting on some of the issues and concerns it raises. An association between a man in his late twenties, looking older, with a girl in her teens, looking younger, even if platonic, would have certainly attracted gossip and innuendo. No matter how often Alastair brushed this aside or ignored direct references it must have concerned him that people were questioning his intentions towards the teenage Naomi. As a local man, leading a drama school, Alastair may have thought he could justify his behaviour – but what if, by chance, he was ever to become famous? What would the public make of this relationship then? What stratagem would he need to employ to keep it quiet?

Alastair's reticence towards the press, especially in his later life, is usually attributed to his fundamental desire for privacy, influenced no doubt by his frequently proclaimed belief in the foolishness of promoting celebrity status. But is it possible that Alastair was wary of dealing publicly with any question posed to him about his early relationship with Naomi? Even Naomi said, 'I wonder now what those friends can have made of our relationship – the tall man looking older than his years and the small, shy girl looking younger than hers.'[13]

Human nature is fairly predictable in these matters and one could easily guess what friends and acquaintances made of this relationship, if only in private thoughts and discussions. Naomi comments, '. . . I don't think it occurred to either of us that our relationship might appear unusual.'[14] One can understand this from Naomi's point of view. Naomi, without a father figure in her life, was receiving attention from a man with whom she was besotted – why should she complain or think anything wrong of it? Furthermore, if Alastair had been in a relationship with Norah then his behaviour towards Naomi would have been seen as paternal and quite natural, but there does not appear to be any evidence to this effect. This leaves some nagging doubts which are not helped by Alastair's insistence on taking Naomi on numerous trips to visit friends where he did little to explain her presence – indeed he often left her sitting in silence on her own.

It is not unknown for a relationship to develop between a student and their teacher, especially in the case of a drama teacher where the coaching can be quite personal, but this often suggests an element of exploitation. The teacher usually has the advantage in terms of age and experience and the student is often compromised by their inexperience. The teacher can offer wisdom and support – something very appealing to a student who might be experiencing an insecure home life. However, a breach of trust can occur if the teacher extends the relationship to the physical; the doting student is particularly vulnerable. Statutory protection exists in the form of the law of consent, which in the 1920s was based on the 1885 Criminal Law Amendment Act. This Act raised the age of consent from thirteen to sixteen. Neither Alastair nor Naomi have ever suggested that a physical relationship existed in their early time spent together, but they did decide to marry as soon as it was legally possible to do so. Without a definitive comment from either party as to when sexual relations first took place (and why would anyone announce that anyway?) one is left simply with conjecture. Even so, it is worth pointing out that it would have been less likely in the 1920s than it is today for a couple to have sex before marriage given the lack of reliable contraception and the social stigma of single motherhood.

3

The Professional Stage Actor

Most of them [Shakespearean roles] were very sinister, slimy and loathsome characters. So sinister, in fact, that after a while they had to be lightened with humour; and it was in this way that, all unconsciously, I found myself playing comedy roles.

– Alastair Sim[1]

The success of his drama school, and the various amateur productions that he had directed and produced, convinced Alastair that he could become a West End director. He wrote for advice on how to achieve this goal to the poet and dramatist John Drinkwater. Drinkwater had been in the audience when Alastair, along with nine other leading members and a chorus of ten, performed a recital of Gordon Bottomley's poems at the Rudolf Steiner Hall in London on 8 October 1929, and had been quite impressed by Alastair's performance. John Drinkwater replied to Alastair on 10 February 1930 saying that he did not know what suggestion he could make in terms of Alastair becoming a producer, but continued: 'The only thing that occurs to me at the moment is that Maurice Browne is I believe organising some rather large scheme of production for his new theatres. If you cared to see him I should be glad to give you an introduction and to tell him that I thought you would be useful.'[2] Not the most glowing of references admittedly, but in those days, casting was often decided on the basis of who you knew and a letter of introduction was invaluable[3].

Maurice Browne was a producer who, along with his wife, Ellen Van Volkenburg, ran a successful theatrical production company. They had founded the Little Theatre in Chicago, which was well known for putting on small amateur productions of experimental plays. Their recent success in London had been the highly acclaimed *Journey's End* and they were now planning a production of *Othello* at the Savoy Theatre. Ellen Van Volkenburg would be directing and Paul Robeson was in place to take the lead. Armed with his introduction from John Drinkwater, Alastair made contact with Maurice Browne and then went to London for an audition.

Alastair returned successful, having been offered the part of the Messenger and various understudy roles. Although it was relatively unusual for someone at the age of thirty to begin professional acting, James Bridie later pointed out: '[Alastair] differs from most members of his profession in having spent two-thirds of his life in living instead of acting.'[4]

What may have appeared to some to have been a difficult decision – giving up his career as the Fulton Lecturer, closing his drama school, leaving behind his life in Edinburgh, and not to mention being separated from Naomi – seems to have been taken by Alastair in his stride. Naomi meanwhile was already forming ideas in her own head as to how she could move to London to be with him.

Alastair formally resigned from his Fulton lectureship receiving in time a letter of gratitude from the University reading: 'Since you came to us we have never had any doubt that the training of our students in speech was in the safest and most competent hands.'[5] He also closed his school of drama and speech training, but for the time being he continued to rent some rooms in Edinburgh as a means by which to keep in touch with Naomi and as a place to house his extensive collection of poetry and theatre books.

Alastair's first professional appearance on stage occurred on 19 May 1930 as the Messenger in *Othello* although he also understudied the parts of Othello, Iago and Roderigo. *Othello* was a well-received production but criticised for the complicated sets that caused off-stage noise during the changeovers. This noise unfortunately overran into the following scenes distracting both actors and audience alike. Further criticism was levelled at Maurice Browne who had cast himself as Iago in the production.

Alastair found accommodation in the house of John Thompson, a fellow member of the *Othello* cast. John lived with his wife near Hampstead Heath and so each day John and Alastair travelled together on the underground to the Savoy Theatre. Occasionally Naomi would visit him and by this time they had, in Naomi's own words, '. . . an understanding'.[6] Naomi was sixteen years old and Alastair twenty-nine.

Although Alastair had settled into a routine, Naomi was far from happy with the situation. She wanted to spend more time with him but a permanent move to London would have been difficult under the circumstances. And so, similar to Alastair's adventurous plan in starting up his own school, Naomi came up with an equally daring means by which to justify a move south.

Naomi had always wanted to be an actress herself and indeed had shown great promise in her school plays, but had no money to pay for tuition fees at a drama school in London. So instead, she successfully auditioned for the Meggie Albenesi scholarship, which paid for her tuition fees at RADA. Thus, in September of 1930, Naomi also took the train south.

Having been separated on and off for several months, Alastair and Naomi were keen to spend some time together, but there were still some problems to overcome. Norah was determined to accompany Naomi to London but since neither of them had much in the way of income, finding accommodation was going to be difficult. The only viable solution was for Alastair, Naomi and Norah to share a flat together. They eventually settled on furnished accommodation in Golders Green.

It must have been an awkward threesome. By Naomi's own admission, she and Alastair were in a relationship together and yet they were now both under the ever watchful eye of Norah. Indeed, it is not clear why Norah followed her daughter to London. One could speculate that she was concerned for Naomi's welfare, but there again, Naomi had every reason to be in London. Furthermore, if Norah had reservations about Alastair's suitability as a boyfriend, it was far too late to do anything about it now, and moving in with Alastair and Naomi was hardly a step to prevent the two from seeing each other. Conversely, it is possible that Naomi was concerned with her mother's welfare – given Norah's fragile mental state. Whatever the reason, Alastair must have felt cramped by Norah's presence, but as we shall see, Norah was to play a critical role in their lives when unfortunate events conspired against them.

As *Othello* proceeded to generate interest in the country, Alastair was keen to look for his next acting job. Ellen Van Volkenburg wrote to him saying that she would like very much to use him again and in October Alastair was offered several roles in *Caviare*, a comedy revue which opened at the Little Theatre in December 1930. A highlight of the revue was a comedy sketch entitled *Wholly Russia* in which Alastair played the Second Commissar. Alastair followed this in January 1931 by playing Vasiliy in a production of *Betrayal* by Leonid Andreyev, and in February, Ellen Van Volkenburg cast him as Cardinal Ferdinando di Medici in *The Venetian* by Clifford Bax, notable for promoting Alastair as a leading member of the cast. James Bridie commented, 'I believe his first hit was as a wicked Cardinal'.[7] *The Venetian* had a very successful run in London and plans were made to transfer the play to America.

The Venetian opened at the Little Theatre in Chicago, and initially received good reviews but by the time they came to play at the Theatre Masque, New York, on 31 October 1931 the critics had turned on the play. After nine performances at the Theatre Masque, the decision was taken to end the tour. The cast packed their bags and returned home to England in time for Christmas.

Wishing to maintain what later became termed as his 'highbrow' approach to the arts, Alastair successfully applied to the Old Vic and received a contract under the leadership of Ralph Richardson. Alastair had once before applied for a job at the Old Vic but had been rebuffed with the caustic: 'Don't take him unless he thinks he's a bloody genius. God knows he doesn't look it'.[8] It was a sweet return.

In the spring of 1932, Alastair began the Old Vic season in the dual roles of Trebonius (a conspirator against Caesar) and Lucilius (a friend to Brutus and Cassius). His salary for such endeavours was a rather paltry £5 a week. This was followed by the role of John Wilkes Booth in *Abraham Lincoln*, the Duke of Venice in *Othello* (although when Ralph Richardson was taken ill with a serious throat illness Alastair took over as Roderigo) and Antonio in *Twelfth Night*. The season ended with Alastair playing Claudius, the King of Denmark, in *Hamlet*.

In August 1932 Alastair and Naomi were married at a registry office. Their honeymoon was a three week break on the island of Sark. Soon after, Naomi became pregnant. The pregnancy however turned out to be a painful one for the young Mrs Sim. Naomi suffered from terrible bouts of sickness which gradually became prolonged and debilitating. The threat to both her life and the baby's life increased to such a degree that Naomi had to be admitted to a nursing home. It was here, after a period of observation that the sad decision was taken to terminate the pregnancy – a decision that would have to be taken again on future occasions.

In the autumn of 1932, Alastair signed a contract for a second season at the Old Vic under the joint leadership of Malcolm Kean and Peggy Ashcroft. The first half of the season began on 19 September with Alastair in the role of Pothinus in a very successful production of Shaw's *Caesar & Cleopatra*. In October, Alastair played the title role – the King of Britain – in *Cymbeline*. This was followed by Duke Senior in *As You Like It*, and Alastair 'looking villainous in a red wig'[9] playing Banquo in *Macbeth*.

The year ended with Alastair and Naomi buying a house in Garrick Avenue, London, using part of a legacy that Naomi had received from one of her aunts. Naturally, given past history, Norah also moved in with them.

On the 23 January 1933, Alastair began the second half of his second season at the Old Vic with *A Winter's Tale,* in which he played Polixenes. This was followed by: Cetewayo in *The Admirable Bashville; Or, Constancy Rewarded*, Sir Thomas Randolph in *Mary Stuart*, Apothecary in *Romeo and Juliet*, Crabtree in *The School For Scandal*, and finally, Antonio in *The Tempest*.

With two seasons' worth of experience of the classics behind him, Alastair decided not to apply for a third season at the Old Vic, but instead took on the character of Carl Salter (a villain) in *As You Desire Me* by Luigi Pirandello. *The Times* wrote that the play 'holds the stage at every turn, completely satisfying the curiosity which it has provoked'[10] and Alastair was singled out for the following praise: 'Mr Alaister Sim [sic] plays the brutal novelist abominably well.'[11] For Alastair's next role he moved from villainy into melodrama by acting in Frank Vosper's *The Rose Without a Thorn*. This production portrayed Henry VIII as an idealist in search of the woman of his dreams and was visited by the Queen on 25 November 1933. The *Stage* rather majestically announced that 'Sir Thomas Audley . . . had dignified exposition from Mr Alastair Sim.'[12]

★

The Rose Without a Thorn brought to an end the first period of Alastair's stage acting career. During this time he had quickly established himself as a competent stage performer adept at playing villainous roles. This may seem ironic given that Alastair is so well remembered today as a comedy actor but as James Bridie once commented, 'it looked for a time as if he would play wicked cardinals all his life.'[13] Clifford Bax wrote to Alastair after seeing his performance in *As You Desire Me* saying; 'It is strange that so charming a man can be, on the stage, so sinister.'[14] Clifford Bax was hoping that Alastair would play the role of Chief Cardinal in a new play he had written (*House of Borgia*) and asked, 'Why should you not make a career in cardinals? If I can get my way, you will be invited to play the chief cardinal who will be, once more, the villain of the piece. . .'[15]. Peter Copley, who would appear on stage with Alastair in two plays in the late 1950s/1960s, put it succinctly when he said, 'Nobody realised then that he was a great comic actor.'[16]

It was the producer, Harcourt Williams, who noticed that Alastair had a natural gift for enhancing any comedic element within his role. Williams suggested to Alastair that he should exploit this strength by moving away from villainy and into comedy. Alastair was not averse to the idea and would later explain, in a verbose manner that was a characteristic of his speeches:

> When you are happy your greatest need is that others should be happy too. And it occurred to me that there might possibly be a sufficiency of others with afflictions similar to my own whom I might help. (Even in my new-found humility I hardly dared to think I was unique.) Also there might easily be untold numbers who, while rejoicing in their clear-sightedness, may have failed to find laughter through the inward eye.[17]

The one drawback was that the move into comedy would inevitably be at the expense of the highbrow theatre that he so venerated.

Some friends such as Gordon Bottomley would find difficulty in accepting Alastair's move away from the verse-speaking idealist that he once was, and yet the transition for Alastair was initially smooth and successful. He even went so far as to 'dismiss Shakespeare and said he would never play a Shakespeare role'[18] – a vow he would keep for thirty years.

This appears to be a typical Alastair Sim trait: a previously dogmatic stance, swiftly circumnavigated when the moment required, into another equally unequivocal position – something we shall encounter on several other occasions during his lifetime. As traits go, it does not define you as a bad person, but it does call on tolerance from those close to you.

Alastair's first important comic role was as Donald Geddes, a comic Scotsman, in *The Man Who Was Fed Up* by Frederick Witney. The play tells of a successful stockbroker, who, tired of the dreary world in which he earns his living, decides to escape it all and enter a monastery. It achieved good notices:

> The piece is pleasantly played by all concerned, especially Mr Basil Foster, who finds great fun in the Stockbroker's disillusionment, and by Mr Alastair Sim, whose truculent Scottish cavalier is always delightfully out of his depth.[19]

The Man Who Was Fed Up was a notable success for Alastair and he followed it up in the autumn of 1934 by two equally good performances in a double bill at the Little Theatre; 'Mr Alastair Sim distinguishes himself in both pieces.'[20] In the first play of the evening, Alastair took on the role of Don Giorgio in the melodrama *The Life That I Gave Him* by Luigi Pirandello. The second play of the evening was *Murder Trial* by Sydney Box. This was a satirical court melodrama where three female witnesses in turn give three distinct personality traits of the prisoner in the dock. Presiding over proceedings was 'Mr Alastair Sim, as the Judge, decorating the final sermon with a very pretty humour'[21] – a precursor perhaps to his television performances thirty years later as Mr Justice Swallow in *Misleading Cases*.

With hardly a break between productions, Alastair accepted the role of Ponsonby, the bank manager, in the comedy, *Youth at the Helm* by Hubert Griffith. The play opened at the Westminster Theatre in

November 1934 with a cast that included Jack Melford, Vera Lennox and O.B. Clarence. *Youth at the Helm* was an immediate success:

> This appears to be that very rare thing – a farcical comedy which, having an idea, neither loses nor belabours it... It is, as good farce must be, consistent in its degree of improbability; its jokes are cumulative, its satirical basis firm in the vanities of human nature, and its incidents of bluff and the calling bluff and the raising of bluff are so ingeniously contrived that they are always credible in their own absurd, but clearly recognizable world... Mr. Jack Melford, Mr. O.B. Clarence and Mr. Alastair Sim particularly distinguishing themselves.[22]

At Christmas, Alastair played the role of the Mad Hatter in *Alice in Wonderland* at the Duke of York's Theatre and also General Wei 'represented most amusingly by Alastair Sim'[23] in *Lady Precious Stream* at the Little Theatre. *Lady Precious Stream* by S.I. Hsiung was described as a Chinese fantasy but although the cast were 'a most distinguished band of artists'[24], the scenery was bare and uninspiring; photographs of the sets show rather bland stages with very little in the way of props to conjure up the essence of the Orient. Nevertheless, the play was well received and even achieved coverage in *The Tatler* on 26 December, when a performance was given at the Chinese Legation for a guest list which included the Polish and Japanese ambassadors.

In February 1935, Alastair revived his role as Ponsonby in *Youth at the Helm*, which by then had transferred to the more prestigious Globe Theatre. Alastair was without an agent at this time and so undertook his own salary negotiations, at which he seemed quite adept, negotiating a salary increase to £20 which was £5 more than the management had initially offered. His performance as Ponsonby received further attention from the attending critics: 'Mr Alastair Sim is once more such an employer as office boys see in their nightmares.'[25] From a rare interview, given in 1938, we have Alastair's own words to describe his role: 'The first big comedy part I had was in *Youth at the Helm* in which I was the bank manager. Here again, the character was really slimy, but the slime was disguised by comedy.'[26]

★

Alastair had been exceedingly busy on stage between 1932 and 1935. Over this four-year period he had advanced from walk-on parts to leading roles and found comedy to be his forte. As a result of his excellent reviews, film offers began to arrive through the post. Now was his opportunity to break into a much bigger market with greater rewards – except that a serious misfortune befell him.

During the second run of *Youth at the Helm*, Alastair strained his back. It was an innocent event at the time. Apparently, Alastair was playacting the fool with some children on Hampstead Heath, when he suddenly felt his back 'go'. Although he suffered some initial discomfort, there were no immediate signs that anything was seriously wrong. Over time, the pain took hold and Alastair found it increasingly difficult to perform on stage night after night. He tried wearing a surgical corset but the pain just grew worse until eventually he was left with no choice but to withdraw from the production. The news was reported in *Theatre World* thus: 'One of the cleverest performances in the sparkling *Youth at the Helm* has unfortunately been interrupted by the calls of a nursing home.'[27] The film roles and now the stage career had to be put on hold indefinitely – Alastair could only wait until the strained back responded to treatment.

Visits to doctors were in vain and for some time, Alastair was without work. A further catastrophe then struck. Alastair's mother, Isabella, died aged eighty-four. She had lived a long and happy life, but even so, Alastair was devastated. The mother he so much adored would no longer be able to share in his future successes. But what future successes? Fate appeared to be conspiring against him just when the opportunity of a film career beckoned. Of more immediate concern was the financial situation. Alastair and Naomi had only just recently bought their house, but since giving up his role in *Youth at the Helm*, there was no immediate income to pay the bills. Under the circumstances, Alastair became increasingly tense and irritable and his mood darkened.

It was Naomi's mother who came to their rescue. Norah's aunts had recently passed away and so she used her inheritance to pay the bills. Alastair would never forget this kind gesture. Later, when he became financially solvent again, he signed a covenant in her favour, which he paid into and increased during her lifetime.

However, the back problem still remained until a chance visit from an elderly friend of Alastair and Naomi's. This friend spoke highly of the recent help she had received for her own back problems from the osteopath Edward (Tom) Hall. In a state of desperation, they called on Edward Hall who diagnosed that Alastair had torn a small muscle in his back resulting in adhesions which were pressing on the sciatic nerve. Hall recommended a form of massage designed to break down these adhesions and relieve the pressure. At the time this was quite an innovative treatment and today Edward Hall is known as the father of modern techniques of osteopathy.

The treatment was a success and as Alastair's mobility and good temperament returned, he began to consider the next step in his career. Initially of course, he had moved to London with the hope of establishing himself as a West End director, but film work offered an exciting new challenge. He hesitated, but only briefly, and then picked up the script to *The Riverside Murder*.

4

'Quota Quickies' and the Early Film Years

I made my debut in *Riverside Murder*. I was asked to play the part of a cockney detective, but rebelled. I had never tried to portray a cockney in all my life. So I persuaded the studio to change the character into a Scot.

– Alastair Sim[1]

In December 1927, Parliament succumbed to pressure from the Federation of British Industries and passed a bill designed to offer support and protection to the British film industry. It was called the Cinematograph Films Act and it stipulated that UK cinemas had to increase the percentage of British films in their screening schedules to twenty per cent by 1937. The intention was to rejuvenate the British film industry in the hope that it could then defend itself against the powerful American studios. The actual result was an expansion in low budget British productions, made to tight deadlines, mostly with new or untried actors and predominantly woeful in quality. UK cinema audiences began to differentiate between films by categorising them colloquially as either 'Quality' or 'Quota Quickies' (QQ) – the latter expected to be poor and a waste of time and money for the cinema-goer. Then again, QQs did provide a rich training ground for British technicians and actors and also allowed for the creation of several new British film studios, although they would not remain British for long.

American film companies quickly realised that the British film industry was too weak to take advantage of the newly passed legislation and more importantly could not be relied upon to meet the statutory quota of British-made films. They responded by setting up their own British film companies. Such an example was the American Fox Film Company (AFFC) who formed Fox-British Pictures, which operated from leased premises in Wembley. Fox-British Pictures were ordered to produce British films at a rate determined by Fox-British's parent company (Twentieth Century Fox) with an eye both on their own major 'Quality' production and the legal requirements of the Cinematograph Films Act. Actors appearing in these QQs were faced with a double-edged sword. It was an opportunity to make themselves known but with material and production values that could wreck a career. Occasionally, even under these circumstances, a QQ would hit the screens that fared well with both audiences and critics alike, such as *The Return of Bulldog Drummond* (1934) and *Dark Eyes of London* (1939).

In 1935 Fox-British put into production a QQ entitled *The Riverside Murder*, directed by Albert Parker and staring Judy Gunn and Basil Sydney. The role of a cockney sergeant in the film was offered to a relatively unknown British actor who had never appeared in a film before but had recently achieved high praise for his comic theatrical performances. His name was Alastair Sim.

Alastair immediately requested of Fox-British that they change the character of the cockney sergeant and make him Scottish (the character was renamed as Sergeant McKay). The irony of this request would not be lost on George Cole who suffered taunting from Alastair for over-relying on a cockney accent for his screen characters. *The Riverside Murder* is a well paced and plotted 'whodunit' although there are several lazy shots where key characters speak with their backs to the camera. As Alastair's first film it is interesting to note his accent – full bodied and without doubt, Scottish in origin. Some have commented that as the decades passed, the accent appeared to travel south, as if with a will of its own. Maybe this was influenced by Alastair's stage and film career becoming based in London; alternatively perhaps as an Elocution lecturer who was conscious of the value of a pleasant sounding accent in the southern counties, he decided at key points in his career to make some minor concessions.

Alastair's screen persona became established almost immediately. Sergeant McKay is the same lightweight Scottish buffoon who would appear in most of his films over the next five years up to and including *Inspector Hornleigh Goes to It* (1940). Sometimes police sergeants, at other times newsmen, but whatever the occasion, Alastair's screen character always seemed to have the same nickname, 'Mac', to speak with the same accent and act in the same manic way.

Quota Quickies were produced in a manner similar to an assembly line and so the production crew and cast would remain together for several films. As a result, the atmosphere on set would often be one of friendly conviviality. *The Riverside Murder* was no exception and the informal atmosphere of filming was to the liking of both Alastair and Naomi. Naomi would act as chauffeuse, driving Alastair to the studios at Wembley, which were a short distance from where they were living at Golders Green, and would then return to pick him up when filming had finished for the day. And so they settled into a cosy routine, as Alastair, armed with a film contract, began to learn his new trade in a series of mostly forgettable films.

Alastair's next film, *The Private Secretary*, produced at Twickenham studios, was an adaptation of the successful stage play by Sir Charles Hawtrey, and stared Oscar Asche and Edward Everett Horton. The producer Julius Hagen was impressed enough by Alastair's first foray into films to offer him a three-year deal. Alastair, without much deliberation, duly added his signature to the contract – an action he would come to regret as the roles he played on screen became increasingly monotonous.

Late Extra followed, somewhat rambling in places, but with a nicely judged romance between James Mason (in his film debut) and Virginia Cherrill. In *A Fire has been Arranged*, Alastair appeared alongside two highly respected comics of their time – Bud Flanagan and Chesney Allen. His final film of 1935, *The Case of Gabriel Perry*, a courtroom drama, starred Henry Oscar in the title role with an early screen appearance by Margaret Lockwood.

Alastair's first film of 1936, the Fox-British *Wedding Group*, is notable for being the only time that Naomi appeared in a film with Alastair. Naomi was given the role of a maid in a Minister's household (the Minister being played by Alastair). She describes her experience thus:

I was told at the beginning that my part would probably last for three days but it spread to thirteen and I had the time of my life. I loved getting up at 6 am, driving Alastair to the studio, getting made up and being dressed and then going to the canteen for a large breakfast before being on the set at 9 am for another day of fun.[2]

Fun or not, this was Naomi's only foray onto the silver screen. Naomi had successfully completed a RADA course and had won a drama scholarship against strong opposition, but now she saw her film career as secondary to that of supporting her husband. Perhaps this sacrifice was an important step in Alastair's success, because in Naomi he acquired a full-time adviser who had first-hand experience of the business. Naomi could not only offer moral support but also filter the screen offers that came his way via his newly appointed agent, Aubrey Blackburn. She could help him prepare for his roles by reading through his lines, and offer suggestions as to how he might play his scenes. Alastair certainly valued this input and during his stage plays would insist that Naomi attended some of the rehearsals in the role of his personal director.

In trying to understand Alastair Sim, it is essential to appreciate the role played by Naomi in both his life and career. Geoffrey Jowitt, who appeared on stage with Alastair during the first two seasons of *Peter Pan* (1941–42 and 1942–43), remembers that Alastair was always closely supported by Naomi:

Naomi came every day to the theatre. She was always very sweet with a nice smile and would say 'hello' to you. She would never interfere in the production, but would stay in his dressing room and help Alastair to change from Mr Darling to Captain Hook. They seemed a very happy couple. I never saw them in a mood or anything like that.[3]

Naomi, like Isabella (Alastair's mother), appeared to have a very clear and unambiguous view of her role in their marriage. Valerie Grove on interviewing Naomi in 1987 said, 'It is her unfashionable but convincing view that to devote herself to Alastair Sim's career was entirely fulfilling.'[4] This appears to have been a very gracious and mature act for a wife who was very young and who could have had her own eyes set on stardom. Naomi wrote:

For myself, the vanishing of my so-called career was the greatest blessing that could have befallen me. It meant that all my interest became centred on Alastair's work which was the bond that made us so close.[5]

It could be argued that such unselfish dedication on behalf of one partner would naturally lead to a close bond in a relationship, but Ronald Mavor[6], who knew them well said, 'Alastair and Naomi were as near to having "one soul in two bodies" as you can get.'[7] Peter Copley, who appeared in a couple of plays with Alastair, remarked that Alastair was 'very dependent on Naomi'.[8] Margaret Wedlake, who appeared in *Windfall* added that Alastair was 'detached from ordinary life but had great reliance on Naomi, his wife, whose support was, I think, invaluable to him.'[9]

Naomi also undertook basic secretarial duties – as Richard Owens (who appeared with Alastair in *Dandy Dick*) recalls:

My two little daughters loved it [*Dandy Dick*] and insisted on sending Alastair a card and had a lovely reply from his wife saying that he was very pleased and thanked them.[10]

It is worth reflecting on the thoughts of neighbour and friend John Howard Davies who said, 'Naomi was a clever lady but Alastair used her when he was offered work which he was disinclined to take by saying "Oh Naomi doesn't like it, so I couldn't do it"'.[11] Alastair certainly valued Naomi's opinion although as John Howard Davies remarked, 'I'm not absolutely convinced it was sound, but there again, it's jolly useful to have someone second read for you and give an opinion.'[12] These comments do not detract from the fact that Naomi provided a key supporting role to Alastair throughout his stage and film career.

Wedding Group was followed by another Fox-British production, *Troubled Waters*. Alastair was still playing safe with Scottish caricatures – this time playing the role of Mac MacTavish (thereby doubling up on his usual nickname). In his next film, *The Man in the Mirror*, Alastair got the opportunity to display his skills with the spoken word.

The Man in the Mirror was a successful light comedy based on a shy businessman's reflection in a mirror coming to life as his alter ego and turning the tables on his business partner. It starred Edward Everett Horton and, perhaps surprisingly for a QQ, used some effective trick photography. The film is lightweight and enjoyable, with some subtle and amusing sexual references. Alastair's role in the film as an interpreter for the Bogus of Bokhara (Aubrey Mather) allowed him to put his phonetic skills to good use as he speaks and interprets a gibberish language into English. Alastair produced a humorous and intelligent performance that proved to be one of the highlights of the film.

Julius Hagen, who had signed Alastair to his contract, suddenly found himself on the brink of financial disaster and *The Man in the Mirror* was the last film to be made at Twickenham Studios under his ownership. The news of Hagen's eventual financial collapse was broken to Alastair while on a skiing holiday in Arosa. The contract Alastair had signed with Hagen now became void, but rather than being disappointed with his situation, Alastair was in fact quite relieved; he had come to doubt the wisdom of being tied into a long-term contract. Indeed, for the rest of his career, he would resist the temptation of being bound by any contractual terms that would limit his freedom to move onto different projects when he saw fit – whether films, such as the *St Trinian's* series where his appearance in the second film, *Blue Murder at St Trinian's* (1956) amounts to a matter of minutes, or plays, because soon he would insist that six months was the most he was prepared to commit to any stage role.

Alastair was certainly being given the opportunity to learn his trade from the comedians of the time. In his next film, *Keep Your Seats Please*, he appeared with the irrepressible George Formby. Directed by Monty Banks and produced by Basil Dean, this is generally regarded as one of Formby's better star vehicles. It was based on the play *Twelve Chairs* written by Ellie Ilf and Eugene Petrov. In the film, the main protagonists have to discover the whereabouts of a fortune in jewels that has been hidden in one of six antique chairs. *Keep Your Seats Please* also featured the song that has become indelibly linked with George Formby – 'When I'm Cleaning Windows'. Alastair appeared third in the credits and played quite a significant role in the film. By this time, Alastair 'had only to insinuate his coy head round the corner of a door to be greeted with roars of delighted laughter.'[13]

Alastair ended the year with top billing alongside C. Denier Warren in the Fox-British film, *The Big Noise*. It was a great accomplishment for Alastair given that it had taken him just two years to accomplish what most actors fail to achieve in their whole lifetime (albeit in the second-rate Quota Quickies). To celebrate, Alastair and Naomi decided to look for a larger house. Under pressure from Norah, they chose a secluded property in Wildwood Road, Hampstead Heath which, because of its size, required daily help to clean and manage. This intrusion of maids into their home life created problems. Unfamiliar faces in the house (and having to manage them) can become a daunting prospect for a young wife. Naomi ceded this responsibility to Norah and instead spent as much time as she could with Alastair. Even so, Norah's influence on their lives was on the wane.

The year of 1937 began with Alastair returning to the theatre to play in Edgar Wallace's 'brilliant revival'[14] of *The Squeaker*. Alastair played a crime reporter who solves a murder at the Leopard Club, a venue frequented by assorted gangsters, fences and crooks. Reviewers praised Alastair's eccentric performance and the *Daily Mail* wrote: 'Chief honours go to Mr Alastair Sim. . .'[15] *The Squeaker* led to a film later in the year that obviously benefited from a higher budget than usual in productions of this period. Edmund Lowe, Sebastian Shaw, Ann Todd and Robert Newton deliver some good performances in a film that stands up to today's viewing.

By this time, it was apparent to all that Alastair had completely moved away from the highbrow as the following observation in *The Tatler* of March 1937 recounts:

> There was a time when Mr Sim used to suppress his native accents and affect a classic style at the Old Vic: now he has come into his own as a comedian on screen and stage, and those who admired his efforts in the Shakespearean purple will rejoice at his triumph in the drama of to-day.[16]

It appears that over the following decade, his classical apprenticeship at the Old Vic faded from memory:

> That long, lean body and baleful eye ruled him out of such classic roles as are essayed by Sir Laurence Olivier. That humorous argumentative

lilt in his voice would have wrought havoc with Hamlet and turned Othello into a coloured comedian. Nor if he did Macbeth could you imagine him being terrified by the witches of the cauldron or Banquo's ghost.[17]

Alastair next took to the stage on 31 July in *The Gusher* by Ian Hay. This was a major undertaking, employing between seventy and a hundred actors, depending on which press item you read. Leading the cast were Coral Browne, Joan Hickson and Jack Livesey. *The Gusher* used a revolving stage that allowed for multiple sets (necessary for the seventeen scenes) although changing between scenes still took time and this tended to prolong the evening. As one reviewer wrote, 'The trouble is not so much that the play is childish, for that is its convention, it is laborious and unexciting. . .'[18]. This may be overly critical, since it had a successful run of 127 performances – closing on the 27 November.

The Gusher was a comedy involving a substantial number of plot twists – shipwrecks, savages, villains, heroes and a gushing oil rig. Alastair, yet again, played the part of a comic Scotsman: 'Mr Alastair Sim, his usual bold and bubbling Scots self, and Mr Cyril Smith are very funny indeed'[19] and 'Mr Sim proves to be a tower of strength on the comedy side.'[20] Alastair, who had years earlier suffered a loss of confidence with regards to his looks, was now finding these same features a great asset as the caricaturists began to promote him with an obvious zeal.

Alastair's first film release in 1937 was the Fox–British production *Strange Experiment* based on the play *Two Worlds* by Hubert Osborne and John Golden, and featuring the one-armed actor Donald Grey. *Strange Experiment* was far-fetched nonsense involving fake pearls and experimental brain surgery – typical ingredients for a QQ. *Melody and Romance* followed and fared slightly better, benefiting from a significantly improved cast including Margaret Lockwood.

Regardless of the help afforded by the Cinematograph Films Act, the British film industry continued to flounder and during this period several more British film studios either collapsed or were forced into undertaking drastic cost-cutting measures. As a result, filmmaking became a disjointed affair. For example, it was not unusual for a film production to be suddenly switched at the last minute to an alternative studio. This would obviously disrupt the lives of all those involved and create untoward scheduling problems. Alastair's next film, *Gangway*, suffered this fate. On 26 February 1937 Gaumont-British closed down the Shepherd's Bush studios and switched production of *Gangway* to Pinewood studios.

Gangway was an important film for Alastair since it established a variation on his screen persona that made him incredibly marketable: '*Gangway* shows him in his first important crazy part, and his lunacy almost steals the picture.'[21] This 'lunacy' is an interesting aspect of his early comedy roles, both on stage and screen. Alastair had developed a dynamic physical form of comedy, played to a fast pace, making best use of his gangly gait and physical looks and appropriately termed 'manic' comedy. Indeed, *Film Weekly* commented: 'Those who remember his early stage days still can't believe their eyes when they see him doing his comedy stuff.'[22] Commenting on an Alastair Sim role today, one would tend to recall his films from the 1950s, when his acting style was more subtle and refined. It can therefore come as quite a surprise and revelation to see him in his early film roles – wild and devoid of the composure apparent in such comedy classics as *The Happiest Days of Your Life* (1950).

Sometime during the filming of *Gangway*, Alastair and Naomi discovered that their house had a faulty drain and that substantial repairs were necessary to rectify damage to the foundations. Rather than live in a noisy, uncomfortable environment, they chose to stay in a country house located near the film studios in Iver, Buckinghamshire. This allowed them to indulge in their leisure pursuits – tennis, horse-riding and countless games of cards, in a beautiful setting. Their experience of this time would influence their choice of home at a later date.

By 1938, Alastair appeared to have found his niche in the film market and was successfully exploiting the need for the injection of manic comedy into otherwise dire British musicals.

At a time when British actors are moaning about the bad condition of the film industry over here, he [Alastair] is whirling from picture to picture with barely a break. Since making a big hit in the Jessie Matthews film *Gangway*, his stock has soared dizzily.[23]

Alastair's next film, *Sailing Along*, was an above-average example of this genre. It featured Jessie Matthews as a barge hand who, in a plot twist devoid of any logic, becomes a dancing star. Alastair's manic role in this film was as an eccentric artist with a penchant for hiding old banana skins in pianos. The highlight of the film was a seven-minute dance sequence with Jessie Matthews and Jack Whiting. Tap, mime, ballet, an orchestra of fifty and a choir of thirty, suggests that *Sailing Along* was aspiring to compete with the great American musicals. Although quite successful at the box office, it was released at a time of developing world tensions. Increasing fear and uncertainty about the future was a constant topic of conversation for the man on the street, and the entertainment provided by light British musicals, though a welcoming distraction at first, began to lie uneasily with the UK population. Furthermore, Jessie Matthews, the doyen of this genre, was beginning to suffer ill health and would indeed shortly retire from musicals altogether.

In *Alf's Button Afloat*, Alastair starred alongside the most successful group of UK performers at that time – the Crazy Gang. He played 'The Slave of the Button' – a genie who could be summoned whenever his master, Bud Flanagan, rubbed a magic button which had been melted down from the original Aladdin's lamp. The trick camera-work is quite effective, but this meant that Alastair often played his scenes alone, and so found little opportunity to develop his friendship with Flanagan and Allen – two comics he greatly admired. *Alf's Button Afloat* committed to celluloid the essence of British music-hall comedy and on release was viewed as 'excellent broad fooling.'[24]

Sitting in the cheap seats, watching a showing of *Alf's Button Afloat*, was a teenage boy mesmerised by the strange looking actor playing the genie. At the end of the film, he watched the credits to learn of the actor's name – Alastair Sim. He hoped one day to meet him. The boy's name was George Cole.

★

In 1934 a film was released in America entitled *The Thin Man*. It was shot in just eighteen days with William Powell and Myrna Loy playing the leading roles of Nick and Nora Charles. Their fast packed dialogue equipped with good-humour, insults and mutual affection appealed to a film audience excited by the sexual chemistry between the leading pair. It provided an antidote to the economic depression and heralded a new era of filmmaking – the comedy thriller. *This Man is News* (1938) attempted to repeat this wise-cracking formula for the British market. It starred Barry K. Barnes as reporter Simon Drake, who finds himself framed for a murder that he predicts, in a moment of drunkenness, to his newspaper editor (Alastair Sim). *This Man is News* was an instant success with British audiences. On viewing today, it curiously lacks a sense of charm even though there is a standout performance by Valerie Hobson as Pat Drake. A sequel was immediately put into production, *This Man in Paris* (1939) involving the husband and wife team tracking down a counterfeiting gang to Paris, but it was less well received and the series came to an abrupt halt.[25]

The *Inspector Hornleigh* series, again built around the theme of a comedy thriller, was based on the radio serial *Monday Night at Eight* created by Hans Wolfgang Priwin. This series ran to three films, all starring Gordon Harker as the Inspector and Alastair Sim as Sergeant Bingham. The first film in the series, *Inspector Hornleigh* (1938) concerned the theft of a briefcase belonging to the Chancellor of the Exchequer containing vital information on the budget. It is a very studio bound production but nevertheless quite engaging as a 'whodunit'. The second film, *Inspector Hornleigh on Holiday*[26] (1939) was a murder mystery set at a seaside hotel involving gangsters and an insurance scam. The third and final instalment of the series, *Inspector Hornleigh Goes To It* (1940), found the Inspector and his Sergeant on the trail of a fifth columnist. Alastair played the Sergeant in a typically dim-witted fashion that provided some light relief in contrast to the dour Gordon Harker. The director, Sidney Gilliat, described the films as:

> ... hybrid propositions because the actor who played the title role was grossly miscast and largely unintelligible. But, being a series, once the cast was established we were stuck with the lot. Sim played Hornleigh's bumbling Scots assistant Bingham and he saved the pictures.[27]

This is slightly disingenuous of Sidney Gilliat; Alastair's comic timing is good but his character is too soppy and inane to save a picture. The *Inspector Hornleigh* films succeed because of the all

round performances of the actors combined with some imaginative
and creative use of cinematography.

By 1939, Alastair had come to realise that his screen roles, so familiar, so superficial and so undemanding, were simply not stretching
him as an actor and indeed, much worse, had typecast him as some
sort of zany comic. He voiced his aspirations at this time in an interview he gave to John Newnham: 'Once, on the stage, I had to appear
in a romantic role – but I made a terrible mess of it. But I want to
do drama again, if it's not too late.'[28] This was a clear indication that
Alastair appreciated his plight and wanted, if possible, to reassert his
highbrow credentials.

The opportunity to 'do drama again' came in early 1939 when
Alastair went to the Malvern Festival and performed in two plays:
What Say They by James Bridie and *Old Master* by Alexander Knox.
Most will agree that *What Say They* is not Bridie at his best. It is a
comedy of university life which 'suffers from not being a farce.'[29] The
London critic of the *Glasgow Herald* wrote:

> Most compensating of all there was Mr. Alastair Sim as a clerk of the
> senate...This was a grand performance in the one character in this play
> which nearly amounted to a part.[30]

Regardless of the success of *What Say They*, the festival had at least
introduced Alastair to James Bridie, a Scottish playwright of some
considerable note. Bridie's major plays up to that point included: *The
Switchback* (1929), *The Anatomist* (1930), *Tobias and the Angel* (1930) and
A Sleeping Clergyman (1933). Although the meeting between the two
men was only a brief one, it was the beginning of an association that
would reap huge success in the 1940s.

The Malvern Festival lasted into the summer. When war broke out,
Alastair and Naomi returned to Wildwood Road and like most of the
London-based community, set about installing an air-raid shelter in
their back garden. In November 1939, during the so-called 'Phoney
War', Alastair went on tour with the comedy *You of All People* starring
Leslie Banks and Margaret Rawlings. The play had arrived at Oxford
and Alastair was staying at the Randolph Hotel when he entered into
an argument with Leslie Banks concerning the upbringing of children. Significantly, Naomi was in the room at the time when Leslie

destroyed Alastair's argument with the comment: 'Ah, but you have no children.'[31] It was a key moment in Alastair and Naomi's life together.

Alastair desperately wanted a child and was prepared to adopt if necessary. The events of the time meant that orphans from the Spanish Civil War and Jewish refugee children were often looking for good homes. Alastair and Naomi visited several orphanages and were vetted by the Adoption Society but Naomi was honest enough to realise that she could not bring up a child that was not hers. Alastair accepted Naomi's decision but the argument with Leslie Banks brought everything to a head. From that point on, Naomi was determined more than ever to give Alastair the child he so dearly wanted.

In addition to *Inspector Hornleigh on Holiday*, Alastair appeared in two other films released in 1939. 'I made a picture called *My Partner Mr. Davis* . . . It hasn't been shown yet, but I believe they are pulling it into shape now and it will probably be released soon'[32] – Alastair at his most diplomatic, for the film, retitled, *The Mysterious Mr Davis* and starring Guy Middleton and A. Bromley Davenport, was something of a mess. It was based on a novel by Jenaro Prieto, in which a man creates the new identity of a business partner in order to postpone the demands of creditors. The producers were aware of the deficiencies in the script the moment filming began and so were faced with an awkward dilemma – either continue the film in its present form and risk a disaster, or make some quick alterations and hope for the best. The result was a panic decision to introduce some manic comedy into the film and so, true to form, Alastair was quickly hired to provide the comic relief. This may help to explain the nonsensical manner in which his character, a lunatic called Theodore F. Wilcox, makes an appearance. As an interviewer reported, 'He [Alastair] still doesn't know of any legitimate excuse for the introduction of the character.'[33]

The second film of 1939 was a Gaumont-produced romantic musical entitled *Climbing High* staring Jessie Matthews and Michael Redgrave. Alastair played Max – a Marxist/Leninist committed to the revolution and in the process of writing his 'bible for the next generation'. The plot, simple but promising to begin with, slowly degenerates into an ending that can only be described as one of the most ludicrous ever written; all the major characters converge on the same mountain top in Switzerland and then begin acting as polar bears.

Both *Gangway* and *Sailing Along* had achieved little in terms of financial success at the box office and as a consequence, the budget for *Climbing High* was substantially reduced at the last moment. The enforced economies resulted in the removal from the film of five musical numbers, without, it seems, much in the way of screenplay rewriting. Filming had begun three months late, which meant that Sonny Hale's contract with the studio had expired and therefore a new director, Carol Reed, had to take over proceedings. Relationships on the set became more complicated when Jessie Matthews fell in love with Carol Reed and out of favour with Michael Redgrave. It was certainly a blessing for all concerned when shooting finished at the end of October 1938.

Alastair plays Max in his usual manic way, perhaps overly manic in this film if such a thing were possible, but at the same time, with a rich, confident bravado. The problem with Alastair's performance should be viewed in its chronological context. Alastair had been playing manic comedy roles on screen for several years and audiences were beginning to tire of the same old thing. The same could be said for Alastair as well. He was faced with the problem: how could he re-establish his credentials as a serious actor?

Predictably, the stark realism of the Second World War temporarily ended the comedy musical. Jessie Matthews, a stalwart of this genre, retired. Only George Formby continued with anything like success, albeit in a modified film format with catchy songs replacing dance routines. The War Ministry commandeered many of the British film studios, including Pinewood, and production became more oriented towards nationalistic propaganda films. Manic comedy was suddenly out of fashion. Not for the first time in his life, Alastair's future looked uncertain.

5

Cottage To Let

Our open house was a very selective one. We never invited anyone
we felt we ought to invite.

– Naomi Sim[1]

Soon after the outbreak of hostilities, Alastair joined ENSA
(Entertainments National Service Association). He was about to go
on tour when Naomi broke the news to him that she was pregnant.
Alastair was thrilled at the prospect of becoming a father but early
euphoria quickly turned to concern as Naomi once again began to
experience terrible stomach pains. One night he returned home to
find Naomi in absolute agony. Alastair and Norah quickly packed
a bag with some of Naomi's belongings and then took her to the
Samaritan Hospital in Marylebone Road. Naomi's ordeal in hospital
lasted several weeks by which time she was desperate to return home
to Wildwood Road. However, London was under the constant threat
of being gassed or bombed and nowhere in the city was safe anymore.

Norah, fearing that something terrible was going to happen, was
particularly insistent that they should move out of London, but like
most Londoners, Alastair and Naomi were adamant that they should
see out the war in their own house. Eventually, the precarious state of
Naomi's health began to sway Alastair towards Norah's point of view
and so when he finished his tour with ENSA he began looking for
safer and quieter accommodation in the countryside. In June 1940

Alastair and Naomi (who was by now six months pregnant) moved into their new house, Egypt Cottage, near Henley. Later that year their previous house in Wildwood Road was destroyed during a German bombing raid – Norah's sixth sense had saved them.

Having made something in the region of four or five Quota Quickies a year for the previous four years, Alastair now settled down to appearing in just one or two films a year – a rate that would continue throughout the next two decades. *Law and Disorder* (1940) an 'entertaining comedy-melodrama'[2] featured Barry Barnes as a young lawyer, Diana Churchill as his wife and Alastair as Samuel Blight, his senior partner. The film, 'thrilling, topical and fast-moving'[3] regaled the audience with a patriotic tale of saboteurs being brought to justice. More nationalistic fervour followed with the stage play *Cottage To Let*, which was billed as the first spy thriller of the war. Cast in the play as a young evacuee was a teenage actor by the name of George Cole.

George Cole was born on 22 April 1925 in South London. Two weeks later, his mother abandoned him. An orphanage beckoned but luckily he was adopted by the Cole family – George and Florence – and brought up as one of their own. Sadly, his adoptive father suffered from epileptic fits which was a result of being a gas victim in the Great War and consequently found it difficult to find employment. Instead, Florence provided for them by undertaking any menial job she could find. There were high expectations in the Cole family that the young George Cole would provide an income for them when he left school, but George had other plans.

Shortly after leaving school at the age of fourteen, George saw an advertisement in the local paper requesting boys for a touring musical called *White Horse Inn*. He passed an audition, and on the same day, packed his bags and left for Blackpool to join the cast as an understudy. George informed his adoptive parents of his decision by sending them the following telegram: 'Gone on stage, back soon.'[4]

George made his first stage appearance at the Grand Theatre in Blackpool in September 1939. The following spring, while still officially an understudy, he accompanied a friend to an audition for the plumb role of a child evacuee in a forthcoming play. Whether by intention or accident, George also managed to secure an audition, which he passed. As a result, it was George, rather than his friend, who was offered the role of Ronald in *Cottage To Let*.

Cottage To Let opened at the Prince of Wales Theatre[5], Birmingham, in June 1940. Of slight build for his age and with a curly mop of dark hair, George was perfect as the child evacuee, bringing to the role a vivaciousness that heartened the dispirited wartime audiences. *The Tatler & Bystander* described him as 'an astonishingly good young actor'.[6] In the cast, playing the character of Charles Dimble, was an actor who had made a huge impact on George when he first saw him on the big screen in *Alf's Button Afloat* (1938). Charles Dimble was played by Alastair Sim.

Cottage To Let, written by Geoffrey Kerr, centred around the enemy's attempt to kidnap John Barrington (Leslie Banks), an eminent scientist. In the spirit of a typical thriller, an assortment of characters act in a variety of suspicious ways until the young evacuee unmasks the real villain – the seemingly innocuous Charles Dimble.[7] *Cottage To Let* was a great success, running for 136 performances. At a time when Britain stood alone, the play captured the spirit of the tenacious British bulldog, as indeed did the small print in the theatre programme, which stated: 'If an air raid warning is received during the performance the audience will be informed from the stage. Those desiring to leave the theatre may do so, but the performance will continue.'[8]

Alastair became fond of the young cockney and saw great potential in his acting ability. It was the attention that a young George Cole yearned for and he was quick to accept the invitation from Alastair to stay for a weekend at Egypt Cottage. The visit was a success, and further invitations followed until George became a permanent 'just visiting' resident. Contrary to a popular myth the Sims never adopted George Cole, George simply moved in with them.

Alastair Sim was a benevolent teacher who drew pleasure from seeing his 'pupils' develop their skills. Alastair took George under his wing and first tried to develop his thinking processes. George recalls walking with Alastair and Naomi and them telling him to go and stand in front of a tree. When he had done so, they informed him that he was in fact standing at the back of the tree. This seems a rather tortuous way of educating a young man to think for himself, and one presumes George was somewhat relieved when Alastair suggested he teach him the rules of chess instead. This George failed at miserably, although he had some success at learning how to do *The Times* crossword.

Despite the difference in their age and experience, Alastair and George drew equal praise from reviewers for their performances in

Cottage To Let. It is possible that George was a natural talent and that Alastair simply gave him the support to allow this talent full expression. Following *Cottage To Let*, George continued to develop his stage and screen career during the war years. He appeared in the film *Those Kids from Town* (1941) and on stage in *Goodnight Children* as Percy King. He then toured in *Old Master* and finally played the role of Percy in *Flare Path*.

Nevertheless, for all his potential, there was one issue to which Naomi and Alastair frequently returned. As George Cole relates:

> It was quite simple really. He and his wife said, 'that voice is fine for an actor who wants to play nothing but cockney parts all his career'. The fact was, they just hated it.[9]

The voice always seemed to remain of cockney origin, even though he gamely attempted other accents, for instance that of a rather faltering Scottish dialect in *The Anatomist* (1960). Even so, although Alastair and Naomi despaired of his accent, it certainly helped George to create one of the most memorable characters of British television – Arthur Daley.

Moving into Egypt Cottage drew comments from some quarters concerning the appropriateness of the relationship between Alastair Sim and George Cole. Friends of Alastair dismissed such comments as nonsense. The suspicious nature of our society means that the public is inclined to arrive at conclusions based on either their own prejudices or the bias of the press, often without recourse to fact. Young actors who stayed over at Alastair's house, and who have contributed to this biography, comment only with gratitude for the generosity shown towards them by Alastair and Naomi.

George Cole was the first of an exclusive group of visitors to the Sim household. Naomi was quoted as saying:

> Our open house was a very selective one. We never invited anyone we felt we ought to invite. A long time ago we cut out all oughts. You have to be ruthless; but then that's the secret of a quiet life.[10]

– and Egypt Cottage provided just that. Rather than a cottage it was actually quite a large building comprising of three smaller cottages, dating from the sixteenth century, joined together. In the summer it was tranquil but during winter, life in the cottage could be an ordeal. There was no electricity – lighting was by old-fashioned oil lamps and candles – and the water was supplied from a well in the garden. Nevertheless, no matter what the season, Alastair and Naomi saw it as paradise – a retreat from the stresses of city life. It would remain their home until 1947.

★

The summer of 1940 was a time of great trepidation and fear for all in the British Isles. Hitler was massing his forces in France in order to strike at the solitary enemy. The air was filled with the sound of warplanes, but life had to go on, and indeed, be created. In August 1940, after much pain and suffering, Naomi gave birth, through a caesarean operation, to a baby girl. Alastair and Naomi named their daughter Merlith – Naomi's middle name.

Egypt Cottage was now full of the joys of a bustling young family. George had the responsibility of keeping the house lit and warm, and in return, Alastair coached him in the art of acting. Naomi was relieved that the ordeal of childbirth was over at long last and Merlith contributed the sounds of a healthy young baby girl. Soon, James Bridie would be a regular house guest and they would all act out the scenes of his latest play in the house or in the beautiful traditional cottage garden. Naomi saw this as the beginning of an idyllic time in their lives. Alastair had successfully established himself as a competent and charismatic film and theatre actor and had come a long way from 'teaching budding parsons how not to speak with a parson's voice.'[11] His star was in the ascendancy.

Cottage To Let ran very successfully throughout the country. Its heroic theme appealed to the anxious wartime audiences and gave them hope for the future. It was thus a natural choice to be turned into a film. Gainsborough Pictures took up the challenge and appointed Anthony Asquith as director. J.O.C. Orton and Anatole Grunwald produced the screenplay and a strong cast was assembled. In particular, Jeanne De Casalis was employed to play Mrs Barrington – a local eccentric, blessed with absent-mindedness, a heart of gold and the unique ability to muddle the simplest of words. Also in the cast was

John Mills, who now took on the role of the 'bad guy', Leslie Banks, who reprised his role as Mr Barrington (an eminent scientist working on a new bombsight) and George Cole as Ronald.

The film version of *Cottage To Let* was well received by the critics and provided Alastair with a high profile, non-manic role. George was especially praised: 'Mr George Cole plays the part of Ronald with a mature sense of character and the right amount of reserve.'[12] Although true to begin with, Ronald's over exuberance does become slightly irritating as the film progresses.

The comedy is perhaps dated – witness the following interplay between Alastair as Charles Dimble and Jeanne De Casalis as Mrs Barrington when Mrs Barrington confuses Charles Dimble for someone else:

> *Dimble*: Madam, you're mistaken. . . I'm Dimble.
> *Mrs Barrington*: Oh, are you? . . . I'm so sorry, but I can't do anything about it now.

Weak? – maybe, but this exchange cannot fail to get a laugh when spoken by these two charismatic screen eccentrics.

George also appeared as a schoolboy in a War Information Film produced at Marylebone Studios entitled: *Nero Save Fuel*. Alastair played the despot ruler and was chided by the schoolboy: 'Don't be like Nero – be a good citizen and *save fuel*'.

At Christmas, Alastair entered into the spirit of the season by playing the roles of Mr Darling and the evil Captain Hook in *Peter Pan*. Also in the cast were Zena Dare, Joan Greenwood and Russell Thorndike. In January, the production went on tour visiting the Kings Theatre in Glasgow, Edinburgh Theatre, the Opera House in Manchester, the Grand Theatre in Halifax and the New Theatre in Oxford. Also in the production was Larry Barnes, who played the Second Pirate and who was also employed as the theatre call boy. Larry Barnes recalls a slightly forgetful Alastair Sim:

> One night, just before Alastair was to go on stage, I noticed his back pocket empty – the pocket in which he should have had his Poison bottle. I quickly rushed back to his room and returned with the bottle in time for his entrance. On another night, Alastair turned to me

and said 'I've got my bottle'. To which I replied, 'Shouldn't you have your cloak on as well?' From that time onwards, I made sure he had all his props and was dressed properly each night.[13]

Larry Barnes, who was fifteen at the time of the production, had the opportunity to witness Alastair both on and off stage. Larry remembers seeing George Cole in Alastair's dressing room, but that room was very much Alastair's domain. Outsiders were not particularly welcomed, although not rudely turned away either. It was just that Alastair greatly valued his privacy. Larry Barnes says:

Alastair would never instigate a conversation outside the dressing room, but never brush anyone off. He was a warm and friendly person who would invite you into the hall but not show you the living room, unless he knew you very well.[14]

Alastair would make a regular point of inviting Larry Barnes into his dressing room on the Saturday matinee, second call, to give him a ten shilling note in appreciation for the work he did as call boy. An example of Alastair's generosity, or perhaps more appropriately, thoughtfulness, occurred during the second run of *Peter Pan* in 1942–43. On the first tour (1941–42), when the show had come to Blackpool, every one of the Lost Boys had been given a free pass to the Blackpool Leisure Beach. However, such passes were not forthcoming during the second tour of 1942–43. Still, when the second tour reached Blackpool, Alastair gave each of the young cast half a crown and said, 'Tomorrow morning, go and have some fun on the Blackpool Pleasure Beach.'[15] Geoffrey Jowitt, who played Nana in both tours, takes up the story:

We got to the pleasure beach early knowing that we had to be at the Blackpool Central train station at 2pm in order to make it back for the matinee. But the pleasure beach didn't open until 12 o'clock. We waited until 12 and then went inside. Well, half a crown in those days would buy five or so rides and it so happened that we were at the top of the Grand National (the big rollarcoaster ride at Blackpool) when I suddenly noticed a clock saying it was 1.45pm. I yelled to everyone and when the ride finished we ran to the tram and got to the station at 2.10pm, expecting the train to be gone – but the guard had held the train, since it was the only one of the day. Cecil King, the producer[16], was fuming when he found out and he started tearing into us but Alastair Sim came up and said 'Cecil, it's all my fault. These children all work very hard and I gave them half a crown each and told them to enjoy themselves at the pleasure beach. Any blame is on me – not them'. And with that, Cecil King lost all his fizz – although it was our fault for not looking at the clock. But he [Alastair Sim] took all the blame – that's the kind of man he was.[17]

One of Alastair's favourite anecdotes during his time as Hook concerns a comment he overheard by an elderly lady leaving the theatre after one of the performances. On being asked what she thought of the play, she turned to her friend and replied, 'A bit far-fetched.'

Alastair enjoyed the role of Hook so much that he would repeat it five times between 1941 and 1968. James Bridie referred to Sim's Hook when he wrote of Alastair's stage personality:

> It is an extraordinary personality – his stage one, I mean. It is friendly but a little macabre, like the nursery characters in which we took horrified delight when we were children. His best creations have very much of the quality of Cruikshank drawings. . . His Captain Hook and his Doctor Knox might have walked straight out of the pages of that extraordinary artist.[18]

Cottage To Let had been a key film for Alastair since it marked the beginning of a transitional period in his acting career. The manic comedy roles that he had made his own had now seen their day along with those of the light British song and dance musical. The war had brought a harsh reality to everyday life, and although audiences would laugh again in the future, now was a time for solemn reflection. This was demonstrated in the costumed melodramas that began to fill the screens. Alastair had to face a stark choice: evolve his acting style or fade into pre-war obscurity.

The decision to make changes was an easy one. The problem was that to be successful, he needed material of a high quality that also matched his style and taste. Yet again, fate would play its part in deciding Alastair's future.

6

Alastair Sim and James Bridie

A pleasant maniac called Alastair Sim.

– James Bridie in a letter to a friend describing his first impressions on
meeting Alastair Sim.[1]

The meeting between Alastair Sim and the playwright James Bridie
at the Malvern Festival in 1939 began a special friendship that would
last until Bridie's death in 1951. They both shared similar views on
life, typifying the 'Scot at his best, independent in his thinking, concerned with moral values rather than class prejudices, resilient rather
than pessimistic.'[2] Bridie wrote:

> The Scot . . . has always taken an almost morbid delight in oddities
> of mind and behaviour. . . The Scot's conversation is full of thowless,
> bloutering nyaffs; of feckless, donnart, doited, havering gowks; of daft,
> glaikit, foutering tawpies; of snuitit generals.[3]

Words no doubt that would have delighted an elocution lecturer
from Edinburgh, and words that found an opportunity for expression in many of Bridie's plays – much to the consternation of the
English audiences. But it was more than just the words. Alastair, who
had spent the past couple of years in one manic comedy role after
another, was attracted by the intellectual rigour of the subject matter
contained within Bridie's works. They offered him the opportunity

to return to the highbrow and thus to refocus his energy on achieving his original goal of becoming a West End director. It also helped of course that Bridie managed to create lead characters in his plays which conformed so exactly to Alastair's personality. As Anthony Cookman wrote in *The Tatler & Bystander*:

> So completely does Mr Alastair Sim identify himself with the leading parts in Mr Bridie's plays that the actor must sometimes wonder if he is not a figment of the author's imagination. On the other hand, Mr Bridie's leading parts have a way of conforming so exactly to the personality of Mr Alastair Sim that the author also may wonder if his imagination is wholly his own.[4]

No one would doubt that James Bridie's imagination was 'wholly his own' but as the *Glasgow Herald* remarked:

> In Mr Sim the enchanter [James Bridie] has a partner more than adequate, a kind of second self that can oversee the stuff and then act it, as if he were the writer's reflection.[5]

Although both men were similar in many ways, ('no man respected privacy more than Bridie'[6]), they had completely different attitudes towards the structure of a play. Alastair was a firm believer in a play having form, whereas Bridie preferred a more *laissez-faire* approach. To Bridie, a play presented a wonderful opportunity for his characters to exchange pithy dialogue on a subject matter of his interest. The final curtain was simply a means by which to announce that the dialogue was over. Alastair was more traditional in his views, seeing the play as a framework within which characters could interact while exploring interesting themes. To Alastair, the final curtain brought the proceedings to a meaningful conclusion. Bridie himself admitted:

> Mr Bridie's critics often charge Mr Bridie with being unable to finish a play. This is a lying charge. Mr Bridie finishes most of his plays: but in his own way, not in theirs.[7]

That was not good enough for Alastair. The effect of this impasse was a constant mental jousting between the two men over the structure of the play; each sure of his ground, each steadfast in his views, each reluctant to compromise. Yet, through this process they forged not only the great Bridie plays of the 1940s, but also a deep friendship and mutual respect. James Bridie described his friend Alastair thus:

> He is a very happy man. He has a wife and daughter who under-stand him and likes playing games of skill like cribbage and poker and games of chance like chess and lawn tennis. He drinks neither beer nor spirits, but he likes a glass of burgundy. He is companionable and, at times, witty.[8]

★

The year 1942 was an important one for the Scottish theatre. James Bridie had long lamented both the paucity of the Scottish theatres and also their lack of expertise in managing their financial affairs. For example, in 1939, the 'Perth Repertory theatre was the only fully professional theatre of native enterprise in Scotland'[9] and the Glasgow Unity theatre had 'scatterbrained finance.'[10] As Bridie's stature grew (he was asked to be the first Chairman of the Scottish Committee of the Council for the Encouragement of the Music and Arts[11]), so did his vociferous support for a national theatre. Bridie gradually won over the detractors and in 1942, and with a budget of only £1,500, plans were put in place to launch a Scottish national theatre in either Edinburgh or Glasgow – although the 'available halls in both cities were inconvenient, uncomfortable and drab.'[12]

The Athenaeum[13], which is in the centre of Glasgow, was eventually selected as the venue for the newly formed national theatre (which became known as the Glasgow Citizens' Theatre, of which James Bridie was the chairman). As with any new venture, it had a nervous beginning: 'There were the wartime difficulties, the shortages of materials and labour . . . the panic of the players when they found themselves facing an inexperienced management and insufficient rehearsal time.'[14] Three years later, after the Bridie-Sim partnership had become a huge success, Alastair was calling for a Scottish equivalent of the Old Vic.

The first production at the newly formed national theatre was James Bridie's *Holy Isle* in which Alastair performed in addition to directing proceedings. *Holy Isle* tells of four diverse members of a civilised society – a businessman, a friar, a queen and a spirited young man – who find themselves castaways on an inhabited primitive island. The Bridie invention is that although they attempt to promote the benefits of their modern values, they are instead won over by the islanders' peaceful and relaxed way of life. *Holy Isle* suffers from the criticism usually aimed at Bridie's work: a good idea that fails to make it to its natural conclusion. As one critic wrote: '. . . if it had been treated with the firm satirical touch that Bridie employs so successfully in the first half of the play all the way through, we should have had a wonderful play, but somehow in the middle Bridie yawns and grins and a certain silliness enters.'[15] In general, the reviews were mixed, with some finding it 'delectable and enlightening'[16] while others, 'music-hall farce'.[17]

Regardless of the success of the play, *Holy Isle* presented another opportunity for Alastair and Bridie to work together and thereby become even better acquainted with each other's strengths and weaknesses. In that context, *What Say They* and *Holy Isle* could be seen as the prelude to the great works of Bridie and Sim that would emerge over the following eight years, beginning with *A Chink in the Blackout* which was subsequently renamed *Mr Bolfry*.

The 1943 production of *Mr Bolfry* begins with Alastair as Mr McCrimmon, a serious-minded West Highland Presbyterian minister, lecturing his niece and two young army men billeted at his house, on the meaning of the Sabbath. The youngsters retaliate against this dry preaching by holding a séance, and to their surprise, they conjure up the devil. However, instead of appearing as a monstrous incarnation of all things evil, the devil is rather a conventional, politely mannered clergyman by the name of Mr Bolfry. The minister and the devil engage in a battle of wits until it slowly dawns on them that they are mutually dependent on each other to justify their own existence. As one critic wrote: 'To prove that the Devil is essential to the Divine purpose and have the Devil himself to do the proving is a typical Bridie thrust.'[18]

Inevitably, the protagonists fall out as their diverse views on morality lead to physical confrontation which occurs off stage. Mr McCrimmon triumphs over the devil, but returns to the parlour in a more thoughtful and reflective mood, less arrogant in his high-held views. The final scene produces some evidence that Mr Bolfry was a supernatural force when his umbrella suddenly rises up of its own accord and walks off stage.

In her book on James Bridie, Winifred Bannister writes: 'Mr Sim's association with James Bridie in *Mr Bolfry* amounted to collaboration. . .'[19] James Bridie, as was his tendency, was completely enveloped in the ideological and philosophical debate that makes up the central theme of the play: Good *and* Evil agreeing that the battle is not so much against one another, but against the indifferent attitude of the young. Such was Bridie's focus on this issue that he gave scant attention to the play's ending. It seemed likely to Alastair that *Mr Bolfry* was to succumb to the usual criticism labelled at Bridie – his inability to draw a promising theme to a structured close.

Bridie's original ending had Mr Bolfry being escorted to an asylum by two white-coated male nurses. Neither Alastair nor Naomi were particularly enthused with this finale since to their mind it left no doubt that Mr Bolfry was a madman and therefore removed the thought-provoking premise that he could be the devil. As a result, a great deal of the play's mysticism and meaning was then lost. Since Alastair was able 'to nudge him [Bridie] now and again with a reminder that some small attention must be paid to the thing as a play'[20] he suggested an idea that both he and Naomi had come up with – the idea of the 'walking umbrella'. Thus in a jocular way, the play was brought to a natural conclusion with an element of the supernatural to leave the audience guessing.

For the academic, John Low (1980) summarises the play as: '. . .a very down-to-earth naturalistic opening to a highly meta-physical timeless centre and back to an uncertain naturalism disturbed by the final fling of the supernatural at the end.'[21] A metaphysical interpretation of the play suggests that Mr Bolfry is the alter ego of Mr McCrimmon. Those ardent supporters of such an intriguing possibility identify the following speech by Mr McCrimmon as conclusive proof: 'If you are, as I think you are, a bad dream and the voice of my own heart speaking evil, I will tear you from my breast if I die for it.'[22] The play is therefore about Mr McCrimmon's battle with the demons within his heart and soul. The umbrella-walking scene is then the metaphysical representation of the devil being exorcised from his soul, rather than the manifestation of the devil's will. James Bridie would have loved such a debate, but what of the audience?

> The audience? It sat rapt and spell-bound as though the theatre were the Royalty, the date 1892, and the occasion Mr Shaw's first play.[23]

Mr Bolfry opened on 3 August 1943 at the Westminster Theatre. Reviews at the time reported: 'James Bridie's latest work is certain to rank as one of the most brilliant plays of the war years.'[24] 'Is the talk good?' asked one reviewer – replying '. . . good enough to make the amateur philosopher inside each of us want to answer back'[25], although other critics described the 'talk' as 'tedious argumentation.'[26] Alastair received praise for his performance:

> Mr Alastair Sim is enabled to draw a richly ironic portrait of a self-confident dogmatist on the edge of what promises to be a most diverting humiliation.[27]

Stage performances during the war years were apt to have their unintentional off-stage effects. John Betjeman recalled in a letter a visit to see *Mr Bolfry* and a bomb falling nearby to the theatre just at the moment when the devil appears. One can only guess what impact this would have had on a naturally nervous audience.

In 1944 Alastair returned to the big screen in an underrated wartime melodrama called *Waterloo Road* (1944). Sidney Gilliat who directed and wrote the screenplay from a story by Val Valentine, cast Alastair as Dr Montgomery – a sympathetic Scottish doctor living in the East End during the blitz. In the ending, the underdog, Jim Colter (John Mills) determinedly wins back his wife Tillie Colter (Joy Shelton), from the conscription dodger Ted Purvis (Stewart Granger). This film no doubt found sympathy with cinemagoers at the time but today seems slightly contrived, although there are plenty of delightful vignettes to keep a modern day audience interested. Sidney Gilliat wrote of Alastair's performance in *Waterloo Road*:

> The part, I think, required a drier, quicker actor and perhaps because it was straight, though quirky, Sim seemed to me too heavy and slow, sometimes deadly slow (though he said 'why do you want me to gabble?').[28]

It is true that Alastair's performance is slow in comparison with the sometimes frenetic pace of the film but equally there is something quite appealing in this character who offers wisdom in an otherwise mad, unfair world. Perhaps more importantly, Dr Montgomery was another role that contributed to Alastair's transition from manic comedian to a more thoughtful actor.

In October of 1944, Alastair teamed up with Bridie again in *It Depends What You Mean*. The play was presented in association with Merlith Productions Ltd – Alastair's own production company. James Bridie wrote that Alastair:

> is one of the best producers in London and the last of the actor-manager-producers of the Irving school. The comparison with Irving is not an idle one. He has much of the impishness, the almost arrogant self-confidence and the artistry of the old man.[29]

It Depends What You Mean started with a short tour in Glasgow, and then transferred to the Westminster Theatre where it ran very successfully for 189 performances. The main characters in the play are members of a 'Brains Trust' – a panel of 'experts' – or more accurately, local dignitaries, who attempt to answer questions posed to them by the general public on the burning issues of the day. The slightly tedious and static nature of this question-and-answer session is enlivened considerably when a member of the audience asks: 'Is marriage a good idea?'. Bridie then weaves his magic as the answers from the panel members bring to the surface weaknesses in their own relationships, and as a consequence, the intended bonhomie of the event rapidly degenerates into accusation and counter-accusation.

The early reviews of the play did not appear to bode well for the future. *The Times* reported:

> Mr Bridie's discussion of marriage is like a part of the brook which goes on forever. . . Amusing, wise, and irritating, it is characteristic but not first rate Bridie. There is not a great deal of scope for acting, though Mr Alastair Sim makes a character of the padre, who takes refuge from reality in an arch simper or a portentous frown.[30]

The following review from the *Daily Mail* was simpler and more in accordance with the play's longevity:'Not for a long time have I heard such laughter in a theatre.'[31] Indeed, the success of the play attracted more than the usual media attention to the work of James Bridie. A full page picture review appeared in the *Picture Post* on 4 November 1944 celebrating an evening in which James Bridie attended the performance and gave a curtain speech to the audience.

In the autumn of 1945 Alastair continued his association with Bridie in a production entitled *The Forrigan Reel*. Act 1 scene 1 of the play occurs outside a highland bothy, perhaps reminding Alastair of his younger days spent wandering the highlands. *The Forrigan Reel* was set in 1740 and followed the exploits of a group of English men and women travelling into the highlands of Scotland in the hope of discovering a cure for their various ailments. It combined comedy – Mrs Grant of Forrigan thinks she is a clock, which doesn't immediately spring to mind as a rich source of humour – with song and dance, in a light-hearted piece that championed a simple theme: the power to heal through dance. The initial run of this 'typical Bridie, both in its flash of charm and its failure to sustain the flash and make a steady fire of it'[32] took place at the Athenaeum in Edinburgh and was produced by the Citizens' Theatre.

The Forrigan Reel met with some early success in Scotland and so the production was transferred to London. Alastair spent nine months searching for a suitable venue, somewhere small and intimate, but without success. In the end, the production went ahead at the Sadler's Wells (the only alternative was the Old Vic). Unfortunately, the size of the Sadler's Wells proved to be its undoing. As Ivor Brown wrote in the *Observer*: 'This mixture of melody and warlocks, periwigs, and tartans, needs a smaller, cosier home.'[33]

Alastair also felt that *The Forrigan Reel* should have been more anglicised. Bridie, of course, would have none of that although a letter dated 4 July 1945 from Bridie to Sim shows how Bridie respected Alastair's suggestions of amendments and concerns: 'I will consider very carefully your suggestions for the new shape of the scene. . .'[34] For once though Bridie stuck rigidly with his dialogue and as a result, the London run was short-lived.

There were in fact two versions of *The Forrigan Reel*. The original version, the one which was received so warmly in Scotland and

Ireland, was based on a Highland tale and had a dynamic Scottish lead (Donald MacAlpin). The language and mannerisms appealed to the Scottish and Irish audiences. The version of *The Forrigan Reel* that failed in London was known as *A Ballad Opera* and had been rewritten by Bridie with the intention of introducing an element of revue into the performance. Ivor Brown made an insightful comment when he wrote:

> ... and Mr Alistair Sim [*sic*], surrounding his bald dome with flaming whiskers, as it were turnip with carrots, goes hirpling and leering and tippling through it all with a proper realisation that his part can be made to seem a great deal better than it really is.[35]

Alastair had acquired a confidence and self-belief that translated into a gregarious and dominant stage personality. Even the most insouciant business could convey a deeper, usually more humorous, interpretation. His time on stage was often the highlight of the performance and in that of *The Forrigan Reel*, *The Sunday Times* made reference to 'Mr Alastair Sim's remarkable bagpipe dance'.[36] Naomi Sim remarked in *Dance and Skylark* that for all its perceived faults by the London critics, Alastair remembered *The Forrigan Reel* with great fondness. Indeed, Alastair would later name his house in Nettlebed 'Forrigan'.

★

On 9 April 1946 there was an announcement in the newspapers that Mr J.A. Rank had once again taken control of Pinewood Film Studios following the de-requisition order by the Government. It was also announced that on Saturday, work was to begin on two new British films. One of these was *Great Expectations*, featuring an all-star cast including John Mills and Valerie Hobson. The other film was slightly more low key – a murder mystery with a modest budget described as a 'hospital story'.[37]

Getting the right person to play the role of the detective in the hospital murder mystery, Inspector Cockrill, was important since the character was written as a quirky, intelligent individual, full of self-belief but flawed. Sidney Gilliat and Claude Guerney, who between them wrote the screenplay, had just one person in mind to play the idiosyncratic Inspector. The script complete, Launder and Gilliat formally offered the role to – Robert Morley.

Gilliat and Guerney felt that Morley had the poise, stature, and just the right amount of eccentricity to carry off the whimsical, thoughtful detective. Robert Morley read the script and loved the part of Inspector Cockrill. He would have accepted the role immediately were it not for the fact that he was currently under contract. This meant he would only become available several months into the planned production schedule. It was impossible to alter the scheduling of the film and so the producers had to search again for their detective. The next person Sidney Gilliat approached was Alastair Sim, 'who promptly telephoned to ask if I [Sidney Gilliat] was mad. I convinced him fairly easily and the only alteration made in the script was to remove a reference to Cockrill's avoirdupois.'[38] And so with the Inspector in place, cameras began to roll on a film that ranks as one of Alastair's best: *Green For Danger*.

7

Green For Danger

Sound Effects: The tapping of a typewriter.
Voiceover: Alastair Sim as Inspector Cockrill.

To: The Assistant Commissioner of the Police, Scotland Yard...

Sir,
The amazing events, which I am reporting, may be said to have begun on the evening of August 17th 1944.
A postman was cycling up Herons Hill on his way to deliver mail at the Hospital. His name was Joseph Higgins. I begin with him because he was the first to die...

– Green For Danger (1946)

Green For Danger (1946) is a skilfully crafted murder mystery that comprises a first rate plot, actors at the top of their form, some occasional light comedy relief, and at times a real sense of menace. The action takes place in the claustrophobic confines of a manor house requisitioned as a Second World War military hospital. The death on the operating table of postman Joseph Higgins (Moore Marriott) is initially treated as an accident until Sister Bates (Judy Campbell) ill-advisedly announces to all and sundry: 'I know who did it!'. Rather predictably a second murder follows, captured by a fine piece of cinematography under the stewardship of Wilkie Cooper.

The murderer, dressed in an operating gown, their face hidden by a mask, stands in a doorway, a long sharp blade at their side. Billowing wind forces the doors to swing to and fro allowing moonlight to intermittently illuminate the spectacle – a beautifully shot, macabre scene, executed under the expert supervision of Cooper who was employed by Hitchcock on several of his films.

The second murder brings the egotistical Inspector Cockrill (Alastair Sim) to the hospital. Sidney Gilliat: 'It is still my own favourite Sim role and of course gained enormously from his rather startlingly late entrance into the story (though we made Sim the first person narrator from the beginning).'[1] Cockrill interviews the suspects – Leo Genn and Trevor Howard playing two doctors fighting over the attentions of Nurse 'Freddie' Linley (Sally Gray) – with unabashed glee at the opportunity it affords him to display his superior intellect. The film's finale takes place in the same operating theatre in which Joseph Higgins lost his life as the circumstances of the first murder are re-enacted in the denouement style of the Golden Age.

Modern day audiences brought up on realistic hospital melo-dramas may find the lack of sophisticated technology in *Green For Danger* mildly amusing. Yet the simplicity of the scenes allows us to instead focus on the emotions of the characters. The inflating and deflating rubber bag (the anaesthetists' means of monitoring the breathing of the patient) combined with close-up facial shots of the surgeons and nurses compels the viewer to become immersed in the oppressive operating room nightmare.

Sidney Gilliat had gone to great lengths to research the difficul-ties, stresses and strains that would have been experienced by wartime hospital staff as well as the surgical procedures that were mentioned in the script. By doing so, he made sure the operating scenes were as authentic a recreation of wartime conditions as possible. Gilliat even employed a theatre sister to check that the instruments and equipment were correctly set out and used appropriately during filming. Trevor Howard, who plays an anaesthetist in the film, prepared for his scenes by watching real anaesthetists at work. Painstaking attention was also paid to the design of the sets so that the walls could be wheeled to one side to allow cameras to film from any angle. In particular, the hospital dance set was a beautiful recreation of the main hall of a manor house and was described by Gilliat as 'a triumph by the art department'.[2]

Green For Danger is based on the novel of the same title written by Christianna Brand. In many respects the film remains true to the book, such as the form of the various murders and the characterisation of the leading roles; a significant exception is Inspector Cockrill. Christianna Brand's version of the Inspector is undeveloped in the book although he does appear testy and arrogant at times. She describes his first visit to the hospital:

> Inspector Cockrill made a tour of the hospital, popping his head into wards and operating theatres in his darting, bird-like way; small and brown and irascible, his shabby old felt hat crammed sideways on his head in the familiar, Napoleonic fashion. . .[3]

– not quite the appearance and mannerisms of the tall, authoritative and mischievous figure of Alastair Sim. Furthermore, the astute and witty dialogue of Inspector Cockrill in the film does not appear in the book. This is a great tribute to the screenwriting skills of Gilliat and Guerney. As Sidney Gilliat recalled:

> In *Green For Danger* (the novel), the part of Inspector Cockrill was pretty dull and characterless and as the story itself was somewhat lightweight, we thought that Cockrill must be beefed up.[4]

Inspector Cockrill is one of Alastair's finest creations. Many will argue that *Scrooge* (1951) is his best screen performance and Chichester the setting for his best stage performances, but in *Green For Danger* Alastair manages to produce a truly enigmatic character. Cockrill is an arrogant man, assured of his own abilities, and yet privately, he is vulnerable and insecure. An example of how Alastair conveys these characteristics is the delightful, purely visual sequence of Cockrill in bed at night reading a crime novel. Cockrill's demeanour takes on a cocky confidence as he thinks he has identified the murderer from just the opening pages. So convinced is he of his infallibility that he decides to skip the rest of the book by turning to the denouement on the last page. Disbelief slowly envelops his whole frame as he discovers that his deduction was incorrect. A wonderful bit of business by Alastair.

Green For Danger was released in 1946 but as Sidney Gilliat recalls 'to the coolness of our colleagues and of the Rank Organisation, in spite of which it was quite a hit[5] and had to be re-booked.'[6] A good point made in the review below is that the audience does not have to engage in the 'whodunnit' element in order to enjoy the film:

> It is possible not to care in the least who murdered the village post-man in a hospital operating theatre after a V1 incident and to give up early the game of eliminating one by one the five or six nurses and doctors who are the suspects and yet to be immensely entertained by all that is said and done on the screen. Mr Alastair Sim as a detective with a rich relish for absurdity whether in himself or in other people, conducts the investigations, and in his hands detection becomes a delicious demonstration of the subtler acts of showmanship.[7]

The film has justifiably become regarded as a classic of the comedy/thriller genre. The V1 rockets date the film precisely; their threatening off-screen presence complementing the eerie unseen menace of the murderer. The drone of the doodlebug engine can be heard on several occasions, sounding similar to a motorbike in one instance, which provides Alastair with an opportunity to display his physical comic genius. There is a palpable moment of heightened tension when the rocket fuel runs out and the engine stops, until the inevitable climatic crash and wanton destruction.

Alastair was in good spirits on the film set. As one of the special effects men recalls:

> During the filming of *Green For Danger*, one scene required Cockrill to hammer on an operating theatre door, as he believed one of the characters was about to kill another. The scene called for him to smash one of the round panes of glass in the theatre doors, and [I] had made a fake pane, which would break easily upon impact. The cameras started rolling, and Sim duly hammered on the door . . . and hammered . . . and hammered; unfortunately it was the wrong pane of glass and refused to break! At this point [I], who had chatted with Sim on many occasions, forgot he was on set and shouted out 'you bloody idiot!' Filming halted, and everyone, including Sim, fell about laughing; many actors would have been aloof, but Sim was one of the few who treated everyone as an equal, and didn't have airs and graces.[8]

Judy Campbell, who played Sister Marion Bates, remembers:

> We took a very long time shooting the scene where I run through
> the hospital grounds in panic; nowadays one would do the scene in
> an actual park, but in those days everything was built in the studio –
> trees, river, the lot [and] in perspective with the hedges and shrubs
> getting smaller towards the edges of the set which meant that some-
> times I had to run with bent knees or run on the spot. On the second
> day, I had to burst out from behind a hedge, the scene took a long
> time to rehearse and we'd already had several takes when Alastair
> arrived. He wasn't in the scene but had come onto the set to see how
> we were doing. I confided to him that I was very anxious to get it
> right next time and feeling nervous. 'Oh don't worry' he said, 'Let's
> give the boys a laugh. I'll go instead of you.' I was appalled! 'You can't'
> I said, 'Everyone will be furious'. But he was determined, and on the
> call of 'Action', he strolled out with his hat and his umbrella and he
> was quite right, everybody laughed, and the tension was eased.[9]

★

Low temperatures combined with heavy snow meant that for many
parts of the UK, February 1947 was one of the coldest months on
record. The film critics that trudged their weary way through snow-
blocked streets and risked icy pavements to see a preview of Alastair's
next film were dispirited not only by the weather but also, like
everyone else in the country, by the austerity of post-war Britain.
Rationing continued, much to the annoyance of a population who
felt they had suffered enough already, and many longed to break free
from the relentless and suffocating bureaucracy. Cinemas, one of the
few places where you could escape from the mundane, at least for
an hour or two, were not helping the cause. Screenings still consisted
of staple wartime propaganda films, interspersed with uninspiring
costume dramas.

The critics took their seats, the lights dimmed, the cinema fell
into a hush and the opening credits of this new film hit the screen.
It didn't take long for them to realise that *Hue and Cry*, a 'joyous
romp among the blitzed sites of London'[10], was of a different breed
to that which they had become accustomed to seeing. This was a

finely judged adventure film with an injection of subtle, yet in places pleasingly eccentric, comedy. This was the first ever Ealing Comedy.

Hue and Cry began in the mind of the British director Henry Cornelius. Cornelius came to 'visualise a situation in which ... hundreds of boys took virtual possession of London for a few glorious hours.'[11] The writer T.E.B. Clarke was given the problem of transferring this visualisation into a workable screenplay. Clarke chose the central characters to be streetwise London kids who crack a code which appears in a weekly comic, revealing the plans of a criminal gang. In frustration at no one believing them they turn for help to the comic's creator Felix H. Wilkinson (Alastair Sim), although for all they know, he may be the dangerous mastermind behind the gang.

Alastair loved the idea of the young using their wits to defeat the scheming activities of nefarious adults. His character in the film is clearly an eccentric, but more refined and tempered than those he played in his manic comedy days. The critics however were still to be convinced: 'Alastair Sim ... tends to overdraw the eccentricity of the character but he has his big moments.'[12] The scene where the children meet with Felix H. Wilkinson for the first time is memorable for its stylish cinematography and air of mystery and danger – especially when Wilkinson walks into the room bearing a tray of drinks that surely must be laced with some sort of devilish poison.

Captain Boycott[13] was Alastair's second film release of 1947. This Launder and Gilliat production, set in nineteenth-century Ireland, told of the uprising of Irish potato farmers against their English landowner, Captain Boycott (Cecil Parker). It is a well-paced film although some of the characters, especially the English, appear as caricatures. Alastair plays a Roman Catholic priest, Father McKeogh (with an Irish cadence to his Scottish accent), in a calm and confident manner that contrasts agreeably with the anarchy of the characters around him. Father McKeogh's intended rousing speech at the end of the film, where he advises his flock in future to boycott anyone who means them harm, appears rather lame and dated on today's viewing.

Captain Boycott is another important film during this transitional phase in Alastair's career. Although rather slight compared with other films in which he appeared, Alastair's role is a purely straight one. This did not go down well with the cinema audiences. As Sidney Gilliat recalls:

On the whole, that bit of casting was an error. The audience wanted to laugh at Sim and was puzzled that they could not – except when he wore a high hat (when they never stopped). Also, he used too much of what I used to call (to his annoyance) his *Vox Humana* for my taste.[14]

Although Gilliat does not go on to explain exactly what he means by this reference to '*Vox Humana*', it can be inferred that Alastair's propensity to express his concerns for humanity in general did not always meet with universal acceptance.

★

Alastair and Naomi began house hunting once again but could not find anything they liked. Eventually they decided on buying a plot of woodland in Nettlebed, Henley, with the idea of having a house built on the land to their own specification. Naomi: 'It's a mixed wood with a great variety of trees, and has largely been untended for years, so there is a fair amount of undergrowth. This makes a perfect place for wild things to live.'[15] An architect was employed and sketches and plans were drawn up, although compromises had to be made in order to meet restrictions in force at the time. In due time, their house was built and they named it 'Forrigan' – after James Bridie's play *The Forrigan Reel*.

They moved into their new home in June 1947. Alastair, a keen tennis player, had a tennis court set aside in the grounds, as well as a makeshift football pitch and an overflow guest house. Alastair was also a fan of all games of skill and chance and so converted one of Forrigan's rooms into a games room. Another room was set aside as a rehearsal room for trying out new plays. Over time, the area around the house changed: 'We cut a glade in front of our house and edged it with rhododendrons and laurels. It runs straight up into the wood and at the top is a large cherry tree with a lot of undergrowth round the base.'[16] Alastair and Naomi loved dogs and so Forrigan also became a home to several young puppies.

This all sounds rather idyllic – too idyllic in fact. Alastair, for all his generosity of spirit, could also be frugal. One of Alastair's friends nicknamed the house 'Bleak House' and described the inside as being rather spartan and not at all a comfortable house in which to live. There was also the problem of Norah. Naomi had matured into a mother, wife and home maker – it was time for her to be free of her mother's reins.

Norah's influence on Alastair and Naomi had already begun to diminish when the plans for Forrigan had been drawn up. Naomi had insisted this time that she did not want the live-in help that had been practically imposed on them previously by Norah's desire for expansive accommodation. The inevitable schism came and Norah, with much ill feeling, moved away to Lymington.[17]

The move into Forrigan coincided with the final preparation for James Bridie's latest play: 'The partnership of Scotland's leading actors has produced a riotous comedy-thriller. . . *Dr Angelus*.'[18] The two major leads were to be played by Alastair and George, but George had not yet finished his RAF duties in Germany. Alastair, in his role as producer, delayed the production and waited for George to return. *Dr Angelus* eventually opened on 23 June 1947 in Alastair's home town, where 'The Edinburgh audience, usually a cautious sipper of the Bridie wit, received *Dr Angelus* with spontaneous enthusiasm.'[19]

Dr Angelus is a parody of a thriller based on the real-life case of Dr E. Pritchard[20] – an infamous Glasgow doctor who, in 1865, was found guilty of poisoning his wife and mother-in-law. Bridie adapted the case into a play, changing the setting to 1919 and giving greater emphasis to the intention of the doctor to collect on the life policies of his victims once they were dead.[21] The signature of the younger doctor[22] (George Cole) on the death certificate is crucial to Dr Angelus (Alastair Sim) successfully claiming the insurance money. As *The Stage* commented so perceptively at the time:

> His [Dr Angelus's] young, much-badgered assistant, who has the death certificate to sign, is played so well by George Cole that I can see agents in the future planning for the Sim-Cole team as a gilt-edged bet.[23]

Dr Angelus is essentially a battle between good and evil, a theme which appealed to James Bridie, as indeed did the performance by Alastair. Winifred Banister wrote:

I sat near Bridie at the first night of the play's appearance in Glasgow, and oh, how he – Bridie – had put in everything he knew of character-drawing – and of Alastair Sim! I felt, as I heard the dry chuckles which meant that Bridie was laughing uproariously inside himself, that I was getting a double dose of enjoyment.[24]

Bridie would no doubt have delighted in the irony of the real case where the junior doctor allegedly professed knowledge of the crimes but a reluctance to report them for fear of being thought unprofessional. The production by Alastair went well and the reviews of *Dr Angelus* were generally excellent. Richard Clowes in *The Sunday Times* described the play as 'brilliant, absorbing, perverse and uncomfortable. . .'[25] and went on to add:

Perhaps the fact that Mr Alastair Sim plays the chief part and directed the piece has something to do with the contradictory emotions it arouses. Mr Sim is an accomplished and resourceful comedian who never permits us to take his villain seriously for long.[26]

The same reviewer also drew attention to a weakness in Alastair's acting style that would gradually undermine his performances for the rest of his career:

Mr Sim's pre-occupation with the, for him, easy scoring of comedy points naturally spoils the dramatic effect of some of the other performances. One cannot believe, for instance in Mr George Cole's young doctor being taken in so completely by his grotesque and posturing partner.[27]

There were now some delightfully poetic descriptions of Alastair appearing in reviews of the time:

The lugubrious, fish-like eyes, the pontifical, unctuous dignity laced with a little querulousness, the soupy voice and the immense command over the tricks of diction and gesture, all make Mr Sim's bravura performance the excuse for a play that says little, wittily enough, but for rather too long.[28]

And:

> Mr Sim's Dr Angelus is six smooth feet of unction, fun, hypocrisy,
> ingratiation, duplicity, authority, sentimentality and sententiousness.
> His leers are as ready as his tears. His smile glavers and gloats.[29]

Dr Angelus transferred to the Phoenix Theatre, London, in July 1947,
where it ran successfully for SIX months – the maximum time Alastair
was prepared to commit to a play. The production made the news, in
a sinister fashion, when a newspaper reported that Mr Fred Stubbing,
the property master, had examined the medicine cabinet used in the
play only to discover that it contained phials of strychnine, cocaine,
insulin, apomorphine and ephedrine. The same cabinet had travelled with the players as they toured Scotland but no one had ever
suspected that it contained real poisons. The story behind the news
was that Betty Marsden (who was appearing in the play as a young
patient) was curious as to the actual contents of the phials. Since she
was married to a doctor, she contacted her husband and persuaded
him to have them sent to the Home Office for examination. It was
then that the ghastly truth came out.

The cabinet, which formed an essential prop for the play, had been
hired from a business dealing in second-hand medical artefacts. They
were able to trace its history back to 1770 but could offer no explanation as to how the poisons had come to be in the cabinet. Today,
this may appear to have been nothing more than a publicity stunt,
but *Dr Angelus* had already established its credentials at the time of
the newspaper article and would run for a total of 195 performances
closing on the 24 January 1948. Indeed, such was its success, that the
BBC filmed a studio production of *Dr Angelus*. Unfortunately no
records exist in the BBC archive about the production.

Larry Barnes[30] remembers seeing a performance of *Dr Angelus*
which drew a tremendous laugh one evening. Alastair as Dr Angelus
was doing a great piece of business with a pipe – dismantling it and
cleaning it thoroughly. Every now and then he would blow down
the pipe just to make sure it was clear. One evening, after Alastair
had gone through his business of reassembling the pipe, he blew
down the stem just as a Ferry outside of the theatre blew its hooter.
The sound effect brought the house down as they say.

★

There can be no doubt that the British film industry is in the throes of a tremendous crisis.[31]

In 1948, a new Cinematograph Film Act was passed which stipulated that British cinemas had to screen at least forty-five per cent of British films as first features and twenty-five per cent as supporting films. It was yet another desperate move by the government and the British film industry to protect the domestic market from the Hollywood studios. Quantity could not compete with quality and most observers realised that the discerning British cinemagoers would simply not pay to see more Quota Quickies. The film magazine, *Picturegoer*, posed the following rhetorical question to its readers:

Do you remember the days just before the war, when so many film programmes were ruined by long and dreary British films, made as cheaply as possible, and forced into cinemas for no other reason than to fulfil a legal compulsion to play British pictures?[32]

It was a point well made, but the British government was determined to protect the British film industry at all costs and indeed increased the pressure further by allowing American producers to take only twenty-five per cent of their earnings out of the country. Many people were suspicious that this ruling might backfire because it had the support of Hollywood. It was a fear well justified as the American takeover of British studios continued unabated. There were also concerns that old British movies would be re-released more regularly in order to make up the quota thereby reducing the choice of the cinemagoer even further. However, there was also another threat to the health of the British film studios; a threat that came from within – the unions – and these would manage to bring to a standstill Alastair's next film *London Belongs to Me* (1948).

London Belongs to Me (1948) was adapted from the novel of the same title published in 1945 by Norman Collins. The screenplay writers (Sidney Gilliat and J.B. Williams) faced the difficulty of transforming an overlong text (600 pages or so) into a manageable 112 minutes of film and the production team were challenged to find a good quality cast who could fit into a tight schedule. Sidney Gilliat was of the opinion that they failed on both accounts: 'to my mind we never tamed the script problems and on top of that, made a couple of casting errors amounting to blunders.'[33] In any event, what transpired was an early-day soap drama, vividly recreating the hopes, fears and aspirations of the inhabitants of 10 Dulcimer Street (the address of the house was used as the alternative title for the film's US release).

Towards the beginning of the film a sinister shadow arrives at the front door of the household. The landlady, Mrs Vizzard (Joyce Carey), opens the door to be confronted by a solemn looking gentleman, wisps of dark hair skirmishing across his domed head, large doleful eyes seeking humble acceptance. It is a wonderful introduction to the enigmatic, depraved and morally bankrupt Henry Squales (Alastair Sim).

Squales is a fake medium, always on the lookout for an opportunity to exploit the gullible. Mrs Vizzard is such a person, longing for a message from her dearly departed husband. Over tea, Squales learns of her inheritance and begins to charm his way into her affections. A wonderful scene occurs when, alone in his room, Henry Squales, in a rare moment of honest, fitful, self-doubt, looks into his mirror and asks of himself:

> 'Henry Squales... Have you sunk so low as to do this thing?'
> (Shaking his head)
> 'There can only be one answer.'
> (Nodding)
> 'Yes you have.'

There is a beautifully delivered line in the film by Alastair as Squales in response to a request for his rent money from Mrs Vizzard. He replies, 'You'll find your rent on the mantelpiece, six pence short – all I could get for my propelling pencil'.

Several anecdotes exist concerning the production of this film. Sidney Gilliat recalls:

> At that time, there was still fairly severe food rationing in Britain and Alastair was openly looking forward to a scene in which a plate of bacon and eggs was set before him. We arranged the scene so that it happened nicely for lunchtime so that he could actually eat the dish.

We waited till he raised a piece of bacon on a fork to his mouth and then I sent the prop man in to whip it away from him with the cameras still turning. His reaction was a joy to watch next day in the dallies.[34]

An interesting example of the problems associated with post-war film-making in Britain was that special permission was required by the producers in order to film a flashing neon sign. The energy conservation laws in force at the time stipulated that the extravagance of illuminated displays was illegal – hence Launder and Gilliat were faced with the dilemma of either having to break the law or submit themselves to the bureaucratic nightmare that was post-war civil service.

Another anecdote concerns the problems of demarcation, which in itself places the film in another social era. Demarcation – the restriction of workers from undertaking tasks associated with other employee union groups – led to a serious dispute over a Christmas tree. One union group assumed responsibility for the tree because of the use of artificial decorations to adorn it; another union group saw the tree as being under their jurisdiction because it was a real rather than artificial tree. This dispute was regarded as so serious a matter by the unions that it caused a halt in filming.

When asked to name their favourite Alastair Sim film, people will often suggest the famous Ealing comedy *The Ladykillers* (1955). Although the role of Professor Marcus in the film was originally intended for Alastair, Sir Michael Balcon, of Ealing Studios, said: 'We're making money with the Guinness films, we're on a run of strength there. It's got to be Guinness.'[35] At that time, Guinness had achieved huge popular success with *Kind Hearts and Coronets* (1949), *The Lavender Hill Mob* (1951) and *The Man in the White Suit* (1951). Nevertheless, when Guinness read the script, he immediately said to the director Alexander Mackendrick, 'But dear boy, it's Alastair Sim you want isn't it?'[36] MacKendrick's reply was 'No', but to this day, people still think that Alastair plays Professor Marcus in *The Ladykillers* and that it is his most memorable screen performance. But there is more to it than just coincidence.

There are some who believe that Guinness was so impressed by Alastair's performance as Henry Squales in *London Belongs to Me* that he decided to use this as the basis for his own performance in *The Ladykillers*. Others suggest that Alec Guinness subconsciously based his character's attributes on those of Kenneth Tynan. There may be more truth in the former since Guinness disclaimed any intention of mimicking Tynan. Perhaps though, some of the confusion lies with the cinematography, so brilliant in places in *London Belongs to Me* (Wilkie Cooper) and very similar to scenes in *The Ladykillers* (Otto Heller) – witness the arrival at the doorstep of both Alec Guinness and Alastair Sim in their respective films.

In the autumn of 1948, Alastair returned to the stage in James Bridie's revival of *The Anatomist*[37]. Alastair took on the role of Dr Robert Knox, an eminent Edinburgh physician, who relied on the nefarious activities of Burke and Hare[38] to provide him with cadavers in order for him to advance medical research into the human body. When asked once why he wanted to act in such a morbid play, Alastair replied, 'It is in the great Scottish tradition of corpses and whisky'.[39] James Bridie described the play as being about the 'shifts to which men of science are driven when they are ahead of their time'.[40] *The Anatomist* contains plenty of soul searching but is slightly undermined by a long first act which contains a tiresome quarrel between Dr Knox's assistant and his fiancée.

Reviewers took delight in comparing Alastair's performance with that of Henry Ainley who played Dr Knox in the original 1930 production. Ainley favoured a 'swashbuckling melodramatic'[41] interpretation of Knox, whereas in contrast, Alastair preferred a temperate performance so as not to detract from the philosophical issues of the play. *The Times* distinguished between the performances by saying, 'Ainley made the doctor . . . seem more of a rogue' and that 'In Mr Sim's interpretation he is unexpectedly innocent of much possible guilt'.[42] Apparently Bridie sided with the Ainley characterisation saying that Knox should be presented as a 'barnstorming tenor'.[43] Other members of the 1948 production included George Cole 'one of Britain's most promising actors'[44] and Molly Urquhart whom Alastair particularly requested for the role of Mary Paterson, the prostitute murdered by Burke and Hare.

The Anatomist was not received well in London with some critics accusing Alastair of rushing his lines. At one point in the play, Knox commands one of his students: 'You will gabble of nothing you have seen or heard or thought this morning'[45], possibly explaining the appearance of the word 'gabble' in several reviews that followed in the press. *The Sunday Times* contributed rather whimsically:

The worst thing to be said about this revival ... is that the best perform-ance in it is Miss Josephine Crombie's in the small part of a servant. It is as if the most entertaining thing in 'Don Quixote' were the windmill, or the most edible part of a particular meringue the spoon.[46]

Putting gastronomic idiosyncrasies to one side for the moment, it is worth reflecting on why *The Anatomist* was such a success in Scotland that it could be revived twenty years after its first perform-ance and yet be so poorly received in London. One possible reason lies in Bridie's continued insistence to use the Scottish dialect even for London performances. Some of the lines must have appeared totally incomprehensible to English audiences, whether 'gabbled' or not. The following dialogue from the *The Anatomist* is a typical example:

Mary Paterson: I'll misguggle your thrapple. I'll mashackerel ye to rights. And I'll no wheesht, Mr. Nebby. Wheesht to a leddy indeed! I'll wheesht ye.[47]

As the *Evening Standard* drolly commented:

One does not engage a Moor to play *Othello*. Authenticity has always been the foe of art, and our London ears would prefer even a bogus dialect which we could comprehend.[48]

James Bridie would have chuckled to himself had he read the above. Bridie enjoyed a wicked delight in portraying the English in his plays as intellectually wanting. His note in *The Anatomist* reads that Mr Raby from Warwickshire is 'English and therefore [a] stupid student'.[49] Those walls built by James II (see chapter one) remain a significant factor in the Scottish psyche. In a composition written by Bridie entitled 'J.M. Barrie', Bridie has a conversation with a Polish Doctor:

Pole: Then you think English audiences are stupid?
Bridie: Not at all. But it all comes back to what you call content. They like a story or a play for its own sake, without bothering about what it is all about.[50]

Bridie would not have purposefully set out to incur the wrath of the English critics since, after all, numerous people's incomes were at stake, but nonetheless he succeeded in doing so in a magnificent manner. The *Evening Standard*:

> If you want to see how a play should not be written, how it should not be acted and how it should not be produced, then you should go to the Westminster Theatre and see *The Anatomist*.[51]

Alastair had directed and produced the play and therefore the responsibility for the production lay heavily on his shoulders. However, the reviews that appeared may have been tainted by the exceptional nature of the first night performance. As *The Times* commented:

> To walk the stage as the notorious Dr Knox of Edinburgh and to be all the while the just elected Rector of Edinburgh University is really more than the flesh and blood of any artist can sustain with equanimity. Mr Sim showed distinct signs of the Pirandellian strain and gave an extremely tentative account of Dr Knox.[52]

Throughout his life, Alastair felt an affinity towards the young. His screen roles such as that in *Hue and Cry* often reflected this affection and his home life was proof that he was prepared to share his world with eager-to-learn young souls. Often such altruism goes unrewarded, but in Alastair's case, the students of Edinburgh University repaid some of the debt by electing Alastair as their new Lord Rector. Naomi writes in *Dance and Skylark* that: 'Alastair was always more proud of being elected Rector – of being elected by the young – than he was of any other honour that came his way.'[53]

The Lord Rector of Edinburgh University was mainly a symbolic post although Alastair had a duty to represent the views and opinions of the students in his role as President of the University Court. When Alastair accepted the nomination to stand for this post he had found himself in a two-horse race with the politician Harold Macmillan. The students, meanwhile, didn't quite see it this way and elected Alastair as their Rector with an overwhelming majority of 1,276 votes.[54] Although one would never wish to question the democratic principles associated with such an auspicious and exalted election, it was reported in some sources that water, flour, fireworks, and dead fish were thrown at all of those planning to vote for Mr Macmillan. And again, without wishing to point fingers, there may have been some truth in the suggestion that the Dramatic Society of Edinburgh University had orchestrated a highly efficient and proactive election campaign that would be the envy of many political parties of today.

The election result was announced just before the curtain rose on the first performance of *The Anatomist*. Alastair sent word to the students of Edinburgh University saying that he was trembling at the prospect of having to address them as their Rector and begged them to be gentle with him. At the end of the evening's production, James Bridie went on stage as was his custom with first-night perform-ances and addressed the audience with 'My Lord Rector, ladies and gentlemen...'.

Alastair's inauguration as the Lord Rector of Edinburgh University took place in April of the following year. The ceremony began in McEwan's Hall and proceeded in a formal procession, compris-ing the University Senate and various other dignitaries, through the University. At least it was intended as a formal procession, but by all accounts of those present, the occasion became increasingly boisterous. The students began cheering in their traditional noisy good-hearted way as Alastair stepped up to give his speech:

> Forgive me if I begin this address on a somewhat nostalgic note. At this moment I am thinking of happy carefree days – no, not here in Edinburgh, but in London, only a few short months ago, when I had nothing to do but play all day, and far into the night. It is certain that I had no thought of having to do anything at all difficult, least of all of having to make a considerable speech to a gathering of learned and scholarly minds, however tolerant and kindly disposed.[55]

The cheering of the students would normally drown out the inaugural speech by their newly appointed Lord Rector. Further distractions were provided by the discarding from the upper balcony of various domestic fowls, feathers thereof, streamers, alcoholic liq-uids, non-alcoholic liquids and the playing of musical instruments by those who were magnificently tone deaf and unfamiliar with the concept of rhythm. On this occasion, the students were slow off the mark. Alastair's opening remarks drew some chuckles, then some of the students actually began to pay attention to what he was saying, and then the rest followed, falling under what the suspicious might have considered a spell of enchantment.

In reality, it was probably a novel experience for the students to hear someone from the entertainment world address them as their Lord Rector, given that the post was usually filled by some notable dignitary from the political, legal or academic field. Perhaps more significantly, Alastair had prepared a special speech for the occasion. Alastair continued:

> There was I, quietly living my own obscure and sheltered life, doing no one any harm, minding my own business, happily cultivating my garden (I speak metaphorically). Then suddenly I am lifted up and spirited back into a world of studious concentration from which I thought I had escaped forever... Now I can well imagine that those of you who have been mainly responsible for setting me in this exalted position are sitting now, in ever-growing trepidation, as to the outcome of your action. If it is any comfort to you, I know exactly how you feel.[56]

Alastair set out two themes within his speech. The first was about 'words': 'Not the utility words of everyday practical affairs, but those abstract words which so subtly affect and distort human relationship.'[57] With malevolent glee, Alastair proceeded to enlighten the students about the 'dark words', words 'which may mean anything, everything, or nothing according to whether they serve with discretion or rule in chaos.'[58] Alastair proposed the following as a test:

> It would be highly interesting to compare what a public speaker was saying with what we knew he was thinking. Words constantly subjected to such a test would soon find honest masters, would soon serve mutual understanding.[59]

An intriguing proposal, which I am sure would meet with some approval today. Alastair's second theme was recounting how he had become a qualified fool:

Here, then, was a life work and a pleasant one. Could I play the fool and know that I was one? Could I wring laughter even from the throats unused to laugh? That is the fool's peak of achievement. In fact, if he can do this more or less consistently he may, without any great loss of self-respect, allow himself to be supported by the community. But, above all, he must see the folly in himself before he holds up the mirror to his fellows.[60]

Alastair ended his speech with:

Students of Edinburgh you have made me extraordinarily happy . . . there is one gift that we do share and will always share – the gift of laughter.[61]

By all accounts, Alastair's speech on the subject of 'words' and the 'qualified fool' was a great success and the students carried him aloft on their shoulders, cheering all the way, to the student's union for the after-speech reception and dinner. Stephen Fry described Alastair's speech as 'quite beautiful in its understanding of ethics and morality.'[62] It certainly showed him to be an articulate, intelligent man, principled and caring about the young, encouraging them to think for themselves. In an interview given by Naomi Sim long after Alastair's death she said:

He saw stupidity as the greatest danger facing the world, and he associated all forms of showbiz – autograph hunting or being asked to judge poodles at a dog show – with stupidity.[63]

There are potential contradictions in Alastair's forthright views. For example, Alastair believed nobody over the age of thirty should be allowed to vote. It is quite difficult to see how one could reconcile Alastair's strong feelings on stupidity and his rather novel views on voting rights. One should not of course take such comments too literally but Alastair's faith in the young sometimes appeared almost unconditional. Those who argue that the 'young are our future' inherently accept that the 'young' will mature and gain wisdom. Alastair appeared to subscribe to a view that this wasn't necessarily such a good thing. Indeed, Alastair's attitude was similar to that of the subtext of *Peter Pan* – and this could perhaps explain why he appeared in Barrie's play five times during his career.

A final note for 1948 was James Bridie's appointment as Honorary President of the Scottish Community Drama Association. It is fitting to record that following Bridie's death, Alastair took on the role until 1961[64].

★

The years 1941–1948 had seen Alastair successfully discard the mantle of being a manic comedian best used in saving a sinking production. Instead, he had gained a reputation for being a thoughtful actor who could bring a cool and assured confidence to a role. *Green For Danger* (1946) played an important part in this transitional period, completing what had begun with *Cottage To Let* (1941). As Sidney Gilliat recalled:

> Sim told me afterwards that the film [*Green For Danger*] had come at just the right time for him as he felt his progress had halted at a big question mark; and at that very time, he had been considering a Canadian offer, with one eye on the States.[65]

Perhaps more importantly was the reaction of the cinemagoers towards *Hue and Cry* (1947). Here was a film which had sparked a desire within many to put the troubled times behind them and laugh. But not only that, the source of the laughter was defining a particular brand of British comedy – a comedy featuring an eccentric. Alastair, the screen doyen of eccentrics, was to find his time had come:

> All of a sudden, the newspapers of our country have discovered what the picturegoers have known for many months, that British pictures have specialized too strongly in gloom. The newspaper writers have shrieked for laughter... And we see the ... spectacle of British film producers panicking to make funny pictures[66].

Alastair was about to be offered the starring role in *The Happiest Days of your Life*.

8

The Happiest
Days of your Life

We had some fun in those days, Sidney.[1]

– Alastair Sim reminiscing with Sidney Gilliat in 1969.

In March 1948, a comedy written by John Dighton[2] entitled *The Happiest Days of your Life*, opened to excellent reviews at the Apollo Theatre. The plot was delightfully wicked and yet deliciously simple – the British Ministry of Devacuation wrongfully billets an all girls' school at an all boy's school. On stage, the ensuing chaos created a magnificent battle of wits between the two opposing heads: Margaret Rutherford as Miss Evelyn Whitchurch, Headmistress of St Swithins, and George Howe as Godfrey Pond, the embattled Headmaster of Hilary School[3].

The foundation of a successful farce is often the plausibility of the situation in which the comedy is taking place. If, in *The Happiest Days of your Life*, one can believe that such an administrative error could occur, then the events that follow are all the more believable – and thus enjoyable. *The Happiest Days of your Life* is set just after the Second World War when buildings were in short supply and therefore, conceivably, a civil servant could accidentally re-house two boarding schools onto the same premises. The fact that they were opposite sex schools was, in post war Britain, all the more epicurean, since it tapped into a sensitive vein within the British psyche. By the late 1940s the authorities in Britain were trying to re-establish pre-war social norms but women were reluctant to relinquish their new-found status – something they had hard earned by substituting for men in many critical roles during the war).The impasse created a tension between the sexes.

Frank Launder saw the play one evening and was convinced that *The Happiest Days of your Life* offered the opportunity for Launder and Gilliat to develop a comedy form to rival that of Ealing. Sidney Gilliat agreed and together they set about purchasing the rights for a film version.The title would stay the same as would the lead female character – how could anyone replace Margaret Rutherford? – but when Frank Launder invited John Dighton to work with him on a screenplay, he stipulated a significant change: Alastair Sim was to replace George Howe in the role of the Headmaster (renamed Wetherby Pond). Filming took place in 1949 at the Byculla School in Hampshire, using a mixture of actual Byculla pupils and students from the Corona Theatrical School, thus imbuing the film with an air of authenticity.The film was released in 1950 and was an immediate success with the public.

The Happiest Days of your Life (1950) begins with a cosy familiarity: the staff – a motley crew each encumbered with a personal weakness – assembling in the Headmaster's study. It seems it will be a typical school year until the administrative error brings the Headmistress of St Swithins, the formidable Muriel Whitchurch (Margaret Rutherford), along with her staff and girls into the male domain of Nutbourne College.

The encounter between Pond and Whitchurch occurs in the Headmaster's study when, during a series of arguments, the Headmaster's chair is both symbolically and literally occupied first by Whitchurch, then Pond, and then finally, a triumphant Whitchurch.The plot thickens when parents and governors of both schools descend upon Nutbourne at the same time.This forces Pond and Whitchurch to concoct a plan to schedule the visiting parties so that each will see only their respective Head running a successful single-sex school. Naturally this goes awry. Parents, governors, boys, girls and teachers all come together in a rousing finale of utter chaos. The film closes with Pond and Whitchurch, the careers of both in tatters, planning to teach in Tanzania.

Critical to the film's success was the casting of Alastair Sim and Margaret Rutherford in the leading roles. Alastair was at the height of his powers, said *Picturegoer*: 'At fifty, he is riding a high wave of popularity.'[4] Alastair appeared on screen as an enigmatic figure, looming larger than life. It took someone like Margaret Rutherford, equally as impressive, to share his scenes without becoming over-shadowed. Naomi Sim commented thus on this clash of eccentric Goliaths: 'They matched each other perfectly during their scenes together when you felt that their mutual anger might cause them to ignite at any minute.'[5]

Like Alastair, Margaret Rutherford delayed her professional stage debut until in her thirties when she also auditioned at the Old Vic. Her film persona as an eccentric was established in *The Demi-Paradise* (1943) and as Madame Arcati in the hugely successful *Blithe Spirit* (1945). Her portrayal of Agatha Christie's Miss Marple in four films, including *Murder She Said* (1961), is a classic example of where the pure eccentricity of the actress overshadowed the actual character created by the author. The point is of course that Rutherford was always going to be playing herself and here we find a notable difference between Margaret Rutherford and Alastair Sim. Alastair's stage performances of the 1940s and '50s (in particular, *Dr. Angelus*, *Mr. Gillie* and *Mr. Bolfry*), and his screen appearances in *Waterloo Road* (1944) *Captain Boycott* (1947) and *An Inspector Calls* (1954), show that Alastair was quite prepared to take on serious roles even at the risk of alienating his fans.

Both Alastair Sim and Margaret Rutherford received CBEs but Margaret went on to win an Oscar for her performance in *The VIPs* (1963) – an award that was to elude Alastair. Margaret Rutherford would appear in one further film with Alastair, the disappointing *Innocents in Paris* (1953), and in one highly-acclaimed stage play *The Clandestine Marriage*. Naomi Sim considered that both Alastair and Margaret 'had a lot in common in that their playing of anything at all was so highly individual. You couldn't employ a Margaret Rutherford 'type' or an Alastair Sim 'type'.'[6]

Not so – the role of the Professor in *Passport to Pimlico* (1949) was initially offered to Alastair but finally played by Margaret. Some might argue therefore that the eccentric, though a peculiar breed of undeniable genius, was essentially interchangeable between the sexes in movies. This augured well for Alastair since the films being made in the 1950s were often centred on the 'eccentric' and so there was plenty of work on offer. Of course the risk was in becoming typecast, the thought of which Alastair abhorred and had taken measures to avoid on two previous occasions. And yet *Picturegoer* declared 'As a screen character actor, Sim has tended to establish himself as an eccentric.'[7]

Rutherford and Sim are renowned scene-stealers and so part of the joy of watching *The Happiest Days of your Life* is seeing these two larger-than-life personalities in a face-off against one another on the big screen. Rutherford, as the Headmistress of St Swithins, makes her entrance in a typically boisterous, determined, and fussy manner. One is left in no doubt that she sits aloft as a great matriarch to her staff and girls. Alastair portrays Pond as intelligent, perceptive (he knows the foible of each member of staff) and witty ('Come in gentlemen,' he announces with a chuckle as he stands behind his staff when they knock on his office door). The audience immediately understands what motivates this man, why he is in control and what he wants out of life; he is clearly defined as the patriarch albeit a rather self-centred one. The humour in the film lies in the contest between the matriarch and the patriarch to determine who rules the roost. Sometimes this seems an altogether one-sided affair – witness the discomfort of Pond, waking up in the bath, having been pressurised into giving up his sleeping quarters to Whitchurch. Pond's vain attempt to maintain dignity in the face of adversity is a recurring theme of this comedy and indeed a polished Alastair Sim trait from the 1950s onwards.

Other notable performances in *The Happiest Days of your Life* are by Joyce 'Call me sausage' Grenfell who plays the part of Miss Gossage as, 'the queen of all galumphers; repressed and upright'.[8] In a film where two imposing characters dominate the screen, it is a curious fact that we seem to know so much about Gossage. This is obviously a tribute to the talent of Joyce Grenfell, who succeeded admirably in producing a well-judged character sketch of a games mistress that seemed so familiar and so right. 'Those gestures. . . '[9], as Alastair put it. Says Joyce Grenfell: 'I gave Miss Gossage a bouncy immature way of walking, too juvenile for her years.'[10] More than that, she provided us with an endearing image of innocence in a school environment in which the children appear more streetwise than the adults. Surely, one feels, it should be the children that are the innocents, but seeing their antics quickly convinces us otherwise. It touched a nerve then, as indeed it does now, although in the 1940s and '50s there was a good reason why children had matured so quickly – the harsh realities of war.

The love interest played out between Richard Tassell[11] (John Bentley) and Miss Harper (Bernadette O'Farell), appears rather lame and obligatory. This is a pity since one feels that the idea of a relationship bridging the sexual divide could have provided a deeper appreciation of the gender issues. Unfortunately, there is never enough time for Tassell and Harper to evolve into anything other than two-dimensional characters.

The Happiest Days of your Life opened to great reviews. *The Monthly Film Bulletin* reported it as an 'uninhibited and energetically handled farce'.[12] *The Times* wrote:

> A genuinely hilarious farce... Miss Margaret Rutherford is the head-mistress, the part she had in the play, and once again she sets before her audience a character well enough drawn to survive even the most preposterous demands of farce. Mr Alastair Sim endows the head master with the exact qualities appropriate to the part; he is pompous, dignified, and ludicrous in turn; an easy target, one feels for the good-natured humour of boys.[13]

The film went on to become one of the biggest grossing films of 1950 and was largely responsible for Alastair topping the British Cinema Exhibitor's popularity poll. *Picturegoer* announced: 'He's bald. He's stoop-shouldered. And he's fifty. Yet he's the top laugh-man of the year.'[14] Alastair was embarrassed by the attention of the media but nevertheless was appearing regularly in film magazines of the time. They gave typical media coverage to his career to date and provided readers with a broad, if not rather bland, description of the man:

> Alastair Sim has blue eyes and is five feet eleven inches tall... He lives in the country and is fond of swimming and playing tennis. When it comes to indoor recreations, he likes to read and is a very keen chess player.[15]

Reporters struggled in their attempt to produce in print any kind of cohesive interview with the reluctant star: 'As for that man Sim – well, there are lots of things that you may never learn about his private life, his opinions, likes and dislikes.'[16] *Picturegoer*, 1950:

> Sim will shrug off (and how that man can shrug!) all attempts to make him talk shop. . . Ask him why his stoop-shouldered, hollow-eyed appearance on a cinema screen instantly raises expectant chuckles, he will reply . . . 'Laddie, I'll no' give away trade secrets. I'm a Scotsman with a living to make.' [17]

Alastair's reticence was nothing new. Geoffrey Jowitt, on discussing Alastair's behaviour towards the general public in the 1940s said 'he would rush from the stage door trying to avoid everyone'.[18] Peter Cellier recalled that Alastair once said, 'what he did on stage was rightfully for the public but otherwise his life was private'.[19] Dora Bryan said, 'Alastair Sim was a very private, but pleasant, nice man'.[20] Avril Angers remarked, 'Alastair, it seemed to me, had nothing to do with "show-biz".'[21] Ronald Mavor, James Bridie's son, observed:

> He was simply uninterested in the trappings of fame and had a positive horror of publicity, not only because he didn't like it, but also from a good Scotch puritanical conviction that it was evil and corrupting.[22]

Even showbusiness colleagues were daunted by the prospect of approaching him. Ronnie Corbett, who once saw him in the BBC canteen during a break in the recording of a *Two Ronnies* programme, said that Alastair was 'quite a formidable soul to go up and have an idle word with.'[23]

Alastair was determined that the press should not make him into a star personality. Friends said that Alastair 'mistrusted the press; he thought they were a bunch of charlatans'.[24] As a consequence, the public was starved of gossipy insights into his life, and yet, rather surprisingly, there seems to have been little fuss made over this issue. Maybe the public didn't want to know what he ate for his breakfast or where he lived and what holiday he had planned. This may have reflected the times in which he lived, when intrusive reporting was frowned upon and scandal magazines were in their infancy. Modern day journalism would no doubt have risen to the challenge of uncovering the latest scoop on Alastair Sim; longed to build him up and then bring him tumbling down with some mesmerising prose on his foibles.

Though the press could lick their wounds and seek out other actors to harass, the autograph hunters were often left feeling disappointed, confused and angry when Alastair shook his head at their request for his signature. Peter Cellier, who appeared with Alastair in *A Private Matter* said 'the trait that I found unaccountable was the fact that he would never, and I repeat never, give his autograph'.[25] A man who reputedly made such careful and thoughtful decisions regarding his selection of film and stage roles and who put so much of himself into nurturing the talents of the young, seemed to completely miscalculate the hurt his refusal to sign an autograph caused his fans. John Howard Davies:

> Someone came up to him and asked him for an autograph for a boy dying of cancer – but he wouldn't sign it. He was absolutely firm on this; he didn't believe in the principal of it – said it was nonsense, immodest and wrong.[26]

Ian Carmichael shares the feelings of many:

> I always thought it rather sad that when he was sitting in a chair out on location doing absolutely nothing, he would still refuse to sign for children.[27]

Dora Bryan, with her feet placed firmly on the ground, remarked: 'I thought he was odd not to sign autographs at the Stage Door. I thought all actors did that.'[28] Avril Angers recalls an incident that occurred when she and Alastair were sitting in a car between takes during *The Green Man* (1956):

> At that moment a little girl, in school uniform, appeared at the window of the car and asked for his autograph. Alastair smiled and said, 'err – no, sorry dear, I don't do that'. The little girl [was] stunned.[29]

The non-signing of autographs became a trademark of Alastair's that often drew comments of disdain from fellow actors, although some, rather wickedly, saw it as an opportunity for a prank. Sheridan Morley recalls a practical joke that his father used to play on Alastair:

> Alistair Sim [*sic*] . . . had a fetish about autographs and used to deliver a ten-minute lecture on the evils of autograph-hunting to anyone unwise enough to ask him for one. In earlier days, it was Robert's [Morley] and Willy Hyde-White's great delight on movie sets to bribe small boys with half a crown to go and demand Alistair's signature, only to watch their little faces glaze over with boredom before Sim was half way through the lecture.[30]

The sad truth of the matter is that it took him far longer to explain away his reasons for not signing than it would have done to simply score his name on a piece of paper.

It is possible that Alastair's refusal to sign autographs was simply the result of a principled man becoming restricted by a self-imposed precedent. Maybe, once he had started a policy of refusing to sign autographs, he found it impossible to go back to signing them without, in his opinion, losing face. This would certainly make sense for someone who was 'stuck with prejudice'[31] as was suggested by his friend, Christopher Fry. The explanation put forward by those who apparently know the real reason is well documented. Evidently, Alastair believed that autograph-hunting was 'a deeply stupid habit'[32] and therefore something he did not wish to perpetuate. The only problem with such an attitude is that it invokes an impression of intellectual arrogance – clearly at odds with the persona of a man who would laugh and joke with everyone on the film set. Alastair's refusal to sign his name in an autograph book was not an attempt to avoid his fans, since, instead of an autograph, he would offer a hand-shake in return, and, according to Alastair, this satisfied their need. Whatever the reason, the shake of the head and an apologetic 'no, sorry', certainly created an impression that he was unapproachable. At best his peer group thought him eccentric, but most thought him disingenuous.

★

Alfred Hitchcock had recently returned to England to make *Under Capricorn* (1949) and was now in the process of casting for his next film *Stage Fright* (1950). One of the characters in *Stage Fright* was to be a senior police officer who was described as having a quirky, endearing nature. The British were good at playing such roles and indeed there were none better at the time than Alastair. Hitchcock was less than convinced. To him, there was an inherent weakness in casting decisions made in English films at that time based around an insular mentality. There is some truth in this criticism. A film of this period would usually include Richard Wattis in a supporting role, or Dennis Price or Eric Barker. In the end though, Hitchcock's scouting agents carried the day and Alastair was engaged for the film.

Stage Fright boasted an impressive cast: Marlene Dietrich, Jane Wyman and Richard Todd, with Alastair playing a 'shrewd, genial commodore who does a bit of brandy smuggling in his weaker moments'.[33] The plot however was too intricate and confusing for the audiences. Even at the time of its release, *Stage Fright* was perceived as a marginal film in the Hitchcock canon. Reviewers complained:

> There is a great deal of aimless camera movement, long tracking shots and slow pans of no dramatic value that merely hold up the action and dissipate tension.[34]

Others were saying: 'Mr Hitchcock, in not making a "typical" Hitchcock film, has made an exceedingly diverting one.'[35] Even so, the film does appear rather tame on occasions with the leading characters failing to bring the plot to life. *The Times* remarked:

> When Eve's father, the eccentric Commodore, makes his appearance, the film changes its course and the rocks recede. The film in other words, ceases to be a Hitchcock exercise in dramatic suspense and becomes instead a diverting comedy brilliantly served by its supporting cast. Mr Alastair Sim brings a rich relish for the oddities and quirks of character to the part of the Commodore.[36]

Modern day reviews of *Stage Fright* comment that 'the characterisation verges too much on English caricature to generate much tension'.[37] Ironically, what was initially believed by some to be the film's saving grace is now thought of as being its cause of ruin. However, not all of the blame can be directed at the British actors. One talking point is Hitchcock's use of the flashback in *Stage Fright*. A cardinal rule in film making is that if such a device is used, then it must be used truthfully. Hitchcock breaks this rule and as a consequence, at the end of the film, when all has been revealed, the audience feel cheated.

On 9 March 1950, the Garrick Theatre played host to the London premier of James Bridie's latest play *Mr Gillie*. Alastair had never been so busy, undertaking, as was by now his custom, to produce and direct the production as well as take on the leading role. At that time the Garrick had a reputation for comedies and the success in the cinemas of *The Happiest Days of your Life* may have predisposed the audience for an evening of light entertainment. Those who had read the Glasgow reviews of *Mr Gillie*, and those who were more familiar with Bridie's style of writing, would have known better.

Mr Gillie is a morality tale – one can tell because at one point during proceedings a major character is accused of 'treachery, hypocrisy, [and] cheap success founded on cynical opportunism and the worship of money'.[38] The central figure in the play is Mr Gillie, a schoolmaster, who encourages his students to take risks in their lives in order to achieve their greatest potential. Initially one sees only altruistic qualities in Mr Gillie, such as kindness, consideration and the desire to see others succeed, but as the play progresses, we learn of the conceit behind his philosophy; the corporeal risk of failure rests entirely with his students. Mr Gillie dies and on the day of reckoning he is granted immortality because he dared to take it upon himself to encourage his students to free themselves from the mundane. *Theatre World* wrote:

> The play is marked by Mr Bridie's customary dry humour and penetrating wit, and Alastair Sim, who also produces the play, gives a most sensitive and telling performance as the remarkable Mr Gillie.[39]

The Times reported:

> It is a part that suits Mr Alastair Sim. He is adept at acting without words, at listening volubly, as it were, and it is his silences as much as his outbursts of impatience and his occasional convulsions of silent mirth that establish the character for us.[40]

And from *The Tatler & Bystander*:

> Mr Sim's restraint in the part produces a vivid, touching and memorable study of a well-meaning man who cannot refrain from releasing birds from their cages even though he knows the cat will in all probability pounce on them.[41]

Though *Mr Gillie* was a reasonable success, 'Mr Sim's restraint' as *The Times* put it probably disappointed the theatre-going public, who were by now well-versed in the Sim comedy mannerisms. As Winifred Banister wrote:

> Four months was as long as London could tolerate their darling Scottish comedian to be playing even the finest character study that had come his way, which goes to show that the London theatre is governed not by good plays or first-rate acting but by a few first-rate players who have that star quality, personality, and yet must not stray from the type or types the audience has assigned to them – for Mr Sim, comic eccentricity or farcically solemn bewilderment.[42]

Both Alastair and Bridie saw reflections of themselves in the character of Mr Gillie. Mr Gillie is portrayed in the play as strongly opposed to the indoctrination of the youth by the bureaucratic State. His desire to see his students attain their potential, or at least be given the opportunity to do so, is viewed by the authorities as reactionary – a man in conflict with the conventions of the time. He is derided by representatives of the social order and indeed towards the end of the play is forced by the education authorities to give up his house; but Mr Gillie maintains his dignity at all times, and more importantly, keeps to his philosophy. Naomi Sim comments:

> It had so much of himself [Alastair Sim] in it – that passionate faith in the young and his belief that they must be supported and encouraged at all times since they were our only hope. I found working with Alastair on Mr Gillie very odd, as if we were rehearsing Alastair himself, rather than a stranger.[43]

Mr Gillie, the fatherly figure, not seeking gratitude, not belabouring past woes, simply there, supportive of his charges – sounds rather like a description of Alastair's father, Alexander Sim. This is the beauty of Bridie's creation, a character that would strike a chord universally. The audience would leave the theatre having empathised with Mr Gillie – his aspirations, his ideals, his self-effacement – either seeing themselves in the role or someone they knew. As one reviewer noted: 'I do not recall another [Bridie character] who has been observed with a more tenderly humorous understanding.'[44]

In Scotland, Bridie took to the stage on the first night, as was his custom, to receive the applause of the audience; but there was no hiding the fact that he was an ill man. In January 1951, he was admitted to the Edinburgh Royal Infirmary suffering from a serious vascular condition. His health rapidly deteriorated and Dr Osborne Henry Mavor died, aged sixty-three, on 29 January 1951.

★

Much has been written in this book of the relationship between Alastair Sim and James Bridie. Bridie provided Sim with material of a quality that allowed Alastair to develop his abilities as an actor and in time, West End director and producer. In return, Alastair brought intelligence and understanding to Bridie's characters and forced the author to attend to the play's structure. There was also the considerable publicity Alastair brought to the productions as a result of his film achievements. This symbiotic relationship was broken with Bridie's death. In the words of Sidney Gilliat: 'When Bridie died, Sim was completely cast down.'[45]

Shortly after Bridie's death, the BBC produced a James Bridie Memorial Programme. Alastair accepted an invitation to contribute to the programme and provided a thoughtful eulogy. Alastair began:

> When I was first invited to make a contribution to this programme I accepted with enthusiasm and alacrity. I was quite sure I could describe the Bridie I knew so that you would understand why and how deeply I loved him.[46]

Alastair's tribute was an affectionate homage, full of praise for his dear lost friend, but also finely balanced:

> For Bridie saw the frightened monkey and the god in every human being, and while he got tremendous fun out of the monkey, he never stopped marvelling at the god.[47]

A man who inspires others is often the recipient of philanthropic inspiration himself. Alastair went on to say, 'I suspect he knew my limitations far better than I did . . . yet he never let up on the encouragement'.[48] After Bridie's death, Sim vowed that 'he would never appear on the stage again . . . then, later, that he would never appear except in a Bridie play'.[49] These were emotional statements from a principled man, though perhaps spoken in haste. James Bridie was a respected playwright of his time, but fifty years have passed since his death and today he is held in less veneration. Sidney Gilliat put the relationship in context when he said that Alastair revered Bridie (who was certainly a brilliant man), though tended to overrate him as a complete playwright.[50]

Bridie had established himself as a successful playwright long before he met Alastair at the Malvern Festival in the late 1930s. Indeed, Bridie even worked with Hitchcock four years before Alastair was involved in making *Stage Fright*. Bridie was, at least to begin with, the senior member of the Bridie–Sim partnership. However, today, while Alastair still gains fans as new generations are acquainted with his idiosyncratic screen performances, James Bridie, who once had three different plays successfully performing in London at the same time, is hardly known outside Scotland. Bridie himself once said 'nobody will know whether Bridie is really good or not till he is dead'.[51] Sadly, history tends to concur with the views expressed by Sidney Gilliat.

Alastair reprised the role of Dr Knox in September 1952 when the Bridie Memorial season opened with a performance of *The Anatomist* at the Glasgow Citizens' Theatre. In 1955 Alastair directed, but did not act in, a stage production called *Misery Me!*, and in 1956 Alastair produced, directed and acted in a successful revival of *Mr Bolfry*. A decade would have to pass before Alastair finally laid to rest the memory of his dear friend.[52]

It is poignant to consider that although 1951 began so disastrously with Bridie's death, it would also provide Alastair with two of his most memorable film performances.

Laughter in Paradise (1951), produced and directed by Mario Zampi, is a compendium of stories about a rich practical joker who leaves a will stipulating that in order for his blood relations to inherit his fortune, they have to behave in a way contrary to their usual character. Alastair plays Deniston, an upstanding member of the community who harbours a dark secret – he writes pulp detective stories. Deniston is challenged by a clause in the will to get himself arrested.

From the beginning of *Laughter in Paradise*, when we hear those distinct dulcet Scottish tones dictating the opening paragraphs to 'Blood Lust', Deniston's latest potboiler, there is an immediate expectation that the cosy world in which Deniston resides is about to be turned upside down. The scene where he has to impart the news to his fiancée, Fluffy (Joyce Grenfell as an over-eager armed services girl), that their forthcoming wedding will have to be postponed due to his imminent jailing, is surreal pathos:

> *Deniston:* 'I have to go away for a month.'
> *Fluffy:* 'Officially?'
> *Deniston:* 'Officially.'
> *Fluffy:* (excitedly) 'For the government?'
> *Deniston:* 'Well, the government will be paying my expenses.'

A highlight of the film occurs on the ground floor of Swan & Edgar's, a department store, where Deniston undertakes some rather obvious shoplifting in order to get himself arrested by the store detectives. Alastair uses such a convincing range of facial expressions and body language to convey fear, hope, astonishment, anger and disappointment, that the scene provides a study in itself of how comedy can be successfully conveyed without the use of dialogue. The sequence is a homage to the silent comedians of the 1920s. Deniston's accidental purchase of a pipe, his stealing and returning of an umbrella ('wrong tartan' he explains), his pinning of a brooch on his lapel, the stuffing of pearls into his pocket – all draw the audience into his increasing sense of frustration at *not* being caught. When the store detectives finally pounce there is a collective sigh of relief – the topsy-turvy situation being ironic, ludicrous and very funny. Naomi recalled that Alastair was particularly proud of his performance in this film, especially the long complicated take of the shoplifting sequence.

Another highlight of the film is when Deniston throws a brick through a shop window. A rather elegant matter of detail is the contrite neatness in the way the brick is wrapped in paper and string. The whole scene is played in the manner by which one would presume such a refined gentleman would undertake such a distasteful task. The ending is wonderfully judged with Deniston knocking a policeman on the head with his umbrella just to make sure that he gets himself arrested.

Picture Show rated the film as excellent, declaring that: 'Alastair Sim gives a brilliant performance'.[53] However, these selected extracts identify a weakness in the film – the Deniston storyline is by far the strongest and therefore overshadows the other stories in the compendium. *Picturegoer* remarked thus:

> It is almost unfortunate that this story is so efficiently and wittily contrived and so aptly cast, for it serves only to throw a harsh light of contrast upon the other three.[54]

The Times was more generous to the other storylines in its review reporting:

> All these are good situations and Mr Mario Zampi the director, very properly insists on treating the film as pure comedy of situation, with no unnecessary brilliance of dialogue but with the kind of skilful character acting . . . that most effectively brings out the humour of the plot.[55]

Laughter in Paradise was made by Associated British Pictures Corporation (ABC) and on general release would have been received with a degree of scepticism by the British public. ABC films were generally acknowledged to be second features – the Quota Quickies of the 1950s. Instead the writers, Michael Pertwee and Jack Davies, wrote a screenplay that was at heart a morality tale but one told with great wit and intelligence. The audiences warmed to the idea of seeing these diverse characters being forced by greed to behave contrary to character, and enjoyed seeing their raised hopes come tumbling down with the twist at the end. The result was that *Laughter in Paradise* became one of the highest grossing films that year.

The studio shots were filmed at the newly built Associated British studios at Boreham Wood in Hertfordshire where: 'The dressing rooms are fitted with telephones for the comfort of the stars, a point that was fully appreciated by Alastair Sim'[56] – cue photograph of Alastair in dressing room with telephone to ear. *Laughter in Paradise* is also famously known as responsible for starting the film career of Audrey Hepburn[57] who had a small scene in the film as a cigarette girl. It also attracted attention for its lavish expenditure by UK standards:

> Nearly a hundred men worked for a fortnight to produce an exact replica of a West End store for one of the scenes in *Laughter in Paradise*. The cost: £1,000. Screening time of that scene: three minutes. Now you know how films become so expensive.[58]

The second of Alastair's films released in 1951, *Scrooge*, is one for which many people feel that Alastair deserved an Oscar nomination. In a letter to James Bridie the previous year he had written, 'It looks very like as if I am going to do *Scrooge*'.[59] Indeed, Alastair had been very keen to take on the mantle of this famous tightwad. The producer-director Brian Hurst confided that Alastair had '. . . put aside other offers so that he could play the part'.[60]

Ebenezer Scrooge is a complex character to play. An actor in the title role has to convince the audience that he has undergone a radical overnight transformation from selfish skinflint to affable eccentric when forced to confront his past, present and future actions. If he fails, pathos becomes overplayed melodrama, and moments of poignancy become unintentional opportunities for humour. Fortunately, as Stephen Fry remarked, Alastair was the 'perfect Dickensian character'.[61] *Picturegoer* added, 'He brings to his characterisation the touches of comedy that Dickens embedded in the miserly skinflint, while not neglecting the dramatic impact.'[62] Not everyone agreed. Compared with later versions, and perhaps the modern caricature of the character, Alastair's interpretation of Scrooge appears neither vindictive nor particularly malicious. Indeed reviews at the time of the release of *Scrooge* commented: 'Sim seems less a "tight-fisted, squeezing wrenching miser" than a dour dyspeptic.'[63] And: 'Sim gives a rich, sometimes moving, often highly comic performance (too comic, perhaps?), but he never really convinced me.'[64] Indeed even before the film had reached the cinemas, George Minter, Managing Director of Renown Pictures, found himself having to defend his decision to cast Alastair in the title role in *Picturegoer* under the by-line: 'Why I Chose Sim'.[65] The essence of the criticism he faced was that Alastair was seen as a comedian by the general public, and therefore not capable of playing such a multifaceted character as Scrooge. Minter defended his position by describing Alastair as 'a comedian and a brilliant all-round character actor' and that Dickens 'obviously intended Scrooge to be a figure of fun, not of fustian melodrama'.[66]

Alastair's manic comedy period had provided him with an opportunity to stretch his physical talents to their extreme, and in so doing, he had become expert in slapstick comedy. There are moments in many of Alastair's films that are clearly derivative of the works of such luminaries as Chaplin, Lloyd and Laurel and Hardy. The example in *Laughter in Paradise* (1951) where Alastair's character taps the head of a policeman with his umbrella in order to make doubly sure that he is arrested — is almost pure Chaplin. Elements of this homage to the silent comedians appear in *Scrooge* — Alastair's dance for joy, his attempt to stand on his head, his fluffing up of his side hair to create the face of a madman. Having said that, Alastair portrays moments of tenderness in a subtle manner that appears neither contrived, nor out of character. The ultimate test is that Alastair succeeds in conveying the contemptuous Scrooge at the beginning of the story along with the joyful Scrooge after redemption without being seen as having played two entirely different characters.

Scrooge also benefits from excellent production values and a good supporting cast. C. Pennington-Richards, who was responsible for the cinematography, shot scenes at Nettlefold Studios in a way that beautifully complemented Alastair's acting. Witness the scene where Scrooge enters his house and walks towards the staircase. The camera is placed to give a perspective that conveys not only the approach of Scrooge, but also approaching damnation. Lighter scenes are equally well shot such as Tiny Tim looking into the toyshop window and the general street scenes in their Christmas glory. The music by Richard Addinsell is inspirational and adds to the eerie sense of the film by interlacing moody themes with traditional English folk tunes such as *Barbara Allan*.

There are many finely judged supporting roles, in particular Mervyn Johns as Bob Cratchit, but a surprising disappointment in the film is Sir Michael Hordern. Hordern plays Jacob Marley in such an ebullient way that what should appear to Scrooge as a fearful apparition becomes nothing more than light comedy relief. As a commendably restrained *Picturegoer* put it 'Michael Hordern is apt to be too theatrical'.[67]

Scrooge received mixed reviews on its release:

> Mr Alastair Sim is an actor with an actor's proper relish for the extremes in character and life . . . his caperings when he wakes from his dreams, his moments of Quilpish defiance during the hauntings; the gusto he brings to the closing scene with Bob Cratchit (Mr Mervyn Johns) are all of the stuff of Dickens . . . and if *Scrooge* is certainly not a masterpiece, nor even a faithful Christmas Carol, it is a brave film with the courage of its romantic convictions.[68]

The magazine *Picture Show* found a timeless quality in the film:

> A heart-warming film, filled with humour, sentiment, and sincerity . . . Beautifully cast and acted, skilfully directed, it breathes a Victorian spirit.[69]

Alastair treasured his performance as Scrooge although it brought him even further unwanted media attention. Interviewing Alastair became somewhat of a game of cat and mouse. To a reporter pretending to be a friend of a friend but secretly seeking an interview, Alastair said:

> Now if you were a Pressman, do you know what I'd tell you? . . . I'd tell you this: I want to go down in history as the actor who always said 'I don't know'.[70]

Alastair was a larger than life personality, powerful in expressing his views, principled, intelligent – a response of 'I don't know' would have been an anathema to him; indeed from someone else he would have seen it as a challenge. Alastair took it on himself to teach the young to think – here was a vocation in life, suited to someone who was a teacher by nature. To Alastair, the world was a fascinating place, from the divine – theatre and the arts – to the mystic – the soul – surrounded by the

unknown – physics and black holes. Alastair despised ignorance and yet
he would regularly use 'I don't know' as a means of distancing himself
from the usual trappings associated with showbusiness; as a means of
keeping his life private. And to this end, he succeeded remarkably well.
As a result, he quickly gained a reputation for being 'uninterviewable'.[71] A film magazine of the time, *The Cinema Studio*, explained to its
readers:

> Visiting newspapermen are always assured of a friendly welcome
> from him. . . But little else! For, when it comes to giving the visi-
> tor something to write about – information about himself, his plans,
> hopes, and aspirations – Mr Sim is a dead loss.[72]

Regardless of its own warning, *The Cinema Studio* sent its reporter to
interview Alastair. The producer of *Scrooge*, Brian Hurst, intercepted
the reporter saying: 'You'll never get him to talk about himself. . .
He's never given an interview yet, and I doubt if he ever will.'[73]
Nevertheless, the reporter tracked down Alastair and asked:

> 'How do you like playing Scrooge?' I asked.
> 'Believe me, I really don't know,' he said with a chuckle. . .

Another film magazine, *Picturegoer*, also visited the set of *Scrooge* and
reported back to its readers in its 'Studio Round-Up' section that
Alastair was 'having a whale of a time' when they arrived, and also
'joking off-set with Michael Hordern' and '. . . roaring with laughter'. It added that 'Alastair admitted to being "happy" about the part.'[74]
Alastair had every reason to be so, for his performance has become
the definitive Scrooge. Indeed Alastair's name often appears in lists
generated by film critics of those who should have been nominated
for an Oscar – but both the 1951 and 1952 Oscars were hotly con-
tested affairs.[75] This was reflected in the annual *Picturegoer* awards
which saw Alastair finish in sixth place – with Kirk Douglas just
beating Mario Lanza into first.[76]

Alastair's third and final film release of 1951 was the satirical *Lady
Godiva Rides Again* (1951). This was an attempt to send up the grotesque vein of beauty contests that seemed ubiquitous in the UK at the
time, but satire does not always satisfy an audience. The critics agreed:

Mr Launder is simply out to score as many points, farcical, fantastic, and sardonic, as he can in his game with an innocent lamb of a beauty queen let loose among the wolves that haunt the film, the advertising and the business worlds.[77]

One of those 'wolves' was played by Alastair – a shock of hair across his forehead, curled and flattering, managing to convey all manner of impropriety. Never could anything be more tenderly seductive, and yet equally as virtuous, as when his character offers to share half his bun with the beauty queen. It was simply a cameo performance by Alastair – as Sidney Gilliat put it '. . . one day's work for fun, or to be more exact, a case of Scotch or something, and a good time had by all'.[78] Alastair was on good form and singled out for praise: '*Lady Godiva Rides Again* would be worth seeing if only for the scene she shares with Mr Alastair Sim.'[79]

The year 1951 was Alastair's last in the role of Lord Rector at Edinburgh University. There was a small announcement in the press that on 6 July, in the exalted company of Air Commodore Sir Frank Whittle, the university presented Alastair with the honorary degree of Doctor of Laws (Hon. LLD). Alastair remained in great demand as a speaker and on 8 May 1951 he spoke at the Cambridge Union debate on a motion regarding the power of the critic. A theme he returned to on more than one occasion was 'Acting, Play-Acting and Personality'. The most detailed of his speeches on this topic was given to the Eton Literary Society. In it he espouses his idea that we begin acting from a very early age, as babies, and so from this point forward we are always astute to the value of being able to hide and camouflage our true intent. One wonders how accurately this was reflected in Alastair's own persona.

Folly to be Wise (1952) was a Launder and Gilliat screen adaptation of James Bridie's play *It Depends What You Mean*. Frank Launder co-wrote the screenplay and directed proceedings and Alastair reprised his stage role as Captain Paris. The play was updated for the film by having Paris organise a brains trust for the troops in order to boost their morale, but as one reviewer wrote 'Bridie's observations on marriage, his digs at the brain trustees, are not amusing enough to sustain the film'.[80]

Folly to be Wise is actually quite an enjoyable, understated and under-rated film. The dialogue within the Brains Trust session does become inane at times (probably one of Bridie's whimsical tricks) but Alastair appears on screen for the majority of the film, driving it forward with an energy fuelled by human goodwill that wonderfully contrasts with the underhand motivations of some of the other films' characters. Behind the scenes though, Alastair was beginning to have an unsettling effect on proceedings. Janet Brown, who plays the part of a Private who asks the panel whether marriage is a good idea, recalls:

> While filming *Folly to be Wise*, if the director had suggested one thing to me, Alastair would still want to 'direct' and would whisper behind the set to do it his way – which was funny but quite difficult, trying to work out whose advice to take![81]

Janet Brown is probably being very diplomatic. Sidney Gilliat gives a different take on proceedings:

> Up to about this time, I don't think one party ever dominated the other . . . but perhaps the rot set in, or the first sign of it, with *Folly to be Wise*. . . Alastair had directed the stage play and had perhaps too much influence on the film casting, which I always thought was not his strongest point. His performers on stage sometimes seemed to us to be capable but dull and/or unattractive. In this department, his rather violent prejudices were apt to come into play. Anyone who smelt a bit too much of showbiz and followed its conventions was apt to feel his disfavour . . . (e.g. Roland Culver . . . whose performance I couldn't ever see anything wrong with).[82]

Indeed, Roland Culver's performance is as good as any of the leading characters. However, as Sidney Gilliat forewarned, the rot had indeed begun to set in.

Alastair's only film of 1953, *Innocents in Paris*, is a rather unsatisfactory compendium of storylines[83]. Alastair plays the British diplomat Sir Norman Barker who contrives to get his Russian counterpart to agree to an economic summit after an extended drinking session at a nightclub. The morning after scene is the most enjoyable part of the film when Sir Norman Barker has to pay for his evening of carousing by offering up his most valuable possessions. Also in the film was Kenneth Williams, playing a window dresser. He commented on the

experience in his diary for Tuesday 16 September 1952: 'Dreary business. Masses of q. degenerates'.[84] One cannot disagree with his first
comment.

★

1950–1952 had been the most successful period of Alastair's career
to date. He had starred in three hit films, *The Happiest Days of your
Life* (1950), *Laughter in Paradise* (1951) and *Scrooge* (1951); he had
worked with Hitchcock in *Stage Fright* (1950), paid tribute to Bridie
in *Folly to be Wise* (1952), and achieved critical acclaim for his performance on stage in *Mr Gillie*. *Picturegoer* regarded Alastair as one
of the best: 'Ann Todd is a top star and there are Trevor Howard,
Michael Redgrave, Googie Withers and Alastair Sim.'[85] Alastair had
also appeared on the opening night of Scottish television speaking
about acting, play-acting and personality. Alastair even achieved royal
recognition when, on 1 June 1953, the Coronation honours listed
that Alastair Sim, 'actor', was to be awarded the CBE.

The offer of the CBE did not sit very comfortably with Alastair.
It meant more publicity, but perhaps more importantly, accepting
it would mean associating himself with an elitist system, something
he disliked intensely. In the end, after much soul searching, Alastair
accepted the award and gave the reason quoted in many different
sources as '. . . in recognition of the number of appalling scripts I
rejected'. It may be just as well that the CBE was not in fact awarded
according to the wisdom of his script selection since he was about
to make some notable failures. Later, when he was offered a knight-
hood, he returned to his principles and respectfully declined it on
the basis that everyone was equal.

Two partnerships had played a significant role in Alastair's success, but Bridie was now dead and Alastair's relationship with Frank
Launder and Sidney Gilliat was beginning to show signs of strain.
Furthermore, regardless of his attempts to stretch himself as an actor
by playing dramatic roles on stage, the public had begun to see
Alastair foremost as an eccentric. His next film would only serve to
reinforce these views, for he was about to play the role of a woman.
But this was no ordinary woman. This was to be an iconic character;
someone who would make a reappearance fifty years later.

9

Miss Fritton and The Belles of St Trinian's

Oh I suppose I'm just a foolish weak woman.

– Alastair Sim as Miss Fritton

The opening cartoon graphics to *The Happiest Days of your Life* had been drawn by Ronald Searle[1] whose series of cartoons describing the grisly antics of a group of unruly and anarchic schoolgirls had become very popular with the readers of *Lilliput* magazine. This popularity had resulted in several books: *Hurrah for St Trinian's* (1947), *Back to the Slaughterhouse* (1951) and *Souls in Torment* (1953). With Ealing in decline, Launder and Gilliat took an inspired decision to turn the two-dimensional Searle girls into three-dimensional characters. The result was the glorious *The Belles of St Trinian's* (1954):

> The caricatures of Ronald Searle really come to life in this joyous, carefree slapstick comedy of life at St Trinian's, a girls' school, the like of which has never been seen before.[2]

Launder and Gilliat approached Alastair and asked if he would take on the role of Clarence, the ne'er do well brother of the headmistress, Miss Fritton. Alastair read the script and agreed. Meanwhile, Gilliat was desperately trying to find a charismatic lead to play the part of the headmistress. Margaret Rutherford might have appeared as a suitable candidate, but she was unavailable. The search was heading nowhere when Alastair proposed the idea that he play both characters. It would mean the use of trick photography, but by the 1950s that was easily achievable. Launder and Gilliat agreed to Alastair's suggestion, and in so doing, presented him with the opportunity to create a character that now lives on in posterity – the somewhat hideous, shrewd and yet benign Miss Fritton.[3]

The Belles of St Trinian's begins with a Sultan sending his daughter to St Trinian's – a private boarding school in Barchester. As the girls return for the new school term, businesses board up their shop fronts, men run for cover and policemen lock themselves in their cells. Clarence (Alastair Sim) arrives at the school hoping to persuade his sister, Miss Fritton (Alastair Sim), to enrol his daughter Arabella (Vivienne Martin[4]) for another term:

> Arabella: Monica Drew wasn't expelled when she burnt down the gymnasium.
> Miss Fritton: The gymnasium was *insured*.

Such an exchange is an amusing inversion of the girl's stories of the 1950s, where traditionally it was the heroine of the book who rescues the girls from the school fire. At St Trinian's, it is the girls themselves who start the fire.

St Trinian's is practically bankrupt. An engaging parallel is provided by the morally bankrupt staff: 'If only I had the courage to give myself up,' announces a beautifully Gothic Miss Waters (Betty Ann Davis mimicking the Charles Butler creation, Morticia Adams). Miss Fritton decides to redeem the situation by placing all of the school's remaining funds on Arab Boy[5] – a racehorse running in the Cheltenham Gold Cup. The fourth-form girls bring the racehorse back to their dormitory for safekeeping but Miss Fritton discovers the girls with the thoroughbred and announces: 'Girls, girls, you know perfectly well that pets are not allowed in the dormitories'. The police are also interested in the goings-on at St Trinian's and so Superintendent Kemp-Bird (Lloyd Lamble) sends an undercover officer, Policewoman Ruby 'Good-Ho Sammy' Gates (Joyce Grenfell), to infiltrate the school as the games teacher. The ending is a happy one with Arab Boy winning the Cup and thus saving the school from closure.

Alastair's performance as Miss Fritton is a parody of all those great aunts who have existed from time immemorial, hence a significant part of the humour is timeless. Naomi described him thus: 'On his high heels he towered over me, the beautifully coifed wig adding to his height and the necessary padding to his girth, a rather monstrous female...'[6] The *Guardian* in contrast suggested 'Sim made no concessions at all to femininity, apart from hauling on a rough tweed skirt and twinset pearls.'[7] Most would agree that this is inaccurate.

Alastair's characterisation of Miss Fritton is a sublimely judged portrait of an ageing female headmistress that manages to fuse the grotesque with the maternal. The mannerisms, especially the walk, and the swirling of the shawl around the neck are feminine gestures, but subtly played and sometimes registering only on a subconscious level. Herein lies the success of Alastair's female impersonation over and above the arguably more physically accurate ones presented in recent Hollywood films such as *Tootsie* (1982) and *Mrs Doubtfire* (1993). When Miss Fritton announces, 'Oh I suppose I'm just a foolish weak woman', the audience knows that quite the opposite is true; but we are not questioning her gender, just disagreeing with her intellectual self-evaluation. George Cole as Flash Harry[8] announces on many occasions 'What a dame!' in total admiration of Miss Fritton. A veneration rightly due if only for the numerous instances in which she avoids the booby-traps left by the mischievous fourth-formers.

It is worth watching *The Belles of St Trinian's* a second or third time in order to concentrate on how Alastair plays his scenes. Those involving him with the schoolgirls have a wonderfully motherly feel to them, especially the way in which his body language as Miss Fritton conveys a real interest in each individual member of the school. A good example of this is when Miss Fritton explains the school's ethos to the new girls with the speech:

> In other schools, girls are sent out quite unprepared into a merciless world but when our girls leave here, it is the merciless world that has to be prepared. That is why we set great store here on physical fitness – lots of games, lots of exercise, a certain amount of food and, above all, lots and lots of fresh air.[9]

Each word or phrase is addressed to a particular girl from the group with touching sincerity. One believes implicitly in the person delivering the speech – not a man in drag, but the headmistress of a girls' school who treasures each of the girls in her care, admittedly mainly due to their economic value rather than for any altruistic reason. Stephen Fry once said of Alastair; 'the best actor I think for looking and listening to people'.[10] This is a perceptive observation for it is Alastair's ability to engage so honestly and intently with the other characters around him that gives such added conviction to his scenes.

The ultimate test for any female impersonator is when their character finds themselves surrounded by women. At one point, Alastair as Miss Fritton, addresses her beleaguered staff while indulging in a subtle female gesture – pinning back her hair. Would a man in drag do this? Obviously not, since the fake hair would be perfect anyway. Hence Miss Fritton is a woman, and an especially perceptive and intelligent one within her self-imposed, closeted world. This is all too clear in the following exchange of dialogue between Miss Fritton and Ruby Gates (Joyce Grenfell):

> Ruby Gates: We're all girl guides, aren't we?
> Miss Fritton: Are we? Some of us may have aspired beyond that happy state, Miss Crawley.[11]

Conceptually, Launder and Gilliat succeeded in offering a brand of humour distinct from the Ealing comedy tradition. Ealing dealt with reality, albeit allowing for eccentricity to evolve within a real scenario. In contrast, the *St Trinian's* films espoused a school system unlike any at the time. St Trinian's is an anarchic environment in which the staff simply co-exist with the girls. The girls themselves are clearly divided into the fourth-formers, whose anarchy is still contained within a tentative framework of good-naturedness, and the sixth-formers, whose passions and ideals are best left unquestioned. The fourth-formers represent the Searle caricature of schoolgirls – a pastiche of the girls in the popular heroic school stories of the time. An interesting element to the comedy is the inversion of the concept that children are innocent. This theme occurs frequently throughout the film with the hockey match embodying much of the mischief to be found in the real world, namely cheating, violence and match-rigging.

One could argue that *The Belles of St Trinian's* lacks the cosy charm of *The Happiest Days of your Life* and is certainly less tightly plotted. Indeed, several characters are left stranded by inconclusive plot diversions. For example, towards the end of the film, Ruby Gates scribbles endless notes on some linoleum and then rides off on a horse without any explanation or conclusion to her action. Inevitably a feeling remains that the film is incomplete. Furthermore, *The Happiest Days of your Life* worked so well because the plot, the setting and the characters were plausible, especially in contrast to the match-rigging, gin-swilling girls of St Trinian's. Nutbourne College could exist somewhere, but St Trinian's? Probably not – one hopes.

Regardless of these criticisms, *The Belles of St Trinian's* became a huge commercial and international[12] success spawning several sequels. *Blue Murder at St Trinian's* (1957) will be discussed in the next chapter since Alastair once again reprised his role as Miss Fritton. The following three films, *The Pure Hell of St Trinian's* (1960), *The Great St Trinian's Train Robbery* (1966) and *Wildcats of St Trinian's* (1980) represented a gradual decline in the quality of the series with *Wildcats of St Trinian's* being an anachronistic embarrassment.

Ronald Searle wrote in 1992 that he had been contracted to work on another *St Trinian's* film but nothing came of this. In July 2003, it was reported that Simon Nye had been signed to write the screenplay of a remake of *The Belles of St Trinian's* with Rupert Everett earmarked as the headmistress. This casting was maintained for the film, *St Trinian's*, which finally made it onto the big screen in the UK on 21 December 2007. Written by Nick Moorcroft and Piers Ashworth, and directed by Barnaby Thompson and Oliver Parker, the supporting cast included Stephen Fry, Russell Brand and Colin Firth, who manages to keep a straight face throughout proceedings as he sends up his own screen personality.

Rupert Everett's portrayal of Miss Fritton is an oddity in that it offers a sexual tension between Miss Fritton and the Education Minister (Colin Firth) that is completely ludicrous and yet presses forward relentlessly, driven by its own self-belief. The characters of the girls are more fully rounded than those in the previous *St Trinian's* films which relied on a straightforward distinction between the fourth- and sixth-formers – when the world was apparently a more simple place. In the remake, the girls are re-categorised to represent the new social demographics of our youth culture, such as Posh Totty, Emos and Chavs (the world now being of course *much* more complicated). Whereas the plot of the original film concerns betting on a horse race, the remake is about a heist, stylishly shot at times, but on a budget that appears to be quite tight. The soundtrack provides an energy that sustains the film especially at the beginning when the plotting meanders. An interesting diversion is in the set piece of the hockey match. The opposing hockey team, a public school, appears to be just as obnoxious, if not more so than the dear monsters of St Trinian's.

Reviews have been mixed. Broadsheets, in general, have criticised the film for its banal plotting and crude sense of humour. Some reviewers have made the *faux pas* in making direct comparisons with the original as if under the impression that nothing has changed in the meantime. This mistake is further compounded by seeming to believe that the film is aimed at adults. All one has to do is to read the informal comments written by teenagers in their own imitable style on social pages on the internet to realise that *St Trinian's* has successfully appealed to their sense of humour. This just leaves some nagging doubts that some of the jokes are too adult-orientated.

Overall, *St Trinian's* will not appeal to the purists and will offend those who recoil at jokes about our drug culture perpetuated on screen. On the other hand, it is not the abject failure that some reviewers have suggested, and achieved respectable figures at the box office. In fact, a new St Trinian's film, currently filming at Ealing Studios, is due for release in December 2009.

Questions were always going to arise regarding Alastair's sexuality when he chose to impersonate a woman. The truth – that it was a different and challenging role – would always be subservient to the perception of deviancy. Whether one would wish to take the step of advertising homosexual tendencies at a time when such admittance was regarded by the state as a crime is a point lost in the murkiness of innuendo. A friend of Alastair's said:

> Alastair was not gay. He was not homosexual. . . If he was gay or homosexual I would have known about it . . . given the long time I knew him.[13]

Another friend remarked, 'I have no reason to think he was homo-sexual – even if he was a little bit the other way'.[14] Although Alastair was not overtly effeminate, he did have a tendency to refer to people as 'darling' with tactile friendliness – in the traditional thespian manner. Far too much can be read into this.

Perhaps of more interest is Alastair's view on marriage. He was once recalled as saying, 'Marriage is very important – to pick the right person I mean and stay with them. One can undertake a bit of bedding on the side.'[15] Taken out of context this could imply that Alastair was unfaithful to Naomi. There is no evidence to support this assertion but Sir Ian McKellen once remarked 'Alastair, as a man, used to know how to get out of scrapes.'[16] Conjecture aside, what it does highlight is how prejudiced and principled Alastair had become. He firmly believed in maintaining the family bond at whatever cost. This belief caused a strain between Alastair and George Cole during George's marriage problems when Alastair was adamant that George should not consider divorce as an option.

★

Alastair had achieved good reviews for both his theatrical and screen work. His face was easily recognisable by the general public and people would pay to see a film in which he headlined. Much to his chagrin, by 1954, Alastair Sim had become a film star. The problem was, Alastair neither enjoyed this status nor wished to play by its rules. Some actors are very protective of their star status and all that it confers, and therefore behave, at least publicly, in a manner conducive to them perpetuating their brand name, which is essentially what being a 'star' is all about. In contrast, Alastair distanced himself from stardom, treating any form of hero-worship with disdain. He was even oblivious to the media through which stardom was communicated. Avril Angers, who was to appear with Alastair in *The Green Man* (1956) recounted the following incident:

As we sat in the location car ... waiting for a shot, I was reading a film magazine. Alastair said, 'What is that dear?' I said 'It's a film magazine'. He looked puzzled and said, 'May I see?' I gave him the magazine and he obviously had never seen the like – he asked, 'Good gracious – are there many of these sorts of things?'[17]

It seems a strange question for Alastair to ask, given that at the time of the quote, he had been in the film industry for twenty-one years. Alastair simply abhorred the thought that the public would spend so much time and money on reading about film stars. Crucially, he saw the idea of hero-worship as clouding the ability of people to make sound judgements. Sidney Gilliat:

> Alastair Sim was a first-class intellect who refused to accept any of the everyday conventions of show business. He eschewed parties, always refused to sign autographs (not as much as being beneath him as that it ought to be beneath would-be autograph hunters) and disliked the usual film publicity.[18]

As Alastair said:

> You know it's awful . . . the things they ask you to do nowadays. . . I mean that only the other day somebody asked me if I would judge poodles at a dog show. Now, because I happen to be an actor does that qualify me to be a judge of poodles? . . . It's all nonsense. . . But I can tell you something even worse. . . Do you know I was asked recently to submit samples of my garden produce for auctioning at a village fair? Now, why in the world should anybody be interested in my vegetables?[19]

So if not exactly a film star, what sort of actor was Alastair? James Bridie wrote of him:

> The little fellows who catalogue actors and who find a pigeon-hole for each of them, high up or low down as the case may be, can't find anywhere to put him. He is not, perhaps, what they call an actor at all, but, I think, something better, if you please, if that is what you mean by actors. He does not go on stage night after night speaking another man's words and contenting himself with, as they say, interpreting them to the audience. The words are his material for creating something out of his own personality. He is not unique in this, only more unusual than most actors would like to think.[20]

A school photograph of Alastair (second from the left on the back row) taken around 1911, courtesy of Margaret Whitaker. His teacher, Margaret Bell, recalled that he loved to recite, 'A horse, a horse, my kingdom for a horse'.

COURT
TAILOR
SIM
HABIT
MAKER

——————————"OUR GIRLS'" COSTUMIERS——————————

Owing to the speedy development of this department, we have found it necessary to transfer our business to **96 and**
LOTHIAN ROAD (as shown above). Here can be seen a large and varied stock of MAIDS' DRESSES, COSTUMES
WRAP COATS, &c., all in the latest designs and shades—the pick of the London Markets.
Our SUMMER SALE is now in full swing **;** every garment has been marked down, and special lines are offered consid
ably under cost price to effect a clearance. ☞ *Please call and inspect our Goods ; we guarantee to give satisfaction.*

Court
Tailor
SIM
Habit
Maker
96 and 98 LOTHIAN ROAD

Above: The Sim's family business circa 1910 as printed in the James Gillespie's School Magazine, courtesy of Anne Inglis and the James Gillespie School. Alexander Sim used to supply the school with their school uniform.

Opposite: Map of Edinburgh (*c.*1920s) and sketches of local scenes relevant to Alastair's time spent in Edinburgh. Courtesy of Brian Quinton.

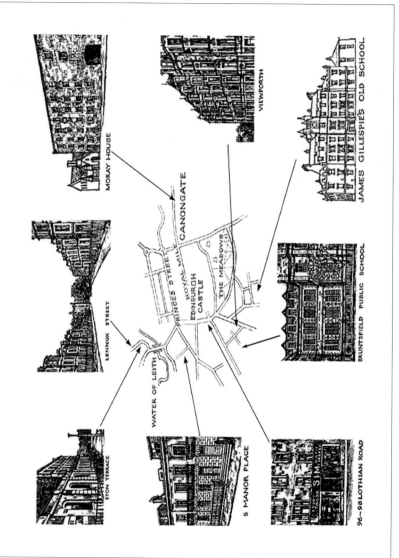

MORAY HOUSE

VIEWFORTH

JAMES GILLESPIE'S OLD SCHOOL

CANONGATE

ROYAL MILE

PRINCES STREET

EDINBURGH CASTLE

THE MEADOWS

LENNOX STREET

WATER OF LEITH

BRUNTSFIELD PUBLIC SCHOOL

ETON TERRACE

5 MANOR PLACE

96—98 LOTHIAN ROAD

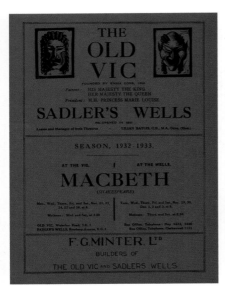

THE OLD VIC

FOUNDED BY EMMA CONS, 1880

Patrons: HIS MAJESTY THE KING
HER MAJESTY THE QUEEN
President: H.R. PRINCESS MARIE LOUISE

SADLER'S WELLS

RE-OPENED IN 1931

Lessee and Manager of both Theatres — LILIAN BAYLIS, C.H., M.A., Oxon. (Hon.)

SEASON, 1932-1933.

| AT THE VIC. | AT THE WELLS. |

MACBETH

(SHAKESPEARE)

| Mon., Wed., Thurs., Fri. and Sat., Nov. 21, 23, 24, 25 and 26, at 8. | Tues., Wed., Thurs., Fri. and Sat., Nov. 29, 30, Dec. 1, 2 and 3, at 8. |
| Matinee : Wed. and Sat., at 2.30 | Matinee : Thurs. and Sat., at 2.30. |

| OLD VIC, Waterloo Road, S.E. 1 | Box Office, Telephone : Hop 5434, 5435 |
| SADLER'S WELLS, Rosebery Avenue, E.C. 1 | Box Office, Telephone : Clerkenwell 1121 |

F. G. MINTER. Lᵀᴰ

BUILDERS OF

THE OLD VIC AND SADLERS WELLS

Embassy

THE MAN WHO
WAS FED UP
by
FREDERICK WITNEY.

Threepence

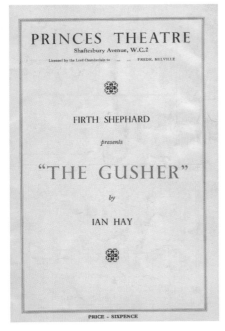

PRINCES THEATRE

Shaftesbury Avenue, W.C.2

Licensed by the Lord Chamberlain to — — FREDK. MELVILLE

❦

FIRTH SHEPHARD

presents

"THE GUSHER"

by

IAN HAY

❦

PRICE - SIXPENCE

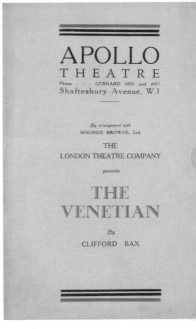

APOLLO

THEATRE

Phone - - - GERRARD 6970 and 6971
Shaftesbury Avenue, W.1

By arrangement with
MAURICE BROWNE, Ltd.

THE
LONDON THEATRE COMPANY

presents

THE VENETIAN

By
CLIFFORD BAX

Four theatre programmes from the 1930s with Alastair in the cast.

A publicity shot (uncredited) of Alastair from 1937.

Two pages of caricatures of Alastair from *The Tatler and Bystander* magazine 1937 and 1947.

Picture Show and Film Pictorial, Vol. 43, No. 1106   July 6th, 1940   Registered at the G.P.O. as a Newspaper

PICTURE SHOW

and
Film
Pictorial

EVERY
TUESDAY

3ᴰ

ALASTAIR SIM • DIANA CHURCHILL • BARRY · K · BARNES

in "LAW *and* DISORDER"

Front cover of *Picture Show* magazine (1940) showing Alastair in the role of Samuel Blight in *Law and Disorder* (1940), courtesy of ©IPC+ Syndication.

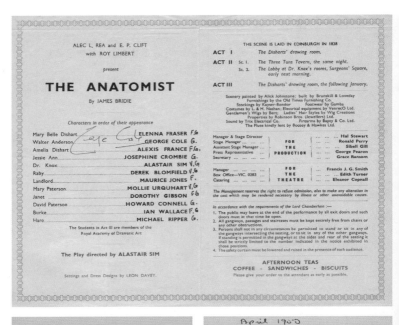
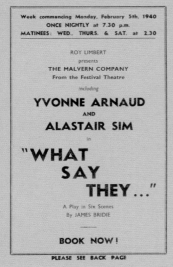
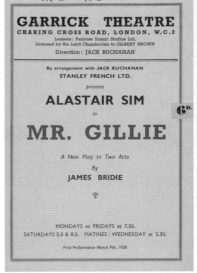

Three theatre programmes during the period of association between James Bridie and Alastair Sim. The programme for *The Anatomist* is autographed by George Cole.

John Vickers

ALASTAIR SIM AS MR. McCRIMMON
IN *Mr. Bolfrey*—JAMES BRIDIE

Alastair Sim as Mr McCrimmon in James Bridie's *Mr Bolfry*. Autographed by
Alastair. Photograph by John Vickers, courtesy of Mrs N. Campbell-Vickers and
the John Vickers Theatre Collection.

Week ending October 6, 1951

EVERY THURSDAY 3½D.

Picturegoer

THE NATIONAL FILM WEEKLY

ALASTAIR
SIM

START READING 'IN TOWN TONIGHT'

see page 10

Front cover of *Picturegoer* magazine (1951). Alastair tops the British Cinema
Exhibitor's popularity poll. Courtesy of ©IPC+ Syndication.

Film still from *The Happiest Days of Your Life* (1950). Alastair, as Wetherby Pond, confronts the formidable headmistress of St Swithins (Margaret Rutherford). Joyce Grenfell (Miss Gossage) fears for the outcome. Courtesy of Canal+Image UK Limited.

Film still from *Laughter in Paradise* (1951). Alastair, as Deniston — author of potboilers — succeeds in getting himself arrested as per the demands of a vindictive clause in a family will. Courtesy of Canal+Image UK Limited.

Film still from *The Belles of St Trinian's* (1954). Alastair, as Miss Fritton, addresses her beleaguered staff. Courtesy of Canal+Image UK Limited.

Film still from *The Green Man* (1956). Alastair, as the assassin (Hawkins), tries to placate the concerns of the vacuum cleaner salesman, William Blake (George Cole). Courtesy of Canal+Image UK Limited.

Several of the theatre plays of James Bridie were filmed by the BBC for television. This shows the coverage of *Mr Gillie* in the *Radio Times*, June 12–18, 1960. Courtesy of the BBC and Glasgow University Library.

Plaque dedicated to Alastair Sim, unveiled in a ceremony by Sir Ian McKellen. The plaque can be found on the wall next to the Filmhouse, located at 88 Lothian Road, Edinburgh.

Sir Ian McKellen wrote:

> It is difficult to categorize his acting but if stage stars could be crudely divided between the 'protean' and the 'personality', between those whose forte is disguise, a varied and soaring daring, and those whose range is deliberately narrower, craftsmen of detail and refinement, then Alastair Sim should be labelled a 'personality' actor.'[21]

There is much truth in Sir Ian McKellen's observation. Certainly Alastair disliked using stage make-up to any great degree, Miss Fritton being the exception, and anyway, there was little he could do to camouflage his distinctive features. Occasionally there might be an embellishment to the hair – witness the debauched, sordid strands in *London Belongs to Me* (1948), the disreputable wisps in *Lady Godiva Rides Again* (1951), or the eccentric tufts in *Scrooge* (1951). Hence disguise was not his forte; and as for being a craftsman, Derek Fowlds once said:

> Alastair was a genius. I never saw him working anything out technically in rehearsal, it just sort of happened. He was so real and truthful and sheer joy to watch.[22]

But as always with Alastair, there is this over-riding sense of contradiction. An acute attention to detail is inherent in all of his work. As Alastair once wrote to James Bridie: 'I am a hell of a fellow for trying to get inside'[23] – a reference to his attempt to understand both the motivations of the character he was playing and also the meaning and themes of the play. Hence even his most superficial of characters had a depth to them, which, given a mediocre film, would often identify his contribution as the highlight, as seen in the five-minute cameo of *Lady Godiva Rides Again* (1951). Though this might be thought of as a natural gift, it brought problems:

> Alastair Sim is just one of those actors who cannot be given a small part without completely upsetting the balance of the whole production. If he played the butler, you wouldn't bother noticing whom he was announcing.[24]

If that was the case with a small part then what of larger roles? There is no doubt that Alastair could, unintentionally, eclipse the rest of the cast. Reviews of *Laughter in Paradise* (1951) noted:

> It is a case of Sim first and the rest nowhere. . . The fact that Alastair Sim dominates an episode which is perfectly designed for him, gives the picture memorable high spots, but only accentuates the negative in the rest of the ingredients of this comedy. . . It is as though the scriptwriters exhausted their ingenuity in catering for Sim and filled out the rest of the picture with second best.[25]

Of course too much analysis can be a bad thing. As Freddie Jones put it: 'Who knows about his approach to acting? His magic was unique and a complete enigma.'[26] And Maurice Denham, who appeared with Alastair in *London Belongs to Me* (1948), when asked to describe Alastair, replied succinctly 'a splendid comic actor'.[27]

★

In a letter to James Bridie, Alastair had once written, 'I really can't be bothered very much with Priestley, though I admit he has occasional visitations from a demi-semi-god'.[28] Such a visitation must have befallen Priestley the weekend he wrote *An Inspector Calls* since it became the next film project for an increasingly selective Alastair. Shooting took place at Shepperton studios with Alastair in the lead role of Inspector Poole, named Inspector Goole in Priestley's play, with all the phonetic undertones. Poole visits the Birling family to request their help in understanding why a girl, Eva Smith (Jane Wenham), has taken poison and committed suicide. Through flashbacks and perceptive questioning, the Inspector gradually reveals how each member of the family holds some responsibility for the poor girl's death.

The film differed from the play mainly in its involvement of Eva. In the play the leading characters constantly refer to Eva though she is never seen, but for the film version, the producers decided that her actual presence was required. Said J.B. Priestley '. . . it isn't enough just to hear about a film character – picturegoers expect to see her as well'.[29] Priestley himself provided the extra dialogue.

The predominant issue as far as the film magazine *Picturegoer* was concerned was expressed thus: 'Please, No laughing at Sim. This is serious. One laugh in the wrong place and you may upset the drama'.[30] Their concern was whether audiences would be able to 'suppress an admiring giggle as those angular Sim features loom upon the screen. . .'.[31] It was a worry shared by the film's distributors and producers, and so the film's publicity department swung into action and tried to make this a positive feature of the film by saying: 'filmgoers have [a] surprise in store for them in the completely uncharacteristic role taken by Alastair Sim.'[32] The film's producer Norman Collins was quoted as saying, 'In this film, picturegoers will see the Sim who made his reputation long ago on the stage, as a very controlled, severe actor.'[33] Although not quite 'severe', Alastair perfectly captures the enigmatic quality of Inspector Poole.

1954 was a year of celebration in the Sim household. One of their 'family' was getting married. Whereas such an event is an opportunity to break free from the family bonds, George Cole felt no such need and chose to live with his wife, Eileen Moore, in a house built near to Forrigan.

Having achieved such huge success in films between 1950 and 1954, Alastair, who justified his acceptance of a CBE on the basis of his script selection policy, managed to make some incredibly suspect decisions over the following six years. His two films for 1955 are noticeable for their mediocrity. The first was *Geordie* (1955), filmed in glorious Technicolor in order to allow the plush Scottish settings to be brought vividly to life. Unfortunately, it is a film over-burdened with genres – drama, romance, sport, travel and comedy. Geordie (Paul Young) undertakes a body-building course and grows into a tall and powerfully built man (Bill Travers) who, on his father's death, becomes head gamekeeper to the Laird (Alastair Sim). Geordie successfully competes at the Highland Games and soon he is heading for Melbourne and the Olympic games.

The first half of *Geordie* is a pleasant enough venture, especially when the Laird takes it upon himself to instruct Geordie in the art of hammer-throwing. This is an opportunity for Alastair to display his physical prowess at comedy. He spins round in an altogether unconvincing manner and launches the hammer in the direction of a passing Reverend (Jack Radcliffe). A weakness is the dialogue, which appears at times positively mundane – the adult Geordie whining at one point: 'I don't want Dad's kilt – I want my Dad.' To give the film some credit, it tries to examine issues of integrity and morality, and ends with an endorsement of wholesome, clean, honest living. One review said: 'Graceless and superficial, it seems to work against the subject a great deal of the time . . . it is sentimental where it should be tender and commonplace where it should be discerning.'[34] Having said that, it is the sheer unpretentiousness of the film that makes it enjoyable Sunday afternoon viewing.

Geordie was followed by *Escapade* (1955) based on a play by Roger MacDougall[35]. *Escapade* featured John Mills as John Hampden, a pacifist, whose obsession for achieving world peace is threatening his marriage. His sons Max (Andrew Ray), Johnny (Peter Asher) and Icarus (a character never seen in the film) steal an aeroplane in order to fly to Europe to present a petition to the four superpowers asking them to prevent future wars.

Alastair made an appearance as the boy's headmaster, Doctor Skillingworth – 'Ruling his boys with quiet firmness, he nevertheless has a deep-hearted understanding of the exuberance of youth.'[36] *Escapade* was a light comedy-drama focussing on the concerns of many during the escalating Cold War. Within the main theme there is an endearing message of both world and family reconciliation as the boys hope that their 'escapade' will reunite their parents. The film was regarded as 'gently and rather effetely whimsical'[37] and flawed by its obvious attempt to exploit the popularity of Alastair. The intention was that 'Dr. Skillingworth comes vividly to life with a quizzical eyebrow, a dash of drolly sardonic humour and, above all, a human touch that springs directly from Sim's superb delineation of character.'[38] This backfired: 'the part of Skillingworth has been expanded to provide some skilful but irrelevant comic interludes from Alastair Sim.'[39]

Andrew Ray had fond memories of his time spent on the set of *Escapade*, saying of Alastair that he was 'a joy to work with'[40] and 'playing scenes with him had an intensity and a reality that I shall always remember and treasure'.[41] The other boy actor in the film, Jeremy Spencer, became a regular visitor to Forrigan. As Faith Evans, friend of Naomi, recalled:

Forrigan with its tennis court, its games room and its makeshift football pitch, became a never-never land, a children's paradise, which
offered a second home to a series of what Naomi called 'unofficially
adopted young ones'.[42]

Jeremy invited Andrew Ray to stay over at Forrigan one weekend.
Andrew Ray continues:

> Alastair was of course a perfect host, even if he did beat me 10–8 in a
> set of tennis! Anyway, that night I must have been shouting in my sleep
> when I was awakened by Alastair's head popping round my bedroom
> door, obviously concerned by my shouting and nightmare noises.
> Being a little disorientated and not knowing where I was, I was abso-
> lutely terrified to see that bald dome and those sad blue eyes staring in
> my direction. I thought I was in the movie *Scrooge* for a moment![43]

Alastair's delight in providing a stimulating retreat for young actors
provoked, on occasion, a backlash of ill-feeling. Such a situation developed over Jeremy Spencer, whose parents – staunch Catholics – were
horrified to discover that their son was being tutored in acting and
life skills by a self-confessed atheist. An angry exchange took place
and Alastair was forced to back down although friends said 'he handled the situation well'.[44] In today's world there might be expressions
of concern made regarding Alastair's behaviour towards impressionable young teenagers. A friend of Alastair's once said: 'Alastair was very
friendly . . . though this could be mistaken for being something more
sinister.'[45] The fact that Alastair was so reticent with the press acts both
ways. Some may see this as his attempt to hide something; others that
he was simply the private man he always said he was.

The weekends at Forrigan became an integral part of Alastair and
Naomi's life. In the 1940s James Bridie would drop in to debate and
discuss the development of his latest play. Naomi wrote 'Those years
in the forties when the author/director-actor relationship between
Jimmy [Bridie] and Alastair was going so well were exhilarating
– something fresh always happening.'[46] In the 1950s the poet and playwright Christopher Fry[47] would stay over for the weekend.

Christopher Fry's son was at a Quaker school in Reading and
became one of the many young visitors to be invited by Alastair to

stay over at Forrigan. It was inevitable therefore that Christopher Fry and Alastair Sim would eventually meet.[48] This meeting developed into a friendship which was summarised by Christopher Fry as 'devoted, affectionate antagonism'.[49] The Frys, along with Alastair's neighbours the Stokes, were frequently employed as the audience in the rehearsal room at Forrigan. All three couples became great friends and enjoyed occasional trips together to one of their favourite holiday destinations, the Welsh village of Portmerion.

Christopher Fry recounted how Alastair and Naomi once stayed with them one summer at their house in Bwlch, Wales. Fry laid out a croquet lawn with hoops and invited everyone to play. Alastair was immediately scornful of croquet – pointing out its associations with the upper classes and how it was not in tune with his social beliefs. After much dithering, he was reluctantly drawn into the game. When it had finished, Fry, his wife and Naomi went for a long walk, returning in the 'early dusk with the moon rising'.[50] On their return, they discovered Alastair still playing croquet – on his own. He had become smitten with the game, having once again circumvented his principles in the process.

Sarah Badel, who appeared with Alastair on stage in the 1960s, said, 'I used to go to stay with him and Naomi at Nettlebed at weekends, which were always informal, great fun and joyous occasions.'[51] Another visitor was Sidney Gilliat:

> I vividly remember Alastair clowning superbly in a mad game of Progressive Ping Pong in his house when the rain had driven us in from tennis. He was an enthusiastic performer at the latter, though the game must not be too serious. In later life, he called his own brand 'Forrigan tennis' to distinguish from anything that might be taken seriously or pretentiously.[52]

Forrigan tennis became infamous among visiting guests since it abided by a special set of rules that would only be imparted to opponents on a need-to-know basis; a set of rules which inevitably favoured the host. John Howard Davies, another regular victim of Forrigan tennis said, with tongue firmly in cheek, 'I used to think he was a terrible cheat'.[53] David Ambrose described Forrigan tennis as 'completely potty'.[54] Another visitor, Peter Copley, recalled:

He enjoyed tennis but never appeared to move, somehow drawing the ball to him, giving it a quick swish and winning the point: put differently, it wasn't really done to beat him at tennis . . . but fate attacked him one wet autumn day when he slipped on the fallen leaves and broke his leg.[55]

Apart from the usual games of chance and skill, Alastair also engaged visitors in a card game called 'Knock', which involved a small gamble. Christopher Fry used to bring a metal box to Forrigan just containing sixpences in order to play the game. Naomi would join in with games of chess and Alastair would take the opportunity to play bridge if such a foursome could be formed.

Also in the garden at Forrigan was a swing seat upon which Alastair would stretch out his full frame and doze. Naomi would come and cut the grass, much to Alastair's consternation: the noise, the damage to the daisies, and Naomi's insistence on doing as many of the household chores as possible. Alastair often told Naomi that she worked too hard and was always suggesting she get help. Naomi, with a similar outlook in life to Alastair's mother, thought nothing of the tasks, and even went so far as to admit that she enjoyed the work. Naomi didn't want anyone assisting them – she still had the memories of the awkward time when Norah had insisted they take on staff at their London house in the 1940s. Naomi was also a considerate hostess. Her friend and literary agent Faith Evans said of her:

> She combined an irresistible naughtiness and sense of fun with an almost compulsive politeness and concern for others. Staying at Forrigan, if you said you had to be in London by nine, she would set her alarm for five.[56].

Although Alastair had a reputation for being introverted when faced with strangers, at Forrigan, he was in his element. He had a keen intellect and was willing to engage in debate with all comers – particularly if it allowed him to provoke a reaction. For example, Alastair would gamely announce: 'I am a communist' – 'because it was more uncomfortable for other people if he said "I am a communist".'[57] Such an expression may not induce much of a reaction today, indeed the speaker would probably be considered as faintly eccentric, but

such a statement in the 1950s of the Cold War was positively antago-
nistic. The irony of the provocation is that Alastair was of the opinion
that wise men did not enter into politics, and throughout his life,
maintained a cool air of disdain towards authority figures.

It is a characteristic of some people who make attention-seeking
argumentative statements that they are simply insecure and seeking
to expose vulnerabilities within others. Alternatively, there might be
a twinkle in their eye as they attempt to galvanise the unwary into
mental debate. Alastair fell into the latter category.

Alastair liked to proclaim 'to be extremely left wing'[58], although
his anti-capitalist stance did not sit too easily with his income from
film and theatre work. But so what if he was astute with his financial
contracts? He did after all show great 'loyalty to people he'd worked
with before'[59], and as for great wealth:

> If Sim had wanted to be a millionaire and if British film companies
> had any sense, our answer to the great American comics would have
> been given long ago. British film companies have not much sense
> and Sim has no desire to be a millionaire.[60]

We have so far a picture of Alastair as a left-wing antagonist who dis-
trusted authority and was dismissive towards politicians. It is all the
more reassuring therefore that having described in the Preface how
contradiction was a word best suited to him, to find that Alastair was
a keen sponsor of various groups that supported the proposition of a
World Government.

In 1947, the Labour MP Henry Usborne established the All-Party
Parliamentary Group for World Government (APPGWG). The first
clerk was Patrick Armstrong, who together with Henry Usborne, set
out the principles by which the Group would be defined. Essentially
the goal of the APPGWG was to draw the general public's attention to
world issues rather than allow them to remain insular and only interested in UK matters. So, for example, the APPGWG proposed changes
to the English educational curriculum in order to have students learn
more about global events. The organisation also supported the creation
of the international criminal court. In 1951 the APPGWG established
the One World Trust whose aim was to create a world where people
lived in peace and security with sustainable economic development.

Alastair was already known to Armstrong as a man whose views were in tune, to some degree, with those of the APPGWG and so Armstrong approached Alastair in the summer of 1951 and asked if he would speak at a mass meeting to attract new members. Alastair attended the meeting but declined the invitation to speak, replying to Patrick Armstrong:

> You see, I feel very strongly that my presence on the platform would be helping to perpetuate the age-old abortive alliance of the obtrusively distractive portentiously supporting the essentially desirable attractive[61].

Given the verbosity of his prose[62] it is with some relief that Alastair goes on to explain in his letter that he felt that his star status would not aid their cause of getting people to think for themselves. The following year Alastair was in correspondence with the Crusade for World Government[63] agreeing to allow his name to be used as a sponsor but wishing to 'avoid becoming actively involved in political complications.'[64]

Of particular concern to Alastair was the title of these movements. Alastair had canvassed opinion from friends and acquaintances and discovered that most people were frightened off from any association with the APPGWG because of the phrase 'World Government'. He raised this concern with the APPGWG. By 1968 this matter seems to have been resolved since Patrick Armstrong was petitioning Alastair to add his name to a list of dignitaries who supported the 2nd Dublin Declaration by the Grenville Clark Institute for World Law. Alastair agreed to this request acknowledging that the emphasis on 'World Law' rather than 'World Government' made the movement more generally appealing to the public.

The APPGWG and One World Trust are still active today with a similar sized membership to that of the 1960s, somewhere in the region of 150 members from both Houses of Parliament. Perhaps the last word on the matter of politics though should rest with one of Alastair's closest friends, John Howard Davies, who said: 'he was genuinely a socialist . . . and a humanitarian.'[65]

Alastair was not a churchgoer and treated religion with 'suspicion'.[66] Peter Copley recalls:

[Alastair] was an unalterable atheist: once on tour... I was standing in the back stage area when Alastair joined me preparatory to making his entrance, saw the local Theatre Chaplain wondering about, [and] said to me, 'Peter, don't let that man near me' and went to play his scene. I was over dutiful and missed my own entrance minutes later and was greatly reprimanded by the magister.[67]

Ronald Mavor added, 'Anything to do with gods and god-men was anathema'[68] to Alastair. Perhaps as a result of his religious beliefs, Alastair decided that on his death, he would allow his body to be used for medical research. His faith, it could be said, was his principles, and these were based upon an endearing belief in the ultimate salvation of humanity by the world's youth. The actress Lucinda Gane said of him, 'Alastair was a man of principle i.e. he refused to give autographs, turned down honours [and] avoided the tackier side of celebrity.'[69]

His character could be playful. Sidney Gilliat recalled when Alastair came to stay at his house:

He used to come in from a morning walk in the garden and literally imitate the flowers so that they could be identified for him. I remember how he somehow elongated himself into a sort of upward writhing and my wife exclaimed, 'That's a Morning Glory!'. And it was. In the next few seconds he similarly mimed various other flowers or shrubs which again we had no difficulty in recognising.[70]

Peter Copley recalls:

He laughed at all the comical situations created with a rich glee – he especially enjoyed jokes with revolving doors, 'Let's do it again', he'd say, 'it's such fun!'[71]

Naomi and Alastair were dog-lovers and also owned some Burmese cats, but curiously, by the late 1960s, Naomi and Alastair had established Forrigan as a breeding ground for a special breed of cat. Margaret Wedlake:

I visited his house in Nettlebed ... with my daughter, to pick up the most beautiful white kitten. Naomi and he had a very special breed (I don't think it had a name) but its offspring populated Berkshire and subsequently West London for years.[72]

But Forrigan could also be an austere place; it was 'completely unshowbizzy'.[73] Alastair was a frugal Scotsman through and through. Never was this more apparent than at his London flat, 8 Frognal Gardens, in Hampstead. The flat was described by one visitor as 'a typical Scottish manse kitchen'.[74] No great expense had been lavished on it and indeed the inside of the flat matched the dour appearance of the mansion block of which it was a part. Alastair would sit at a sturdy table with a bowl of oats for breakfast and then smoke all day. Although he was renowned for his love of Havanas, he had a strict order by which he smoked his cigars. In the morning it would be a cheaper brand, and only gradually, as the day passed, would he allow himself the luxury of smoking a Havana. His smoking was certainly a vice he enjoyed: 'Alastair Sim has . . . vanished Jove-like in clouds of cigar smoke.'[75] Richard Owens, who appeared with Alastair in *Dandy Dick* remembers: 'I felt very honoured when he gave me one of his large Havana cigars during the rehearsals of *Dandy Dick* and I treasured it for years.'[76]

Alastair was a regular at his club, the Garrick, where he 'prowled behind dark glasses . . . heading for the bridge table which drew him as a dog is drawn to aniseed. He would pause to gaze quizzically down, or, out of the blue, launch into a panegyric of modern youth'.[77] Throughout his life, Alastair was a true champion of the young generation, 'passionate in conversation about youth and its potential for the future'.[78] He was certainly not naïve so as to think that they were always right, and on occasion, found 'it necessary to correct some of their misapprehensions – but these would be misapprehensions inculcated by adults.'[79] Alastair felt at ease at the Garrick, though 'probably spoke his mind too often. . . Though he never spoke his mind gratuitously – something always had to provoke him.'[80]

★

By 1956, Alastair had spent some considerable time mourning the loss of James Bridie and was now relatively upbeat about the prospect of returning to the stage. He returned to the theatre to direct *Misery Me!* – projected as being 'a sophisticated comedy rather than one of rustic humour'.[81]

Misery Me! was set in a mountain hotel in Arcadia and featured George Cole as a young man who finds himself employed by two men (Colin Gordon & Clive Morton) to murder each other. To complicate matters even further, also in the hotel is a suicidal young lady (Yvonne Mitchell). Needless to say, the young man murders neither and instead wins the girl. *Misery Me!* began a four-week tour in February before opening in London at the Duchess Theatre on 16 March. Alastair took his seat on the first night with mixed emotions. It seemed odd not to have his friend Bridie around and he wondered what Bridie would have made of the production they were about to witness. As with all first nights, it was a tense affair. The critics were also probably unsure as to what to expect from a man who had been in a self-imposed theatrical exile for the past five years. The curtain rose on *Misery Me!* and the actors took to the stage. It did not take long for the audience to become restless. A critic for The *Illustrated London News* reported: 'I noticed the producer of *Misery Me!*, the ever-delightful Alastair Sim, sitting, bowed, among the first-night audience.'[82]

Three days later on 19 March, the production manager[83] E.P. Clift announced that *Misery Me!* was ending early – that very day in fact. This was the cue for a surprising amount of protestation by members of the public who wanted to see the production. After a frantic reconsideration, a complete U-turn was taken and the following announcement appeared in the *Daily Mail*: '*Misery Me!* will not be coming off as was announced earlier today after 5 performances.'[84] Even so, the desire of diehard fans to see the production could not save its fate. *Misery Me!* limped on for a further couple of weeks and then, after only twenty-eight shows, the curtain was finally brought down on the production.

Alastair's foray back into the theatre had proved disastrous. Those people who thought that he could succeed without Bridie were proved wrong. One can see why therefore, in the following year, Alastair chose to play safe and resurrect some of his former Bridie glory days.

In August 1956, Alastair revived James Bridie's greatest success – *Mr Bolfry*. The performances took place at the Aldwych Theatre under the auspices of Alastair's production company Merlith Productions Ltd.

Alastair chose to direct the production and also to play the role of Mr Bolfry – a change from the 1943 production when he played Mr McCrimmon. George Cole took the role of Cohen, originally played by Harry Ross, and Sophie Stewart returned to reprise her role as Mrs McCrimmon[85]. The production opened on 30 August and was an immediate success. It closed on 1 December having run for 108 performances.

Also in the same year, Alastair returned to the film limelight once more in a wonderful Launder and Gilliat comedy–thriller entitled *The Green Man* (1956). Alastair played an assassin (Hawkins), once retired, but now back in business. George Cole plays a vacuum salesman William Blake who gets caught up in proceedings and the glamour is provided by Jill Adams, attired so provocatively in some scenes that the film was classified as 'Adults Only' in some countries.

In order for Hawkins to discover the itinerary plans of his next target – an important merchant banker, Sir Gregory Upshott (Raymond Huntley) – he woos Sir Gregory's secretary, Marigold (Avril Angers). The publicity department made much of this ill-fated romance between Hawkins and Marigold going so far as to declare of Alastair: 'His First Screen Kiss – after 20 Years in Films'.

The kiss is intentionally deceiving and any discussion of romance is entirely superficial. Indeed, Hawkin's accomplice does away with Marigold and dumps her wrapped body into the trunk of a car. On discovering this, Hawkins exclaims indignantly: 'You're not putting her in there! She was my fiancée' – said with such touching tenderness that one cannot help but laugh at the absurdity of the situation. The discovery of the body leads to a scene where the unsuspecting William Blake tries to convince Hawkins to phone for the police. Alastair made the scene appear fresh and natural by telling George Cole at rehearsals:

> Forget about lines. Just do your damnedest to get to the phone and say whatever you would say in the circumstances and I will do the same and manage to prevent you.[86]

The focus of the film switches to a hotel called 'The Green Man' where Hawkins is planning to assassinate Sir Gregory by planting a bomb in the lounge radio. Another visitor at *The Green Man* is

Charles Boughtflower (Terry-Thomas), who plays a philandering husband who suspects his wife is onto him. Terry-Thomas recalls:

> I told the producer Frank Launder, I didn't think the part was impor-
> tant enough for me. In the end I agreed to do it. I found George
> Cole one of the easiest people in the world to work with, and it
> was an experience to collaborate with Alastair Sim. You never knew
> exactly what he was going to do, and neither, I felt, did he![87]

There is also a veteran female musical trio, who accidentally contrive to stand in the way of Hawkins' dastardly plan. This allows for several moments of high comedy as Hawkins attempts to ingratiate himself with the women. Alastair is superb as he tries to convey his utter enjoyment at their atrocious musical renditions while plying them with drinks. The arrival of William Blake and Ann Vincent warning the occupants of the bomb plot leads the film to its frenetic conclusion.

The opening sequences, specifically written with Alastair in mind, are strangely reminiscent of Alec Guinness's performance in *Kind Hearts and Coronets* (1949). Even *Picturegoer* remarked: 'Sim moves into Alec Guinness territory'.[88] A territory he might share, but it would be very difficult to argue that Alastair was anywhere near as great an actor as Alec Guinness. The reference by *Picturegoer* is to the fact that at the beginning of *The Green Man*, Alastair is shown in various disguises, plotting the downfall of a series of despots. However, he never sustains these as characters – as Guinness so successfully does in his masterpiece *Kind Hearts and Coronets*. In fact, there are several instances within *The Green Man* where one senses that Alastair is performing well within himself. The hardened eye may even suggest that Alastair is simply going through the motions. He seems tired and drawn at times. Avril Angers offers an explanation:

> Alastair was, I think, mostly seen in black and white films, looking
> morose [and] lugubrious, but in fact, with rosy complexion and
> bright blue eyes, he was quite different in the flesh.[89]

Strange though this may seem, the tinted lobby cards used to advertise his films often coloured his eyes brown and therefore it would be doubtful if many people were actually aware of his true eye colour.

More significantly, the working relationship between Alastair Sim and Launder and Gilliat, had begun to break down. The problems that arose during the filming of *Folly to be Wise* were about to reappear – and multiply.

During pre-production for *The Green Man* Alastair informed Launder and Gilliat that he would like to direct the film. Sidney Gilliat, though concerned about Alastair's lack of experience of film directing, realised that they could ill-afford to upset their leading man and so they acquiesced to his wish. This was only the beginning of their problems. Unionisation was rife in the UK at that time and since Alastair was not recognised by the unions as a film director, they quite simply refused to allow the production to go ahead.

Launder and Gilliat were forced to negotiate with the unions. The outcome of these talks was that Alastair would direct on probation, with a co-director, who would be a union member. They selected Robert Day, who was regarded as a highly competent camera operator, to take on this arduous, mainly diplomatic task.

Although the intricate matter of dealing with the unions had been resolved, there now came the sensitive issue of casting. A meeting was arranged during which Launder and Gilliat put forward their suggestions and then Robert Day contributed his ideas. The meeting took a turn for the worse when Alastair announced that he was completely against both sets of proposals and put forward instead his own preferred alternatives. These were disputed by the other three men. Disagreements broke into private rows, and private rows turned into open quarrels. After one such quarrel, Alastair resigned as co-director.

One can imagine the consternation felt by Launder and Gilliat at these developments. Having attempted to placate Alastair and meet his difficult wishes, they were now faced with the inexperienced Robert Day in charge of direction and the possibility that Alastair might withdraw from the production altogether. Various options were considered, including cancelling the film. This would have incurred only a moderate cost to the production company given that the film was still in pre-production. However, although Alastair could clearly be difficult at times, he was always loyal to his friends and indeed freely accepted that he owed much of his film success to Launder and Gilliat. Though he was annoyed at what had happened, he gave assurances that he would honour his acting commitment.

The film was given the green light, but there still existed the problem of whether Robert Day was sufficiently experienced to handle a disconsolate Alastair Sim. Launder and Gilliat had their doubts and so asked Basil Dearden to take on a supervisory role in the production.

This hiatus probably explains why Sidney Gilliat wrote:'*The Green Man* was a low budget picture which we probably ought to have taken more care over... Alastair was fun in it, but was never in fact in his old high spirits.'[90] The US publicised *The Green Man* as:

> The kind of picture the British have a way with ... things like very merry murders ... very unusual characters ... very sly sex ... and all combined in an uproar of laughs and suspense.[91]

The 'sly sex' remark clearly referred to Jill Adams and her bedroom attire. The US press book helpfully provided more information:

> With 36'-23'-36' measurements, it was inevitable that Jill be dubbed the 'British Marilyn Monroe', a term she hates, insisting that she needs to lose half-an-inch around the waist.[92]

The release of *The Green Man* in 1956 coincided with the end of a six-year period that had seen Alastair achieve huge popular and critical acclaim. But there had been costs – the loss of Bridie as well as his deteriorating relationship with Launder and Gilliat. Worse times were ahead. A television commercial was being planned for a product that would become indelibly linked with him, much to his disgust and annoyance. It would stain his public persona and accompany his decline from screen stardom. It would cause him public humiliation and he would become the butt of many a school playground joke. The product ... baked beans.

Sim v Heinz:
the Faltering Years

ALAS! MR SIM HAS NO SCOPE

– Cecil Wilson, *Daily Mail*[1]

The omens looked good for 1958. Alastair decided to produce and take the leading role in a new comedy by William Golding entitled *The Brass Butterfly*, which began its tour on 24 February at the New Theatre, Oxford. He played a Roman Emperor 'sprawled comfortably across a marble throne on the terrace of his island villa.'[2] The Emperor is wise to the hollowness of the pomp and circumstance of his position, if also slightly beholden to it, but is a genuinely benign man with an affable nature, willing to defend the status quo. A Greek inventor, Phanocles (George Cole) attempts, with a great deal of scientific rationale, to interest the Emperor in his latest anachronistic ideas. These include: the first steamship, a bomb[3] (though the Emperor fails to appreciate its destructive potential, instead seeing it as a useful way of producing big holes in the ground) and a pressure cooker. The Emperor, a gourmet at heart, is particularly intrigued by the idea of a pressure cooker and the opportunities it could afford him for cooking his fish, but even more enthusiastic about the inventor's sister, Euphrosyne (Eileen Moore[4]) whom he attempts to match with his son. This love match saga and a further plot involving a revolution fails to bring any real urgency to proceedings and the play meanders to the final curtain.

The Brass Butterfly had been developed from a short story by William Golding entitled *Envoy Extra-ordinary* and could not sustain the jokes for the entire evening. Even though the play closed after thirty-six performances, one reviewer wrote:

> Mr Alastair Sim is great fun as the tolerant but astute old pagan, and he deepens the comedy by suggesting a genuine paternal tenderness for a boy whose judgement he mistrusts. It is a relaxed and yet precisely pointed comic performance.[5]

Alastair openly acknowledged the difficulty he was facing in finding someone who could write roles of the quality that Bridie had produced for him during their successful years working together in the 1940s. A significant addition to this problem was the expectation of theatre audiences who, by the late 1950s, had become accustomed to a diet of Alastair Sim comic performances in films such as *Laughter in Paradise* (1951), *The Belles of St Trinian's* (1954) and *The Green Man* (1956). Such audiences would arrive at the theatre with preconceived ideas of the entertainment they were expecting, namely comedy, even if the play had not advertised itself as such. Alastair's situation was a difficult one. On one hand he could throw himself into a serious role and hope to re-establish his credentials as a highbrow performer, or alternatively, he could seek refuge in what he knew best – the comic look of angst and bewilderment. Alastair chose the latter, relying on acquired mannerisms and perfected timing to produce distinctive, yet unoriginal performances. The critics, who were so lavish with their praise at the beginning of the decade, became restless. It was time for one or two of them to voice their concerns.

They did so on two fronts. First, by questioning Alastair's staid and repetitive acting style, and second, his skill as a director. Under the headline: 'ALAS! MR SIM HAS NO SCOPE', Cecil Wilson, of the *Daily Mail*, wrote that Golding's play had brought Alastair back to the stage to face:

An uncomfortable mixture of cheers and boos. . . Mr Sim, who finds little scope this time for behaving like a bishop on the razzle . . . directs the play with – for him – a heavy hand.[6]

Alastair appeared to deal with his vulnerability in a sensible, logical way: 'I stand or fall in my profession by their [the public's] judgement of my performance, and no amount of publicity can dampen a good one, or gloss over a bad one.'[7] In the main, mildly critical reviews were the exception. Most incorporated an indulgent, sycophantic air – something that would grow increasingly monotonous as Alastair's stagnation became more apparent. The reverence appeared heartfelt in many instances but all this did was postpone the critique.

Alastair had closed down his school in Edinburgh, resigned from his lecturing post and moved to London in the 1930s with a burning desire to direct in the West End. He had not only achieved this feat but had also won great critical and public acclaim for his acting performances both on stage and screen. Alastair's retirement in 1958 would have seen him depart the theatrical arena with his head held high, his dignity intact, but staying on and producing increasingly stale performances, ran the risk of a laboured, embarrassing decline. But for the moment, such difficult decisions had to be put to one side. It was time for Alastair to dust down his oversized brassier, add the iconic bird's nest coiffure to his head and undertake a short reprise as the Headmistress of St Trinian's in *Blue Murder at St Trinian's* (1958).

Some hold that *Blue Murder at St Trinian's* is the best of the *St Trinian's* series but there are two significant reasons why *The Belles of St Trinian's* should hold this accolade. The first lies in the narrative structure. Whereas *Belles* follows a conventional narrative style, with a clearly defined plot, organised sequentially, *Blue Murder* appears episodic in nature: a UNESCO competition, a marriage bureau, hidden loot, undercover police officers and a crooked bus company – and therefore less satisfying overall. The second reason concerns the reduced screen presence of Miss Amelia[8] Fritton (Alastair Sim). Alastair appears in two brief scenes, one at the beginning of the film when Miss Fritton is shown incarcerated in Holloway, and finally at the end of the film when she greets the successful return of the jubilant girls from their European jaunt. In *The Belles of St Trinian's*, Miss Fritton provides a central character around whom events can

transpire in a cohesive and rational way – even though the environment itself is somewhat exceptional. Her absence for the most part
from *Blue Murder* leaves an unfocussed film clearly suffering from
the loss of a strong leading character.

'Was the joke worth repeating?'[9] asked *Picturegoer*. The answer is
yes – if only for the nicely judged love affair between the bus manager Romney (Terry-Thomas) and Ruby Gates (Joyce Grenfell),
full of misplaced angst and transparent deception. *Blue Murder at St
Trinian's* was the last film in which Joyce Grenfell and Alastair Sim
worked together.

★

The Brass Butterfly and *Blue Murder at St Trinian's* may have appeared
on paper as a respectable contribution for 1958, but the reality was
somewhat different. Alastair's stage career had stagnated and his film
career was in decline. Although he had survived the demise of the
light British musical in the 1940s and the dour wartime propaganda
movies, a new wave of filmmaking was in production that appeared
to have no need for his talents. Ealing comedies – those quintessential British movies, epitomising the underdog sense of humour,
subtle and self-effacing – were rapidly becoming obsolete. Taking
their place was a new film genre which promoted realism with
regards to violence, drama and comedy.

Even by the mid-1950s, the increased violent content in films was
already the subject of much media coverage. *Picturegoer* ran a portentous article in 1955 entitled, 'Let's stop this Violence' in which
it said, 'The violence-packed films now out, or coming out, make
the prewar Cagney-Bogart beat-ups look like smooth interludes for
children's television.'[10] Drama was typified by films such as *Look Back
in Anger* (1959) and *Saturday Night, Sunday Morning* (1960) in which
the establishment had become a legitimate target of pent-up frus-
trations. The eccentric was no longer a mildly amusing, bumbling
buffoon, so caricatured in British comedies over the previous twenty
years, but usually a social outcast of sinister intent.

It is a matter of great debate as to how beneficial or damaging this
period was to the British film industry. The kitchen-sink dramas,
with their emphasis on drab authenticity, were a statement by the

directors that they intended to reflect life in its reality, devoid of the cosy fantasy world of Ealing. There was an underlying cultural tendency to view such films as progressive. Cinematography was skilfully adapted to present scenes in a stark fashion, devoid of any fantasy embellishments; something that could provide insight into the deeper motivations of the characters, but at the same time appear abhorrent to an audience looking for light escapism. Indeed, such a response would act as a motivator in its own right and lead perversely to the production of films with the sole intention to shock. Light escapism became an anathema to filmmakers wanting to be taken seriously for their art.[11]

Comedy began to reflect permissiveness. To begin with, it was simply a moving image of the traditional seaside postcards of Donald McGill. These relied on innuendo and a healthy appreciation of the lighter side of sex – even grandmothers might find the saucy seaside image amusing. There was no intention to offend, simply the opportunity to introduce a topic that had hitherto remained fairly circumspect. The success of the *Carry On* films, and their increasingly unsubtle attitude towards sex, simply reflected the times.

The reality so far as Alastair was concerned was that the idiosyncratic roles he so favoured, and indeed had become so adept at playing, had become extinct. There was no demand anymore for the staged farce. The eccentric was no longer the catalyst, no longer the focus of the comedy, but a person to laugh at rather than laugh with. If anything, the new filmmaking era of realism portrayed the eccentric as senile and degenerate, expelled from normal social groupings and left isolated, enveloped in mockery. He might have been a murderer, psychopath or child molester, or the manifestation or representation of a sadly inefficient bureaucratic system. This was no place for Alastair, his time had passed, but he was not alone. Ian Carmichael, who appeared in two films with Alastair commented dryly in his autobiography: 'The film scripts that had swamped me between 1955 and 1961 stopped almost as suddenly as they had started.'[12] Alastair Sim, a man who abhorred violence, who rejected the idea of stardom, who loathed the concept of stupidity, faced an uncertain future.

When decline occurs, it is sometimes graceful and reflective, and at other times, accompanied by ridicule. Things were about to get ridiculous for Alastair Sim.

★

Summer 1958. Alastair was enjoying the company of friends one day, when one of them recalled something odd they had seen on television the previous evening. A television advertisement shown in between programmes had featured a voice-over which sounded distinctly similar to those familiar dulcet tones belonging to Alastair Sim. The friend turned to Alastair and enquired of him: 'Why have you decided to perform in a commercial?'[13]

It is important in today's age of ubiquitous product placement and z-list celebrity endorsement to understand the provocative nature of this question. Commercial television in 1958 was still in its infancy, and yet, there had already developed a general consensus that television advertising was a low form of art – if not the lowest. Accepting work in a television commercial, even that of a voice-over, implied that the actor had reached the end of their career and had sold out their principles in a desperate final attempt to cash in on their name.

Alastair, a man of principle, was naturally perplexed that someone, especially a friend, should suggest he would do such a thing. He protested his innocence and enquired as to the nature of the product being advertised using his voice. The reply – baked beans – did not lighten the moment. Indeed it was reported in the resulting court case that even though Alastair made it clear he had played no part in the commercial, there were many people who simply did not believe him.

Several months previously, Heinz had approached Young and Rubicam Ltd and requested they develop an advertising campaign on commercial television for their famous baked bean product. Young and Rubicam went to work on the brief and by the summer of 1958 they had produced six 45-second commercials of cartoons in a pen and ink style, with titles such as 'Living like a Lord'. In the cartoons was a character who Young and Rubicam assured was not based on anyone in particular, but whose voice, it would have to be said, was uncannily similar to that of Alastair's. So similar in fact that the majority of people who saw and heard the advert naturally assumed that it was indeed him. This assumption was incorrect, of course, since the voice belonged to the talented actor Ron Moody, who had already gained a reputation as being a good mimic of Alastair. However, 'In evidence, he [Ron Moody] denied that on this occasion he had used his impersonation of Mr Sim's voice'.[14]

Alastair was extremely annoyed. His first reaction was to try and stop the commercial but of course by then it was too late – it had already begun airing on television. Even worse, from his point of view, was that the adverts were proving to be very successful. So much so, that he was quickly becoming the butt of many a baked bean joke. When Alastair entered a restaurant called Simpson's, the manager came up to him and said, 'Ah Mr. Sim, I know what you want. You don't want roast beef. You want baked beans'.

Alastair wrote to Heinz requesting that they withdraw the commercial due to the personal embarrassment it was causing him, but they refused. Indeed further calumny was inevitable given that there was a whole series of adverts to be aired. Alastair felt he had no choice but to resort to legal action. He instigated a claim for libel and passing off[15] against Young & Rubicam Ltd, but first he requested a temporary injunction against the commercials to prevent them from being shown on television until after the court hearing. On Thursday 18 December 1958, arguments for an interim injunction were heard in the case Sim v H.J. Heinz Co Ltd and Young & Rubicam Ltd. A case that could have easily featured in its own right on stage in the West End.

Sim v H.J. Heinz Co Ltd and Young & Rubicam Ltd

The Setting: The High Court of Justice

Act One: The Injunction

The Cast
In the chair: Mr Justice McNair
Appearing for Alastair: Mr Guy Aldus QC & Mr JNB Penny
Appearing for Heinz: Mr Peter Bristow
Appearing for Young and Rubicam: Mr Gerald Gardiner QC & Mr Helenus Milmo

Sim v H.J. Heinz was destined to become a celebrated farce in its own right, not only because of its comic nature – a judicial case between the well-known actor of eccentric roles, Alastair Sim, and the staple diet of the masses, baked beans – but also because of the media attention it drew. Perversely, this would count very heavily against Alastair during the hearings. Indeed, even when the court case began, the more he tried to justify his action, the more ridiculous his position seemed to become. Mr Aldus, acting on behalf of Alastair, tried to clarify the position of his client: 'My client hates this case. He dislikes all publicity. He would never advertise a baked bean.'[16]

Beneath the somewhat farcical surface of such statements, there was a very important issue at stake. Alastair considered his voice a trait or trademark, and as such, an important asset. To have this asset devalued by its association with a product such as baked beans could jeopardise his career. Indeed, his friends and colleagues had already 'expressed the opinion that if he allowed his voice to be used in this way he was doing something beneath his dignity as an actor.'[17]

Mr Justice McNair listened to the pleas for the injunction but rejected the claim and a date was set for the case to be heard before three judges. The adverts continued to be broadcast, thus adding to the publicity over the dispute.

Act Two: The Interlocutory Appeal

The Cast
In the chair: Lord Justice Hodson, Lord Justice Morris and Lord Justice Wilmer
Appearing for Alastair: Mr Guy Aldus QC & Mr JNB Penny
Appearing for Heinz: Mr Peter Bristow
Appearing for Young and Rubicam: Mr Gerald Gardiner QC & Mr Helenus Milmo

Their Lordships began the hearing of the interlocutory appeal on 5 February 1959. Mr Aldus, acting for Alastair, described him as: 'a well-known stage and film actor and a distinguished ornament to that profession who . . . had a very distinctive voice and manner of speaking.'[18] There is no record of how Alastair felt at being described as an 'ornament' – one could but guess.

Advertising agencies inherently understand the value of creating a brand name. Branding creates product differentiation, which in turn allows for higher pricing and more sales. To brand a product requires distinctiveness, something which can be attained by creating an association between the product and a well-known actor or personality. The problem is that hiring a famous actor can be expensive, and so a sound-alike often makes more economic sense. Copyright laws are inadequate protection from the use of such mimics since such laws are used predominantly in the expression of ideas. Hence they apply, for example, to books, songs and films. Copyright is therefore not infringed when a new piece of work is presented in a way that sounds like an existing performer. It can however be applied to a look-alike where there might be misrepresentation of the product, but to a sound-alike being used over an existing brand name in a new commercial? The issue was and still is complex because there are no clear legal distinctions between a look-alike and a sound-alike. Undoubtedly a famous singer would be protected in this context since their voice is distinctive, but with actors, it is usually their faces that are regarded as their distinctiveness.[19]

Lord Justice Hodson saw the case in an entirely different light, perceiving the adverts as benefiting Alastair by attracting media attention. This was not the point. Alastair neither wanted, nor liked the publicity. The issue was much more serious. Alastair's counsel, Mr Aldus, tried to make the point as transparent as possible by saying: 'He did not wish to prostitute his art by advertising baked beans.'[20]

Even at this early stage it was clear that the case was not going well for Alastair. The judges were particularly concerned with regard to the wider consequences of Alastair winning. They were fearful that the creation of such a precedent would invite a rush of cases brought before them by less distinguished actors attempting to benefit from the resulting publicity. Before they knew it, their courts would be packed to the rafters with has-beens (no pun intended) attempting to rekindle a lost career by accusing all and sundry of stealing their voice. Even so, this issue could have been settled relatively quickly, but there remained much badinage to be had by all.

Lord Justice Wilmer asked whether these advertisements were still continuing so that he might watch them that evening on television. Alastair's counsel replied that they had received no information from

Heinz suggesting that Heinz had any intention other than to continue with the adverts – in layman's words:'yes'. Both sides did agree
that an important issue was whether or not the voice in the advert
did actually sound like Alastair's. One presumes that a fairly reasonable test would have been to compare the two voices, but mirth and
merriment is something to be savoured in the High Courts. Enter
Professor Fry:

> Professor Fry, Professor of Experimental Phonetics in the University
> of London . . . stated, 'the cartoon voice had a greater preponder-
> ance of low frequencies arising from a pronounced pharyngeal
> resonance. . .' whereas the plaintiffs voice 'had more high frequency
> components produced by greater head resonance.'[21]

After much frowning, a rather droll Lord Justice Wilmer enquired of
the court in general:'Do you know what all that means?'The court
erupted into laughter. Alastair's counsel, who one presumes was better disposed to appreciate the ritual humour of the judges, and so
could have found an agreeable riposte, instead responded: '[I've] not
the slightest idea'. Mr Aldus QC then suggested that 'the test was
not whether the broadcast would deceive a professor of phonetics,
but whether it would deceive a substantial number of normal persons who lived in the country'[22] – as opposed, one presumes, to the
abnormal persons living in the country.

The proceedings then moved on to financial matters. Alastair's
counsel identified that the cost of dubbing the commercial with an
alternative voice was approximately £1000 – a small amount compared with the total cost to Heinz of the commercial which was
£180,000. It seemed a compromise might be in the air. Counsel
for Alastair said that there 'had been a recent letter intended to be
conciliatory in which the defendants said that . . . they had now
made a seventh film with a different voice which they said they
liked better'[23] – the sarcasm at the end of the letter no doubt adding
to Alastair's overall sense of humiliation.

Mr Gardiner declared that the court had yet to see the commercials – a somewhat obvious detail that had been raised earlier but
had not been acted on. It would have been highly unusual for ITV
to have screened all of the offending adverts in one go, one after

another, in one evening, and so arrangements were put in place to allow the judges to watch the commercials the following day. But then Lord Justice Wilmer exclaimed, 'But we have never heard the plaintiff's voice'. A strange statement given Alastair's film successes by that time.

The dialogue continued:

Lord Justice Wilmer to Mr. Aldus: 'You would not object to film being identified as excerpts of Mr Sim's voice?'

Mr Aldus said that he did not know whether the excerpts would be fair examples of Mr Sim's work.

Lord Justice Morris: 'Not if they showed him as a Scottish bishop?'

Mr Aldus 'Or possibly a woman.'[24]– referring of course to the *St Trinian's* films.

Act Three: The Ruling

In the chair: Lord Justice Hodson, Lord Justice Morris and Lord Justice Wilmer

The following day, 6 February 1959, the court dismissed the case – Alastair had lost. The judges were too fearful of setting a precedent whereby anyone wanting publicity could take a company to court for allegedly copying their voice. Offering succour to Alastair, Lord Justice Morris, in reference to the Heinz Baked Beans commercials, declared: 'From now on, no one will think this is the voice of Mr Sim.'[25] Lord Justice Morris seemed to be inferring that everyone was reading the reports of the court case in *The Times* which may have been somewhat optimistic. There followed a technical discussion regarding whether the hearings had been open or closed. It seems that no one was particularly clear on this matter and then Lord Justice Wilmer offered a parting shot:

The jury may think that the publicity of these proceedings has done the plaintiff quite a lot of good.[26]

On the contrary, it had not. Alastair was despondent at the outcome. His argument was based on sound principle, and yet, it had been implied that his sole intention had been to seek publicity. In conclusion, the court refused to accept that, for someone such as Alastair Sim, in the entertainment industry, his voice could be defined as a property. The one consolation was that Heinz later announced through its solicitor that it 'would use a different voice in order not to step on Mr Sim's toes.'[27]

The Heniz court case, perhaps mostly forgotten by now, provided at the time a rich vein of comedy material. The last ever radio episode of *Hancock's Half-Hour*, broadcast on 29 December 1959, was entitled 'The Impersonator' and featured someone attempting to mimic Hancock's voice in an advertisement for Cornflakes.

★

Over the period of the baked bean fiasco, Alastair had been working on several film projects that would prove to be his last for over a decade. These consisted of the ill-chosen, *Left Right and Centre* (1959), where his performance is the highlight of a thoroughly anachronistic film; disappointing adaptations of heavy dramatic stage plays, such as *The Doctor's Dilemma* (1959), *The Millionairess* (1960) and *The Anatomist* (1961); and *School for Scoundrels* (1959), a film that brought to an end a decade of gently mocking, self effacing British comedy.

Left Right and Centre (1959) is a dated-looking Launder and Gilliat comedy even by 1959 standards 'that takes a knock at British politics'.[28] It starred Ian Carmichael as a television game show panellist who stands for the Conservatives in an election but in true farcical style, falls for the Socialist candidate, Stella Stoker (Patricia Bredin). The problem with the film is that it frequently invokes the impression that love is a splendid revelation that occurs spontaneously, accompanied by a little bit of soft focus and light music. All well and good for the early 1950s, but the swinging 60s were about to happen and audiences wanted sex and realism, not blurred images of fluttering eyelashes. Even Alastair in, 'an outstanding and hilarious portrayal'[29] of Lord Wilcot, 'a poverty-stricken member of the nobility who throws his stately home open to the public'[30], describes the romantic couple in the film as 'nauseating'. Most of the audience would agree. *Left Right and Centre* is the sort of film that provided conclusive proof that the 1950s, with its coy references to romance and sex, were about to be consigned to history.

Ian Carmichael offered these impressions of working with Alastair:

> I felt very nervous of him at the beginning. Although I had the lead part, he was very much my senior in years and experience. I had heard tales that he could be a bit difficult to work with. I was to find that this was far from the truth. I found him amiable, friendly and, as you would expect, very professional. He might have been more dictatorial when working in the theatre, but that I was never to experience.[31]

Behind the scenes, things were not quite so amicable. Alastair's relationship with Launder and Gilliat had reached a nadir.

Sidney Gilliat, as director, had always felt that Alastair had a tendency to slow down scenes. In *Waterloo Road* (1944), Gilliat felt him 'slow, sometimes deadly slow'[32] but up to *Lady Godiva Rides Again* (1951) he had usually succeeded in speeding him up. At the time of the *St Trinian's* films (1954–1957), he thought him 'tending to be slower than ever'.[33] However, by the time *Left Right and Centre* came to be filmed, it was not only the speed of Alastair's delivery that was irritating Sidney Gilliat:

> In our last picture with him [*Left Right and Centre*], which I directed, we did not see eye to eye about his part. Also, while never having been exactly conscientious about learning his lines, Alastair now seemed uncertain even as to which scene he was in, which led to me throwing the script at him and walking off stage to cool off.[34]

The crux of the problem, from Alastair's point of view, was his desire to appear spontaneous whenever he was in a scene; this was not something new. Larry Barnes, Second Pirate in the 1941 production of *Peter Pan*, said of Alastair's performance as Captain Hook:

> Alastair's technique was beautiful. If he threw his cloak across his shoulder on a certain line, he would do it every night on that line and it would never appear mechanical.[35]

Janet Brown recalls of her time on stage with Alastair in the 1950s
and 1960s:

> Alastair loved the actor to be free of the 'book'. He was always saying
> 'Put it down, don't worry about the words – just get the feel of what
> you are doing'.[36]

One can appreciate how this technique might work well on stage.
There is, after all, a serious risk that an actor's performance can
become stale due to the repetitive nature of daily performances.
The introduction of spontaneity helps to overcome this problem.
On the other hand, Sidney Gilliat, as director of the film, quite
reasonably, wanted Alastair to know his lines and to perform them
as directed. Gilliat put this to him. Alastair's response was typically
opaque. Gilliat recalls:

> He had an irritating way of telling you that he could not be sponta-
> neous if he learnt his lines beforehand and when you asked him how
> he managed on the stage, he would reply 'Ah! . . . that was a very dif-
> ferent matter'.[37]

Left Right and Centre was supposed to include a deathbed scene written by Sidney Gilliat with a great Wiltshire character in mind called
Tiny Alexander, who, on his own deathbed, would bellow to visitors 'Come into the death chamber!'. Gilliat wanted the scene to be
played with irony and a black sense of humour. Alastair was adamant
that he would not play it in this manner, saying to Gilliat, 'Death's
not funny'.[38] As a consequence, the scene never made it into the
final cut of the film. Sidney Gilliat suggested that Alastair's stubborn-
ness towards this scene might well have been due to the deep loss
he still felt for his dear friend James Bridie, even though it had been
eight years since Bridie's passing.

Just as the loss of Bridie had brought to an end a run of auspicious stage performances, *Left Right and Centre* was the final film
in what had been a hugely successful film partnership between
Alastair Sim, Frank Launder and Sidney Gilliat. Sidney Gilliat
explained the importance of his and Frank Launder's association
with Alastair thus:

It may seem odd that Launder and I were perhaps the only filmmakers who exploited – if that's quite the right word! – Sim's odd spectrum of comedic gifts at all fully (though far from exhaustively).[39]

Significantly, with Bridie gone and the fruitful partnership with Launder and Gilliat at an end, Alastair was without the two main catalysts that had sparked and sustained his career for the past two decades. He was now on his own.

Alastair's final films of this period began with *The Doctor's Dilemma* (1959), another Shaw adaptation[40], where Alastair and Robert Morley played a pair of fraudulent doctors. The film's heavy emphasis on ethics and morality made for a dour evening's entertainment that reviewers found 'a trifle dated'.[41] As *Picturegoer* put it: 'The fault of the film is the fault of G.B. Shaw – his characters are merely mouthpieces for attitudes and causes he championed.'[42]

The Doctor's Dilemma also starred Dirk Bogarde as Louis Dubedat, a young man suffering from consumption, and Leslie Caron, his wife. The film opened to good reviews in America where Dirk Bogarde was singled out for high praise. In Britain, the story was slightly different. On the film's release, the Rank production offices began receiving a large number of telephone calls from cinema managers across the country reporting on the strange behaviour of the general public. Apparently, moviegoers would arrive in the cinema foyer, look at the lobby cards and stills from the picture, and then walk out of the cinema in disgust. The film distributors quickly commissioned market researchers to look into this matter. Their survey concluded that *The Doctor's Dilemma* was perceived by many as being the fourth film in the hugely successful *Doctor* series that starred Dirk Bogarde in the role of Doctor Simon Sparrow. Those entering the cinema foyer were dismayed at seeing images of Doctor Simon Sparrow in period costume and were convinced that they had been the victims of a marketing ruse. They left the cinema in anger and some even held Dirk Bogarde personally responsible for their disappointment. Under such circumstances, *The Doctor's Dilemma* could only fail at the box office.

School for Scoundrels (1959) featured Ian Carmichael in the role of Henry Palfrey – one of life's losers. Palfrey undertakes a course in lifesmanship run by Stephen Potter (Alastair Sim) in order to win the delectable April Smith (Janette Scott) from Raymond Delauney (Terry-Thomas).

School for Scoundrels opens in a quaintly reassuring way with a train arriving at a station in a scene reminiscent of *The Happiest Days of your Life* (1950). However, whereas *The Happiest Days of your Life* marked the beginning of a decade of quintessential British humour – during which time a woman's reputation would be ruined if she were caught in a single man's bedroom –*School for Scoundrels* brought that decade to a close. British comedy would never be the same again. Even the actors felt that the set was subdued, although there were some extenuating circumstances.

The producer, Hal E. Chester, had problems in financing the film and although he gave the production the green light, towards the end of the shoot money began to run out. Hal Chester was left with no choice but to mortgage his house in Hampstead in order to finance the final days of filming. The financial worries were exacerbated by the director, Robert Hamer's, drink problem – which in turn was not helped by Terry-Thomas's desire to spend his lunchtime drinking in the company of Hamer. Indeed, Hamer was so drunk on one occasion that Hal Chester had to direct the shoot for that day. And finally the script, written by Peter Ustinov, was considered to be too British and therefore unlikely to be understood by American audiences. Consequently there was a significant amount of script doctoring undertaken in order to bring in more American-friendly jokes.

Under such circumstances one would not be surprised to find *School for Scoundrels* a mess, but it is in fact a rather pleasing comedy with Alastair on good form. In an early scene he addresses the new intakes on his course of one-upmanship with the pomposity of a superior, but also emphasises his human side by careful and pronounced eye contact. This is suggestive of the scene from *The Belles of St Trinian's* (1954) when Miss Fritton addresses the new girls. It also allows for an explanation of the *raison d'être* for Potter's course on one-upmanship and consequently an opportunity for the main theme of the film to be expressed: 'Adam bit into that apple . . . at which moment, the first loser was born.'

Another early scene has Palfrey visiting Potter in his office. As the two of them discuss matters, a maid comes into the room and places a tea tray on the table between them. Ian Carmichael recounts of the scene:

I seem to remember his [Alastair's] apparent reluctance to handle props unless it was absolutely essential. I was the guest, he was the host, and yet it was I who was instructed to pour it out. He didn't want to handle it. A lifemanship ploy emanating from the character, or an abhorrence of handling props? I don't know, but I certainly got the impression that there was quite a bit of the latter. [43]

In *The Millionairess* (1960), Alastair appears alongside two international giants – Peter Sellers and Sophia Loren. Alastair played the part of Sagamore – a rogue of a solicitor to the world's richest woman Epifania Parerga (Sophia Loren). The love interest was provided by Dr Ahmed el Kabir (Peter Sellers), an Indian doctor, devoted to the poor and disinterested in her wealth. 'A fairy tale story with a fairy tale ending'[44] claimed *Picture Show*. Alastair was extremely fond of Sophia Loren and they immediately became friends. Peter Sellers, on the other hand, was very edgy on the film set. This was not surprising given that he had fallen madly in love with Sophia Loren, but apparently he was also incredibly nervous in the presence of Alastair. Alastair took it on himself one day to calm Sellers down and so began discussing with him his admiration of *The Goon Show*.

Although the performances are very good, the Bernard Shaw adaptation is disappointingly mediocre; the love interest fails to convince and the colour appears to have been laid on with a trowel.

Alastair's final film in this period, *The Anatomist* (1961), was a low budget production of a Bridie play. Designed for television, it was filmed at Elstree Studios on three sets[45] that corresponded to the play and adhered very closely to the original text. Watching the film is therefore a fascinating means by which to have some experience of those Sim/Bridie stage productions of the 1940s. The earlier debates on the comparisons between the 1930 and 1948 stagings of *The Anatomist* now at least form the basis for some discussion. Is Alastair too reserved, or is his performance more in keeping with a barnstorming tenor? Is the language incomprehensible at times? Is Mary Paterson misguggling Mr Nebby's thrapple? Who knows? Unfortunately George Cole reveals a rather suspect Scottish accent and is unconvincing in his attempt to impart the sincerity of his feelings for Mary Belle Dishart (Jill Bennett). Diarmuid Kelly and Michael Ripper are impressive as Burke and

Hare, managing to construe an inordinate amount of menace in their tightly shot scenes.

★

The year 1961 brought to a close a film career that had, ten years previously, seen Alastair topping polls and winning widespread critical acclaim. Alastair, who had never wanted to be a movie star, and whose love had always been with the theatre, laid to rest the ghost of James Bridie and returned to the stage.

In December 1959 Alastair directed *A Clean Kill*, a murder mystery staring Peter Copley, Helen Christie and Dandy Nichols, which ran successfully at the Criterion Theatre for 140 performances. Alastair's daughter Merlith[46] was the assistant stage manager. Peter Copley's recollection of the play offers a fascinating insight into Alastair's approach as a director:

> He had a theory about directing: provided you rehearsed Act 1 up to performance point, Acts 2 and 3 would follow. Act 3 scarcely needed rehearsal at all, so completely would the cast understand their functions, relationships and so how to handle the Act 3 plot resolutions – Alastair carried the principal to extremes. With *A Clean Kill*, at the end of the first three days of rehearsals, we had only reached page 9. Hugh Latimer, a gentle actor, but who perhaps lacked the manoeuvres necessary to live with Alastair's method, was exhausted and sweating. Meanwhile, the as yet unused cast had had three days sitting and watching. Rachel Roberts, a fine actress . . . but with an emotional Welsh temperament, was no longer grumbling discreetly but audibly objecting to not being used and, even more audibly, repeating, 'Cheeky bugger, cheeky bugger'.[47]

In January 1961 Alastair surrounded himself with friends and family when he directed and appeared in the comedy *The Bargain*. He played an elderly solicitor who faces embarrassment and humiliation when he becomes the victim of a blackmailer. Peter Copley, who had appeared in *A Clean Kill*, was now becoming more familiar and adept at dealing with Alastair's style of directing:

He was meticulous about moves and, once they were settled, expected us all to abide strictly by them as being the moves essential to play the scene correctly. He once said, however, perhaps not publicly, that having achieved the correct playing of a scene, you could then abandon the moves or vary them as you spontaneously felt. I had a scene in *The Bargain* where he was alone in his solicitor's office and I joined him: one night, instead of coming on and speaking from the door, I crossed the stage and spoke from the other side of his desk. I saw a wicked look in his eye and away he went on a variation of his own. He brilliantly proved his point by still playing the scene perfectly, but I was left stranded in a corner – He was so much more skilful than I was.[48]

The Bargain further exposed the repetitive nature of Alastair's acting style. His stage performance would involve a certain amount of shoulder shrugging, whimsical looks of bewilderment, an entreaty for fairness, mock innocence and a succession of double takes – all beautifully timed; all seen before. Peter Copley gives a flavour of those customary and characteristic comedy tricks:

In *The Bargain* he had a scene where he returns to his empty lawyer's office having suffered some life-threatening humiliation. He did so little, he stood behind his desk quite still, and you knew he was sick with exhaustion, and fear and humiliation. He clearly has a thumping headache, opens a drawer, takes out a bottle of aspirin, shakes out two pills, closes the bottle, puts it back in the drawer, picks up the two pills, realises he has no water and no source of water without leaving the room. His resolution to swallow them without water, the monumental, sustained effort to do so, and the final achievement but without any sign of achievement or relief was sublime.[49]

Alastair was an intelligent performer – an intelligent man. He was acutely aware that predictability was beginning to plague his performances and so decided to re-establish his credentials by a surprise return to the Old Vic in *The Tempest*. One evening, over dinner with Sidney Gilliat, Alastair explained in detail some of his ideas for his interpretation of Prospero:

He saw Prospero as always performing little tricks and illusions with his left hand – magic being so much a part of his nature that he indulged in it almost absentmindedly, so much so that he simply couldn't stop without an effort.[50]

Rather than find a new challenge, it appears that Alastair had chosen the one Shakespearean character that fitted his acting style so snugly. On 29 May 1962, thirty years after his first employment at the Old Vic, Alastair appeared on stage in *The Tempest*. His obituary remarked of his performance as Prospero:

He saw that redoubtable magician as a gently irascible, circumspect housemaster, speaking in his customary aerated purr and finding some unlooked for, yet typical, emphases ('Thou *hast* slept well!' he told Miranda).[51]

Alastair, a past master in elocution, had been developing a skill whereby he emphasised an unlikely word or short phrase in a sentence in order to give a logical sentence structure a rather illogical and nonsensical feel. There appeared to be meaning, because the combination of words made grammatical sense, but one could never be certain of their interpretation.[52] Alastair was using the power of words; a power he had explored in his Rectorial Address in 1949. It was a skill he would continue to develop further over the forthcoming years and use to good effect in his role as the Bishop in the film *The Ruling Class* (1972).

Although Alastair had put much thought into his interpretation of Prospero, Peter Copley had doubts: '. . . he played Prospero and was strangely laborious and unmagical.'[53] The critics were equally unimpressed. Kenneth Tynan wrote rather tartly in his review for *The Observer*:

The Tempest is remarkable mainly because of its Prospero. Rather than play the part Alastair Sim chooses to reconnoitre it, you might think him a tentative pantomime dame standing in for Tommy Cooper, the music-hall magician whose tricks never work.[54]

The image of a tentative pantomime dame is one that contains an immense amount of ridicule. The pantomime dame is supposed to be lavish in appearance, flamboyant in nature but above all, a grotesque entity. To describe therefore a pantomime dame as tentative is to deride the performance while at the same time mocking the physical attributes and mannerisms of the performer. It was a disparaging review, but more were soon to follow.

In July 1963 Alastair directed and acted in a new comedy, *Windfall* by Michael Gilbert. Alastair played the role of Alexander Lindsay, a housemaster at Ramsfield, a public school. Also in the cast were Douglas Muir as Major Gunn and Margaret Wedlake as Margaret Lindsay. Alastair's daughter Merlith played his daughter (Jean Lindsay) in the play. *Windfall* 'toured for 13 friendly weeks, then came into London and lasted a friendly month. . .'[55] A certain fab four were also on tour. Margaret Wedlake: 'I think we were pretty successful though, and it was a pity the Beatles burst on the scene in a tour at the same time!'[56] It is somewhat amusing to consider how an Alastair Sim production in 1963 might have been competing for the same audience as the Beatles.

Margaret Wedlake found Alastair's direction:

> . . . curiously contradictory: in rehearsal, much time, as the director, spent on making actors do little things like miming the turning of a non-existent doorknob, while in performance, allowing himself considerable liberty of movement and business. . . [57]

How would one sum up Alastair as a director? Dictatorial? Intimidating? Selfish? Pedantic? It is true to say that Alastair, as a director, polarised views. There were those who responded well to his methods and those who hated them. He was also extremely prejudiced, disliking some actors for the oddest of reasons but remaining remarkably loyal to those whose talent might have been exaggerated. What is also known is that you could ill afford to get on the wrong side of Alastair. Once he had lost confidence in someone, either a director or fellow actor, that was it, he would dismiss them, as we will see. Furthermore, directing Alastair towards the end of his career was virtually impossible. The best anyone could do was to make a subtle suggestion, using the most diplomatic of terms, maybe employing Naomi as a go-between. These are the characteristics of a very difficult man.

At Christmas, Alastair reprised his role as Captain Hook. This was the fourth time he had donned the wig and wielded the hook, and he would do so for a fifth and final time the following year. John Standing[58] expressed a view shared by many: 'There will never be a Captain Hook like him. He was definitive – very frightening and very funny.'[59] Although this might have been true of Alastair's previous three seasons as Hook, by the 1960s, his interpretation of the evil captain had become rather tame. An analysis of *Peter Pan* would lend itself to raillery given that the play is a traditional Christmas pantomime and therefore not to be taken too seriously. Over-acting is *de rigeur*, but Captain Hook has to command a degree of villainous respect in order to generate tension between himself and the hero, and perhaps more importantly, between himself and the audience. Without this tension, there is no need to side with the underdog hero, no need to shout, 'He's behind you!' at the prescriptive times, and no need for children to peek into their wardrobes and look under their beds before they go to sleep at night. Fearful moments lose their impact, comic moments are nothing but a diversion, and the children lose interest. *The Times* critic wrote:

> Mr Alastair Sim is a Captain Hook for adults only. He underplays in an amusing way, but the lack of terror which he engenders is the only improbable thing about the evening.[60]

Alastair had settled into a style of acting that was largely a caricature of his previous performances. The pantomime dame had re-emerged only this time *in* pantomime; yet it was still the wrong interpretation of the part.

While co-stars such as James Mason, Margaret Lockwood, John Mills, Trevor Howard, Stewart Granger and Peter O'Toole developed along more traditional lines of stardom, working their way up to headlining star, Alastair's promise in the early 1950s began to evaporate as critics recognised that his performances lacked originality. As much as Alastair would have wished to describe his characters as individual creations with idiosyncratic mannerisms, they were all too frequently blessed with the same mannerisms. Some critics were wise to this fact and commented that 'films were merest vehicles for his comic mannerisms'.[61] The familiar Sim chuckle or chortle would introduce or end a line in many of his films, as would the flourish of his handkerchief to wipe his nose, only to be returned, haphazardly, into his top pocket. Such an action identifies a nasal complaint universal to all the characters he played. A small piece of business maybe, but used far too frequently.

Yet not all was lost. A pantomime audience is characterised by a mixture of children and adults, and it was Alastair's rapport with the adults in the audience that made his final two Hook interpretations so successful. Indeed, his latter performances in *Peter Pan* had unwittingly identified a way in which he could reclaim some of his past success. Alastair needed a role that was pantomimesque in nature, within a play aimed primarily at adults, in a role in which he could exploit his natural gift of comedy and in an environment where he could interact with the audience. The question was whether such a role and environment existed. Alastair would have to wait two more years to find out.

Alastair ended this period of his career with a mixed bag of performances. At the beginning of 1964 he played Shylock at the Nottingham Playhouse and then toured as Freer in *The Elephant's Foot*. The latter was a disaster and Alastair demonstrated contriteness by blaming himself for having made some crucial casting blunders. How prescient was Sidney Gilliat? In the following year he recorded *She Stoops To Conquer*[62] by Oliver Goldsmith and appeared at the Edinburgh Festival, in *Too True To Be Good* by Bernard Shaw. The play was well received:

> Among its delights are Dora Bryan's Cockney-genteel Sweetie. . .
> Alastair Sim as the enraged Colonel Tallboys smartly rapping her over
> the head with a tartan parasol . . . and the upstanding puritan sergeant
> is robustly played by George Cole.'[63]

Dora Bryan regarded Alastair as a 'brilliant performer'[64], though understandably she was a 'little in awe of him'.[65] On 22 September *Too True To Be Good* switched to the Strand theatre and the next day, the following mild reproach appeared in *The Times*: 'Mr. Sim could, as a matter of fact, allow himself a little more boisterous freedom than he chooses to take.'[66]

The film career had finished, Tynan had described Alastair as a 'pantomime dame', and the critics now seemed prepared to say we have seen this all before. Alastair's performances, though charming, were a predictable series of angst-filled expressions, sandwiched between sign-posted double takes. The critics were on to him now, openly challenging the performance of a man who had once earned so much respect and admiration for his performances in *Scrooge* and *Mr Gillie*. Something had to happen to revitalise his career or he would land up as a curio, a one-trick pony, or at worst, a has-been.

The catalyst to Alastair's first period of success in his acting career had been the looks and manic actions so much in demand on stage and in film in the 1930s. The catalyst to his second period of success had been the formation of two partnerships – one with James Bridie and the other with Launder and Gilliat. The catalyst for his third and final period of success would be the theatre itself – or more precisely, the type of stage.

The square-on stage, the standard feature of most theatres, produced an unequivocal separation of the actors from the audience. This division was essential in many respects when presenting a play since it defined the boundary between reality and fantasy – similar to the use of a red curtain in a cinema. A square-on stage meant that the setting was very formal and the atmosphere within the theatre generally reticent. In contrast, the thrust stage, dated but steeped in tradition, jutted out into the audience, blurring the distinction between audience and actors thereby creating an intimate setting for the evening's proceedings. Although the gains of the thrust stage were clear, there was also a risk attached to the informality of the setting. The audience might refuse to suspend disbelief and instead become restless and critical. A thrust stage was therefore a high-risk strategy, but with the right actor, someone with presence and charisma, it could be a hugely successful means by which to engage the audience in a rollicking good comedy.

Significantly, a thrust stage was about to be built in Chichester.

II

The Chichester Festival Years

His brilliance balanced the grotesque with the utterly real, the pathos of the character's self-deception with the psychological truth, wit, and self-revelation of the master that he was.

– Sarah Badel, who played Miss Fanny, describing Alastair's portrayal of Lord Ogleby in *The Clandestine Marriage*.

One evening, Leslie Evershed-Martin, twice mayor of Chichester, was watching a BBC programme called *Monitor*. In the programme, Sir Tyrone Guthrie was explaining how he had created a theatre in Ontario in accordance with the Greek and Elizabethan style whereby the audience sat around an open-thrust stage. He said he had favoured such a design because it created an intimate atmosphere between the actors and the audience, encouraging and indeed endorsing, audience participation – especially in the comedies. All very good for Ontario but Chichester was not exactly renowned at that time for its love or support of the theatre. True there had once been a Roman amphitheatre, but more recently, the original town theatre had been replaced by a shopping mall.

Thankfully, Leslie Evershed-Martin was not a man to be beaten by the public's love of retail therapy. He resolved that a theatre would be his cultural legacy and crown his lifetime achievement in serving

Chichester. As a result of his determined efforts, plans were put into place and in 1962, the Chichester Festival Theatre (CFT) opened its doors under the guidance of Lord Olivier.

Laurence Olivier found the demanding task of managing three theatres – the CFT, the Old Vic and the National Theatre – quite exhausting, and so in December 1965, Olivier stepped aside to allow John Clements[1] to become the new director of the CFT. John Clements was well aware that the open-thrust design of the theatre meant that the success of a play was often dependent on the personalities of the actors involved in the production. They had to be charismatic, willing to engage with the audience, and confident enough to deal with any heckling. John Clements had a particular actor in mind whom he considered ideally suited to these conditions.

The friendship between Alastair and John Clements dated back to the early 1930s when they both appeared in *Caviare* and *The Venetian*. Perhaps more significantly, they shared the same London club – the Garrick. In 1966, John Clements asked Alastair if he would be interested in playing the ageing lotharian Lord Ogleby in *The Clandestine Marriage* by David Garrick. Alastair responded positively to the invitation and set about considering how he could incorporate his idiosyncratic personality into the play.

John Clements now attempted a double coup. In December 1965 he had began making overtures to another well-known British eccentric, whom he had good reason to believe would complement Alastair in the production. Margaret Rutherford, who had stood up to Alastair, if not almost eclipsed him, in *The Happiest Days of your Life*, had recently been suffering from a bout of depression, sadly a frequent occurrence in her later life, but was on friendly terms with John Clements. Through careful diplomatic negotiations, he gently persuaded her to take part in *The Clandestine Marriage*. Margaret Rutherford gamely acquiesced, although at seventy-five, one could not have expected a virtuoso performance, and the reviews reflected this fact: 'Margaret Rutherford . . . gives a mild and subdued performance.'[2]

Alastair put a lot of thought into how he was going to play his scenes. Sarah Badel, who played Miss Fanny in the production, recalled:

Alastair played the lecherous old Lord Ogleby . . . and had come to the first rehearsal with every detail of the performance meticulously worked out. He took a great deal of trouble to assist me in the timing of the scene that we had together and showed me exactly what he was doing whenever my back was turned so that the playing of the scene was a true partnership and a joy to perform.[3]

In the scene referred to above, Alastair, as Lord Ogleby, attempts to seduce the young Miss Fanny. The performance is at risk of being seen as perverted, but as Sarah Badel recalls, 'the delicacy of his comedy ensured that never for a moment did that element creep in and the audience adored it.'[4]

There was a problem however. John Clements was concerned that Alastair's final entrance was taking too long. In *The Clandestine Marriage*, Alastair (Lord Ogleby) appears at the top of a three-tiered staircase wearing a nightcap and gown. He then proceeds to totter anciently down the stairs. Clements felt that the tottering, though amusing, slowed down the pace of the play – but how to broach the subject with Alastair? It was only after first previews, that Clements passed a note to Alastair saying his 'final entrance was taking too long'.[5] The next evening, Alastair appeared at the top of the staircase on cue as usual, and then dramatically fell down the three tiers – accompanied by roars of laughter from the audience. Most would agree that this was a novel way of speeding up the descent. Every time Alastair fell down the stairs, he always managed to land on his feet. Sarah Badel, who witnessed this act of self-sacrifice every night said, 'Nobody had appreciated his talents as a gymnast and we watched him do it night after night without ever harming himself.'[6]

The Clandestine Marriage was hailed as a great success:

Alastair Sim as Ogleby gets much his best effects in the early scenes, straight out of bed, a surgically-belted Earl trying to coax his palsied limbs into a semblance of gallantry.[7]

Alastair had responded tremendously well to the challenges of the intimate theatre and the audience had responded in turn with rapturous applause and laughter. Alastair was back in the limelight once more.

In 1966, the BBC began preparing for a new television comedy series which was to be set in a courtroom where various moral debates could take place around the stories of A.P. Herbert, such as 'Are Englishmen really free?' and 'Is every man's home his castle?' The producer of the show, Michael Mills, approached Alastair to see if he was willing to undertake the role of the presiding judge – Mr Justice Swallow. It might sound unlikely that Alastair would consider an offer to appear in a television situation comedy but Alastair liked the works of A.P. Herbert and 'they got on very well together'.[8] Perhaps also at the back of Alastair's mind was the thought that such a role would provide him with an excellent opportunity to caricature the law courts. Thus in some small way, he could seek revenge on the judicial system that had so humiliated him over the Heinz Baked Beans affair in 1959.

Rehearsals got under way and on Tuesday 20 June 1967, at 7.30pm, the first episode of *Misleading Cases*, entitled *The Negotiable Cow*, was aired on television. A star actor, such as John Le Mesurier, Eleanor Summerfield and Irene Handl featured in each episode alongside the regulars: Roy Dotrice as Albert Haddock, who would appear before the judge each week with a case usually concerning a moral question, Thorley Walters and Avice Landon. Alastair played Swallow as a slightly naïve, sometimes slow, other times shrewd judge, who watched over the court intrigues rather more in the manner of a concerned spectator that as a presiding magistrate. Swallow's irritating characteristic was to interject into proceedings with the apologetic air of one mystified by the technical jargon, although the jargon was often everyday conversational terms.

Misleading Cases offered a satirical interpretation of the judicial system which appears, even today, all too true – a judge completely out of terms with the modern way of life. It was an immediate success combining 'two uniquely English qualities, odd law and eccentrics'.[9] Alastair's performance received good reviews:

> Alastair Sim, who appeared first as a magistrate and then finally as a judge of a court of appeal, where he presided sympathetically over the scenes of Mr Haddock's victories, was a joy.[10]

Misleading Cases ran to three series. The first two series, produced in 1967 and 1968, were in black and white, while the third series, produced in 1971, was in colour. In total there were nineteen episodes, each of thirty minutes' duration. The last episode was aired at 8.30pm on Friday 10 September 1971. Playing the part of a financial expert in the last episode was John Cleese: 'He [Alastair] seemed very friendly – indeed avuncular – but in a quiet way. Distinctly low-key, but charming.'[11]

Although Alastair appears at ease in his performances in *Misleading Cases*, he was very uncomfortable with television work. The director John Howard Davies recalled: 'he thought it rather forced'.[12] The problems that had led to Alastair's deteriorating relationship with Sidney Gilliat reappeared during the three-season run. John Howard Davies, who directed the second and third series had to contend with the fact that 'Alastair took a dim view about learning his lines.'[13] Also, Alastair's loyalty towards past colleagues meant that he made casting suggestions to John Howard Davies that were somewhat contrary to those in the mind of the director. Alastair tended to cast actors and actresses whose company he enjoyed; it gave him comfort to do so and created a pleasant working environment in which to spend his life. As a result, John Howard Davies sometimes found himself having to manage a difficult situation carefully in order to avoid a blatant miscast. Even so, Alastair was on good form during the series and John Howard Davies remembers how 'I used to look forward to going to work with him.'[14]

Everything has a life cycle; a situation comedy is no different in this respect. The premise of *Misleading Cases*, eccentric and original to begin with, began to look a bit tired during the second series as the moral debates started to become repetitive. A.P. Herbert wrote an episode but it was of such poor quality that the production team could not use it. Unfortunately this created some ill feeling and at the end of the third series, the decision was taken not to plan for a fourth.

In the summer of 1967, Alastair appeared in *Number 10* – a stage play that was to become embroiled in its own political row. *Number 10* opened on 29 August 1967 at the King's Theatre, Glasgow and was chosen to represent British drama in a festival in Toronto. Financial backing was originally provided by the Board of Trade but at the last minute they decreed that the subject matter of the play was politically incorrect for Canada and so withdrew their sponsorship of £5,000. Nevertheless the two-week run took place in Canada to great success, making a net profit of £51,000.

Number 10 is based around a political crisis that arises when the president of an African state illegally takes control of a British mining factory. The Prime Minister's task is to mediate between the British Foreign Secretary (John Gregson), who wants the incident referred to the UN, and the Defence Secretary (Michael Denison), who wants immediate action taken by the British Armed Forces. Alastair plays the Prime Minister 'like a benevolent headmaster watching over unruly pupils, but his familiar brand of bumbling geniality fits the part surprisingly well'.[15] A political play rather aptly brought the spotlight to bear on the actors' own political biases. Alastair 'I'm very left-wing you know'[16] Sim was poles apart from the right-wing attitudes of Michael Denison. This antagonism found an outlet in the stage production: Alastair would undertake a bit of business just as Michael Denison was delivering a line. Denison retaliated by doing likewise in return. Potentially this could have been disastrous, but the two sparring partners seemed to raise their game to meet the challenge, and *Number 10*, which finally closed on Saturday 10 March 1968, was regarded as a very successful production.

Hot on the success of *Misleading Cases*, Alastair was enticed to undertake further television work. On 15 June 1968, a weekly serialisation of *Cold Comfort Farm* by Stella Gibbons was transmitted on television. In the production, Alastair played the part of Amos Starkadder. Freddie Jones as Urk Starkadder recalled:

> I was thrilled to meet him and I recalled remembering a piece of invention that I had so admired in *Green For Danger* to which he replied 'Ah! I can't invent anymore!'[17]

Alastair's career and popularity was on the rise again. To confirm such status, he sought another challenge – to reclaim the post of Rector of Edinburgh University. However, whereas since the late 1940s his views regarding the philosophy of folly had hardened, those of the students' had not:

> Mr Alastair Sim . . . appealing for a return to responsibility in the rectorship and self-respect in the university. He is unlikely to find many students going with him.[18]

The result of the vote supported this supposition and the journalist and television personality, Kenneth Allsop, was elected to the post.

Although the students had turned their backs on him, his theatre fans remained ever loyal. Alastair now repaid that loyalty with what many believe to be his finest stage performance – the 1969 Chichester Festival production of Pinero's comedy *The Magistrate*. Also in the cast were Patricia Routledge, Christopher Guinee, John Clements, Michael Aldridge and Renee Asherson.

The Magistrate is a well-constructed nineteenth-century farce telling of the scrapes that befall Mr Poskitt (Alastair Sim). It was a role that suited his mannerisms perfectly. Renee Asherson recalled:

> Alastair gave such a definitive performance in *The Magistrate* that it was impossible to believe that Pinero hadn't written it with Alastair in mind. I remember that one night Patricia Routledge and I made our first entrance and I fell flat on my face. Alastair took it all in his stride and thought it was an intended piece of business.[19]

Renee Asherson's choice of phrase 'it was impossible to believe that Pinero hadn't written it with Alastair in mind' is very interesting because it sounds very similar to the quotes levelled at James Bridie during the 1940s. Maybe by this time Alastair had realised that no one could replace Bridie and that he had to look to the past masters of comedy to achieve success in the present day.

Patricia Routledge who played opposite Alastair as Agatha Poskitt says of his performance:

> He was at his peak. When he reached that pitch of obsession with a situation, however absurd, there was nothing he could not do with those staring eyes, that jabbing finger, the swoops and wobbles of his voice. Playing opposite him taught me so much.[20]

Peter Copley:

> Alastair could convey the agony or catastrophe in a way so painful to watch and still so funny. He was unique in this capacity. His performance in '*The Magistrate*' was unbearably painful and the funniest there ever was – one of the great bits of acting.[21]

The Magistrate was extremely successful, breaking all box-office records at the Chichester Festival. The production moved to London and began an equally successful run at the Cambridge Theatre in September 1969.

> Leading them is Alastair Sim, and no one else in the world can be so outraged, so embarrassed, so baffled, so hurt, and so sly as Mr Sim. Everybody is larger than life – Mr Sim is positively gigantic – the result is simply a delight.[22]

Hugh Leonard writing in *Plays and Players*:

> And, at the moment when falsehoods mount in an obscene pyramid as *The Magistrate*'s career teeters on a cliff edge, Mr Sim's stricken, finally still face seems to age before our eyes. This is a great farce performance.[23]

Although he goes on to add: 'Alastair Sim's performance was so gloriously funny that one resented not being able to hear every word.'[24] Naomi, in 1931, making her first tentative suggestion to Alastair of how to improve his stage performance, had identified that his voice did not always reach the back of the circle. Alastair had a tonsil operation around that time that had improved things, but forty years on, age was beginning to dampen his ability to project his voice.

Sidney Gilliat went to see *The Magistrate* one evening and afterwards wrote a letter to Alastair congratulating him on his performance. Alastair immediately replied with an invitation to lunch at his club. Gilliat recalls:

> It was quite like old times. The play was Pinero's *The Magistrate* and he was at the top of his form, as indeed he was at our lunch. We discussed making a film about it, but technical and other difficulties, nothing to do with either of us, got in the way.[25]

Alastair added to *The Magistrate* a favourite scene from *London Belongs to Me* (1948) – the scene where Henry Squales admonishes himself in the mirror with, 'Have you sunk so low as to do this thing? . . . (shaking his head) There can only be one answer. . . (nodding his head) Yes . . .

you have'. Alastair used a similar invention for when Mr Poskitt returns home after a disreputable night out on the town. Gilliat recalls:

> He [Alastair] said to me at our lunch, 'Of course you recognised that
> as having been lifted from *London Belongs to Me*?'
> I said, 'Yes, I had.'
> 'I suppose I ought to have written to Norman Collins and apologised
> for pinching it,' he said.
> 'Not to him. To me. . . That line wasn't in Collins's novel. I put it in
> the script myself.'
> 'Ah! Did you then?' he said. 'We had some fun in those days, Sidney'.[26]

Sidney Gilliat and Alastair Sim finished their meal in a happy reverie of past times. The work they forged together in the '40s and '50s will entertain people for many years to come. It was the last ever meeting between the two men.

Alastair's stage performance as Mr Poskitt was nothing short of a triumphant success. Actors that follow in this role are forever compared to hiss performance at Chichester. A wonderful opportunity presented itself for this stage production to be captured for posterity when Cedric Messina, on behalf of the BBC, approached Alastair with an offer to record the play. Alastair was initially impressed with the idea and entered into preliminary negotiations although when the finer points were discussed, it became apparent that Cedric Messina wanted to recast all of the roles except for that of Mr Poskitt. Alastair, who throughout his career, always felt a deep sense of loyalty towards his fellow cast members, could under no circumstances accept a recast and so withdrew his support for the project.

A production in which Alastair might have appeared around this time but for a very sad incident was *What the Butler Saw* by Joe Orton. Orton was looking for an eccentric to play Dr Rance in his latest play and had initially wanted Ralph Richardson for the part but then had second thoughts and decided instead to request Alastair for the role. Sadly, before the play could go into production, Joe Orton was murdered.

★

The 1970s began inauspiciously with William Douglas Home's *The Jockey Club Stakes* at the Vaudeville Theatre. *The Jockey Club Stakes* is a fast-paced, convoluted affair, involving race-fixing and horse-doping, and unsurprisingly, the reviews tended to be slightly dismissive:

> Murray Macdonald's production also operates effectively on the musical-chairs principle of never letting anyone remain seated for more than three minutes at a time.[27]

Alastair had achieved such acclaim with his Chichester performances that critics now seemed prepared to accept his idiosyncratic acting style as if in the manner of someone greeting an old friend:

> However, the evening has a saving grace that can be summarised in two words: Alastair Sim. As the senior Jockey Club steward, Mr Sim displays all the conspiratorial shoulder-heaving glee, the exaggerated bonhomie and the lugubrious dismay for which he is justly famous.[28]

His obituary highlighted his performance in an ultimately disappointing play by remarking, 'Delightfully bantering work as the Marquis. . .'[29].

The time had arrived when critics were no longer interested in offering an honest critique of his performance. Everyone knew that he would run through his usual repertoire on stage and the audience loved him the more for it. Woe betide any director then who would dare to suggest to Alastair some alternative business. In Alastair's next play, the director Robert Kidd, rather unwisely, tried to do exactly that.

In February 1972 Alastair appeared at the Cambridge Theatre alongside Michael Bryant and Stanley Holloway in *Siege*, the first stage play by David Ambrose. The action takes place in an upper-class club in St James and begins with Willy (Alastair) asleep in his chair, clearly enjoying a humorous dream. Sidgwick (Stanley Holloway) enters with a tray of drinks and 'one feels in the capable hands of a team of light comedy artists deftly prepared to beguile us for a couple of happy hours.'[30]

Unfortunately, *Siege* was not a successful production all round. The script over-employed a plot device, identified by Charles Lewsen of *The Times* – 'wrapping an exciting idea in the framework of a dream is a good way of diminishing it.'[31] The lighting of the stage also received criticism as did the direction by Robert Kidd. Kidd was in a difficult position. Alastair was by now such an established stage actor that any direction, if offered without a certain amount of diplomacy, could cause offence. Alastair had a good sense of what he could do and indeed, what he was best at doing. At seventy-one, he was beyond the need to stretch himself as an actor, and instead was content to deliver his famous angst-ridden look of despair on cue. This was, after all, what his public wanted to see. Robert Kidd, on the other hand, wanted Alastair to try some new business befitting the character he was playing. Alastair considered Kidd's suggestions to be outside of his range; he said so, and then dismissed Kidd as a 'silly little man'.[32]

Robert Kidd's position was made even more difficult during dress rehearsals when Alastair's stalwart, trusted defender, Naomi, sat in the circle offering her own brand of advice and direction. Alastair eventually made it clear to Robert Kidd that he was only interested in what Naomi had to say, belittling the man further. Although Alastair's fellow actors may not have entirely agreed with him over his dispute with Kidd, they nevertheless remained on his side. As usual, Alastair reciprocated this loyalty. When Michael Bryant felt that his salary was insufficient during the rehearsals for *Siege*, Alastair stood by him and supported his request for a rise.

The venue was also wrong. David Ambrose considered *Siege* a 'chamber piece'[33] and therefore wanted a small intimate theatre in which to set his production. Unfortunately, the only theatre available at the time was the Cambridge Theatre – a relatively large theatre and therefore not particularly suited to a small three-man production.

The other, perhaps more telling factor against *Siege*, was the union strife in the country at that time. *Siege* found itself a victim of the three-day week, during a period of time when electricity was in short supply due to the strikes within the power industries. Although the production went ahead, even press night took place under restricted lighting conditions. It comes as no surprise therefore to learn that the lighting of the production received criticism. The three-day week also affected audience attendance. Theatregoers were reluctant to travel out in the evening and, even if they did so, found all the amenities were affected by the strikes. In general they stayed at home and gathered round their candles, or took an early night. Even amongst all this strife, Alastair still received his customary good reviews: 'The incomparable Mr Sim is puckish, sceptical, deft and enchantingly resourceful.'[34]

Also in 1972 Alastair returned to television to give an impressive performance as General Suffolk in the television play *The General's Day*. *The General's Day* was set in a seaside resort and featured Alastair as a retired, amorous and slightly alcoholic general who is aghast to realise that his daily help intends moving in with him – even worse is the fact that she intends bringing her pet parrot. Annette Crosbie[35] played the part of a caring schoolmistress, sympathetic to his plight. The broadcast was well received: 'The sum total was wholly convincing, and there were a hundred lovely touches on the way.'[36] And:

Alastair Sim's General moved from a military crispness through explosive moments to a crumbling ebullience as the events of the day and the drink took their toll.[37]

The film work that had dried up so conspicuously with the onset of the 1960s began to re-appear. Alastair's first film role for ten years was the part of a Bishop in the film *The Ruling Class* (1972).

The Ruling Class mixes sweet subtlety with gaudy ghoulishness and overlays this with a satirical wit which now appears dated and at times juvenile. Jack Guerney (Peter O'Toole) – a paranoid schizophrenic who believes he is God – inherits a title and thwarts his family's attempts to have him classed insane by throwing himself wholeheartedly into the role of Lord of the Manor. As his mental health deteriorates, he finds sanctuary in the House of Lords. On being asked to explain the plot, Alastair replied, 'I am an actor. . . I play parts. . . That is enough. . .'[38]. Just as well really since the plot is mystifying at times.

Alastair played the Bishop of Lampton – a doddering, senile man, 'a confused and maladroit lump of episcopality who manages to forget the lines from the marriage service.'[39] This is not entirely accurate. In the scene in question, the Bishop is marrying Jack to his bride and is urged to 'get on with it' seven times. Panic and anxiety ensue.

Alastair employed his skill with the spoken word to good effect in this film. He had previously developed a speaking style whereby he would emphasise certain words not particularly deserving of such attention, in order to produce the curious effect of giving meaning where there is none, and where there is supposed to be meaning, making it nonsensical. This effect can be witnessed at several points during the film, thereby making the message of God unintelligible which, given the satirical nature of *The Ruling Class*, is probably the intention.

Apart from this, there is something disappointing about Alastair's performance in *The Ruling Class*. There are various fumblings and falls that convey the ageing senility of the Bishop but these are performed in such a music-hall manner that they lack conviction. Alastair's Bishop is the antithesis of his brilliant portrayals of Scrooge, Wetherby Pond, Inspector Cockrill, Mr Gillie and Mr Bolfry. Instead it was a clear sign that the Chichester Festival performances, though warmly received, had encouraged a return to the manic performances of Alastair's earlier films.

The Ruling Class received high praise for the way it openly challenged the class system. This was brave and ground-breaking, but as is so often the case with satire, the passing of time has reduced its impact. Peter O'Toole was nominated for an Oscar and some of the other performances, Arthur Lowe in particular, are excellent. In contrast, the sound quality is at times raw, as could be said of the annoying songs that punctuate the film. At the end of *The Ruling Class*, one feels neither enlightened, nor sympathetic to any of the issues raised. Alastair, on the other hand, his politics in tune with the message of the film, loved *The Ruling Class* and in particular adored Peter O'Toole whom he thought hilarious.

In early 1973 Alastair appeared as Dakyn alongside Dorothy Reynolds, Derek Fowlds and Peter Cellier in the stage play *A Private Matter*. It was a poignant moment for Alastair since the play had been written by Ronald Mavor – James Bridie's son. *A Private Matter* examines the strains within the Black family when an Oxford Don visits their home intending to write a biography of the late General Black. It had first been presented in Nottingham in 1972 under the title, *A Life of the General* without Alastair in the cast. The Nottingham run was a success and so it transferred, in the following year, to the West End, opening on 21 February at the Vaudeville Theatre London with Alastair now in the cast.

Finding a director with the necessary panache, confidence and diplomatic skills to direct Alastair was always going to be difficult. At this stage of his career, it was no longer the case that any director could be appointed without prior consultation with Alastair and the nod of approval. Ian McKellen was brought to Alastair's attention because he had been enjoying some success directing in regional theatre at that time. It also helped that McKellen shared the same agent (Elspeth Cochrane) as Ronald Mavor. There was one other crucial factor. As Sir Ian McKellen recalls: 'I had to be approved by Alastair . . . but I had youth in my favour.'[40]

Ian McKellen was appointed director and began rehearsals with the cast. Naturally Naomi sat in her usual place making her own notes and observations. With some relief for all concerned Alastair appears to have got on well with his young director although as Sir Ian McKellen later said of his experience: 'Alastair took my direction only when he'd checked it out with Naomi.'[41]

The cast were also very friendly and the atmosphere in the dressing rooms was one of good spirits. Although Alastair was seventy-two, Peter Cellier remembers that he 'seemed to have a better memory, more energy and inventiveness than the rest of us put together'[42] and adds:

He was of course a truly charming person to work with, the only difficulty being to refrain from laughing outright at his superb comic timing.[43]

Another actor in the cast, Derek Fowlds, said that Alastair taught him to 'take the day in with you'.[44] Derek Fowlds explains:

I was very badly affected with hay fever and thought I would have to miss a performance. Alastair insisted I went on and when he first met me on the stage, he said, 'Ah, you are the son who suffers badly with Hay Fever'. . .You see I had taken the day in with me.[45]

The critics were again generous in their praise of Alastair's performance:

Mr Sim fills out the role of Dakyn with gleeful mischief, innocent solicitude and the suggestion of intellectual incisiveness.[46]

Ronald Mavor was perfectly placed to comment on Alastair's attention to detail:

> He always . . . ticked me off for forcing my own ideas on to the characters in a play. . . 'I hate to hear the author speaking through a play,' he said. And when we were rehearsing *A Private Matter* he would again and again argue that during such-and-such a speech one of the other characters must be reacting in such-and-such a way. 'Yes, it's a serious speech,' he would say, 'but can't you see, Anthony thinks it's a load of rubbish!'[47]

Ronald Mavor considered that Alastair's robust defence of an individual's right to express their opinion, even if they were only a fictional character in a play, reflected his fundamental belief about mankind in general. In addition, Alastair firmly believed that everyone should have the opportunity to make the most of their life. Of course, these are the same beliefs asserted by Alastair in the play *Mr Gillie* by James Bridie. However, as Bridie makes clear in his play, Mr Gillie is a flawed individual.

Although *A Private Matter* enjoyed some success in London, in general the reviews were rather lukewarm: 'The subtlety of Alastair Sim shows up, but cannot fulfil, the pretensions of Mr Mavor's play.'[48]

Criticism of the play was practically guaranteed when it came to light that Ronald Mavor had given an interview in which he had compared himself with Ibsen and Molière. Some of the critics were antagonised by such arrogance in a young writer. Harold Hobson of *The Times* responded, 'I call this a bit thick', but went on to question whether the comparison was an 'elaborate Scottish joke'.[49] This, of course, would have been in keeping with the Bridie tradition. There was also some feeling that Alastair took on the role out of respect for the memory of his old friend – and perhaps against his better judgement.

Later in the year, Alastair was enticed once more to return to Chichester for John Clements's farewell show *Dandy Dick*[50]. 'Alastair

Sim, flapping and shaking like a swollen-headed stork'[51] played the
role of the Dean in Pinero's comedy. *Dandy Dick* was another great
Chichester success and after the festival ran at the Garrick Theatre,
London. Irving Wardle in *The Times* announced:

> Mr Sim now resembles the aged Stanislavsky, and every gesture he
> makes is entirely his own property: the whole wrist flapping where
> another actor would point a finger, expansive arm movements, timidly
> retracting into hugging himself. . . In its combination of innocence
> and unconscious guile, this is the most perfect Pinero performance I
> have seen.'[52]

The 'perfect Pinero performance' was the result of much planning.
Lucinda Gane, who played Salome, said:

> Alastair was very demanding of rehearsal time but only in order to
> perfect his role. Every comic moment was planned and refined to
> produce the classical effect. His performance was 'choreographed' in
> every aspect.[53]

Richard Owens who played Norah Topping in the production adds:

> He always gave the impression that any comedy business he invented
> was completely spontaneous. I used to watch one scene as I was
> awaiting my entrance and it seemed new every time.[54]

These comments are similar to those made by Larry Barnes regarding Alastair's performances in the 1940s – nothing much had changed
in the intervening years. Alastair appeared as a relaxed actor on stage
or screen, effortlessly delivering his lines, but of course every nuance
had been meticulously planned out in advance. Ronald Mavor, who
directed Alastair Sim in *A Private Matter*, recalls:

> Seeing him rehearse a role in a play was to see a great artist, and a
> great clown, at work. And the secret . . . is to care enough: to care
> enough about those three words, that gesture, really to work at it and
> get it right. Of course, one must also have the vision to know what
> right is.[55]

The Chichester Festival years had been a triumphant time for Alastair. He had successfully re-established his reputation as one of the great comedy actors of his generation. Of course the performances were far too snug to the Alastair Sim stage and screen persona to be regarded as a challenge, but they delighted audiences without fail. As his obituary said:

> Even if he was inclined to repeat such effects as his tentative, disappearing smile, audiences delighted in the friendly ruefulness with which he established so many parts.[56]

Film success had also been achieved in *The Ruling Class*. Unfortunately, all was not well with Alastair.

Alastair's health up until this point had been relatively good. Apart from his back injury in the 1930s, a broken leg endured on the tennis court and a hernia operation, Alastair had in general been a fit person. But he had lived during a period when smoking was considered the social norm rather than the unhealthy exception. There were warnings, certainly, of the ill effects from too much smoking, but during the '50s and '60s there was still some scepticism regarding the link between smoking and cancer. Even so, Alastair, speaking in 1951, seemed aware of the potential dangers he faced:

> 'Well now, I'll tell you something.' Here he held up his cigarette for me to see. 'Cigarettes,' he said mysteriously. 'Do you realise now we really shall have to cut down our smoking? I suppose you read in the newspapers about this new complaint said to be caused by too much smoking?'[57]

Sadly, typifying the principled yet curiously contradictory man that he was, because of the harm they caused, Alastair would never offer someone a cigarette or keep them in his house. Instead, he smoked cigars – swapping one vice for another. Having spent decades smoking cigars and cigarettes, Alastair was now about to face his greatest personal battle – that with cancer.

Escape to the Dark: the Last Years

You know I wouldn't be surprised if this gets me one day.[1]

– Alastair, referring to his cancer.

As Alastair approached old age, Naomi made sure that all household chores were taken care of since, 'Alastair disliked physical labour.'[2] Later, Naomi would turn to writing and contributed articles on animals, nature and octogenarian life to *The Oldie* magazine. John Gibbons, who was editor at *The Oldie* at the time, met with Naomi at several luncheons. He described her as 'charming, modest and unassuming with a deep understanding of people.'[3] Naomi was also interviewed about her life by Ned Sherrin on the radio programme *Loose Ends* and contributed to several television programmes about Alastair's career.

On 29 April 1975, Alastair starred alongside Ron Moody and Dandy Nichols in *The Clandestine Marriage*. The director was Sir Ian McKellen, who commented on Alastair's approach to his craft:

Much of his precise planning is done in private so that rehearsals are a testing-out within the scheme of the play or a scene, moments of business which have been conceived at home. Nothing seems left to chance and yet his finished performance varies night after night in detail.[4]

However, Alastair was now seventy-four and although the mind was willing, the body was less so. Try though as he might, he was unable to repeat his successes of the 1960s and early '70s. Some people even went so far as to describe the revival of *The Clandestine Marriage* as 'disastrous'[5], but this is too harsh. *The Clandestine Marriage* had a short, successful run at the Lyceum, Edinburgh, and then transferred to the Savoy Theatre, London. Maybe the critics were aware that they were in the presence of a great British comic-actor who was in the twilight of his life and career, since the reviews that appeared in the press were genuinely warm and sympathetic:

> Alastair Sim, as a noble Lord ready to sacrifice love for kindliness of heart, is inexhaustibly rich in nods and becks and wreathed smiles.[6]

> Mr Sim's marvellous Ogleby, which presents the portrait of a senile lecher without a trace of the macabre. Hauled on speechless and palsied by his valet, and dumped hiccoughing in a chair, he presents all the symptoms of blind vanity in a wrecked body without ever evoking the shadow of death's head.[7]

There is poignancy in the second review concerning Lord Ogleby's physical degradation 'without ever evoking the shadow of death's head', for Alastair was not well. David Ambrose described a visit to Alastair one evening in his dressing room after a performance of *The Clandestine Marriage* and finding a 'shagged out old man, totally exhausted.'[8] The truth of the matter was that Alastair had recently spotted an ulcer under his tongue, and after consulting with a doctor, had been diagnosed with cancer.

Alastair decided to fight the cancer but also to continue with his work. His hopes were initially raised when the cancer retreated, but this was only a temporary respite. It quickly reappeared – and worse, it began spreading to other parts of his body. Sir Ian McKellen recalls:

> One night after a late supper at the Caledonian Hotel where we were both staying during the run of *The Clandestine Marriage* at the Lyceum Theatre, we were waving off Mr and Mrs Ronald Mavor. He was smoking a cigar. He breathed in the night's chill and said, 'Oh Ian, I don't want to die'.[9]

This must have been one of the rare occasions when he spoke of his illness since, according to Naomi, Alastair avoided discussing his cancer and the radiation treatment, thinking it self-indulgent, and the subject of death, mawkish. Naomi even went so far as to say that at times he even refused to believe that he was dying; but given that he had also resigned himself to the fact that a miracle was needed to cure his cancer, one suspects that Alastair was just putting on a brave face for the sake of those dear to him.

Although Alastair could draw no comfort from religion, he strongly believed in the power of the human consciousness and considered the world to be far more complex than we could possibly imagine. There is a sense of naïvety in Alastair's views, since he also liked to believe in the powers purported to be held by Uri Gellar. Even so, after Alastair's death, Naomi very cheerfully reported that Alastair was still very much with her – his spirit moving things around Forrigan.

In the summer of 1975, Alastair's general health began to fail. When *The Clandestine Marriage* came to a close in July, he was admitted direct from the Savoy Theatre to the University College Hospital. On the following Wednesday, he had a prostate gland operation. Alastair tried to remain optimistic for the future and continued with as many projects as his doctors would allow. He would appear in David Turner's *The Prodigal Daughter* for television and three more films before he died.

In 1975 Alastair appeared in *Royal Flash* – a film replete with British character and comedy actors: Joss Ackland, Alan Bates, Lionel Jeffries, Roy Kinnear, Michael Hordern, Oliver Reed and Alastair as Mr Greig. *Royal Flash* featured the exciting and dramatic exploits of the irascible Harry Flashman, played with vigour by Malcolm McDowell, but was ultimately a disappointing adventure yarn.

In 1976 Alastair made his final television appearance in a well-received production of *Rogue Male*. The screenplay writers, Frederic Raphael and Clive Donner, successfully created a mood of gloom and depression that permeated the film, accentuating the star performance by Peter O'Toole. The television adaptation was fairly faithful to the book, with two exceptions. The first was to make it more obvious that Captain Thorndyke is attempting to hunt down Adolf Hitler, before he in turn becomes hunted. The second was to create a new character – 'Alastair Sim's Earl, an admonishing figure boiling gently like an amiable lobster in a Turkish bath.'[10] It was a role that Alastair enjoyed playing;'The Earl provided a jolly last role for the great and irreplaceable Alastair Sim.'[11]

Alastair's final screen appearance was alongside Peter Barkworth, Maurice Colbourne and Susan Tebbs in a Disney production entitled *Escape from the Dark*, otherwise known as *The Littlest Horse Thieves*. Alastair played Lord Harrogate, the owner of a Yorkshire coal mine[12], whose new manager decides on modernisation at the expense of the old ponies – 'Even competing with children (three of them) and animals (over a dozen), he steals scenes.'[13]

By the summer of 1976, Alastair was beginning to feel very weak. The glands of his neck were now rife with cancer and there was nothing that anyone could do to prevent it running its course. Even so, Alastair remained optimistic, discussing with Naomi his plans for the rest of the year. He wanted to make the most of the little time that was left to him. Sadly, that time amounted to nothing more than days.

When it was apparent that his health was finally failing him, he was admitted to the University College Hospital. Hours passed by, during which time he drifted in and out of consciousness. Naomi sat by his bed holding his hand, remembering the day when her teacher, Miss Attwell, had introduced her to the man who was to play the Priest.

On 19 August 1976, Alastair Sim passed away.

Alastair had left two express wishes. One was that his body should be made available for medical research, and the other was that there should be no memorial service. A man who had been at pains to avoid publicity at all times during his life was equally as concerned that his death should draw as little attention as possible.

Alastair's obituary in *The Times*[14] was entitled; 'Idiosyncratic comedian of stage and screen' and in memory of Alastair rather aptly quoted Puck:

Things do best please me that befall preposterously.

★

The comments of love and affection from those who knew him is overwhelming evidence of the high regard in which Alastair was held, both professionally and personally. From his peer group, Derek Fowlds (*A Private Matter*, 1973): 'I will remember him always with much warmth and love and lots of laughter.'[15] Lloyd Lamble (Superintendent Kemp-Bird, *The Belles of St Trinian's*, 1954): 'A kind and thoughtful man.'[16] John Standing (*The Clandestine Marriage*, 1975): '[I] simply adored him – he was brilliant and totally outrageous.'[17] Peter Copley (*The Bargain*, 1961): 'He was of good heart and kind spirit.'[18] Peter Cellier (*A Private Matter*, 1973): 'A truly charming person.'[19] Larry Barnes (*Peter Pan*, 1941–42): 'I never heard a word spoken against Alastair – he was universally loved.'[20] Geoffrey Jowitt (*Peter Pan*, 1941–43): 'I don't think he could have had an enemy in the world.'[21] Richard Owens (*Dandy Dick*, 1973): 'Warmth, generosity and delicate ebullience.'[22] George Cole: '[He was a] deeply caring person about everything, great fun with a passion for teaching young people to think for themselves.'[23]

In fairness, this biography has also identified Alastair as a man who sometimes became trapped by his principles, some of which were ill-conceived and, quite frankly, ridiculous. He was at times prejudiced and as a director would impose rules on others that he himself refused to abide by. His acting ability was limited, prone to a repetitive style that lacked originality. He would proclaim a belief in something simply to antagonise and to provoke a reaction. In short, at times, he could be a difficult man to be around. Perhaps most people forgave him these weaknesses.

Furthermore, book sales are so driven by exposé style writing that there is an unhealthy expectation from all parties concerned that a biography should focus on the macabre, the risqué or the deviant. There is potential in such a book on Alastair – Man of twenty-six, lecturer and priest actor, seduces schoolgirl of twelve! – but such headlines of gossip magazines often bear little resemblance to the truth. We could dwell, for an unhealthy time, in a discriminatory way, on Alastair's desire to nurture young talent, the invitation for young actors to stay over at Forrigan, the so-called adoption of George Cole. But the desire for such information simply reflects the fact that altruism today is regarded with distrust; seen more as a folly than as a virtue. Suspicion is the new social currency. And there is undoubtedly game to be had by examining the hypocrisy of a man who shunned showbusiness and its stupidity and yet often infused the same qualities into the character he played on screen.

Instead, it is worth reflecting on the fact that Alastair Sim was associated with some of the key British films of the past fifty years. Alastair starred in the first ever Ealing Comedy, *Hue and Cry* (1947), alongside the Crazy Gang in *Alf's Button Afloat* (1938), in the Hitchcock thriller, *Stage Fright* (1950) and the social satire *The Ruling Class* (1972). The eccentricity of his character, whether originally scripted or of his own doing, would have the audience warm to him whether he was the villain, Hawkins, in *The Green Man* (1956) or the enigmatic detective in *An Inspector Calls* (1954) and *Green for Danger* (1946), or indeed both, as Charles Dimble in the film and stage play of *Cottage To Let*[24] (1941). And the irascibility of his nature was never more so apparent than in one of his most memorable roles – that of Miss Fritton, the female headmistress of the notorious St Trinian's school for girls.

In his obituary, *The Sunday Times* wrote:

> His general gait and gangling lope, his vast dome of a head wobbling, uneasily, his sunken eyes swivelling wildly, he was the very model of a mad professor in a children's comic; and out of this singular physical equipment emerged a voice which yelped and gurgled, spluttered and gushed like water from a pipe full of air-bubbles, yet which seized upon passing words and caressed them with a long incredulous amazement.[25]

Alastair Sim will be remembered for his performances in films that provided a brand of humour that is both gently self-mocking and quintessentially British. His private life was guarded and he sought little public recognition. One wonders therefore how he would have responded to the dedication of a plaque by Sir Ian McKellen on Edinburgh's Filmhouse cinema near to where Alastair was born.[26] Alastair may have interpreted this outward sign of popularism as a foolish, stupid act – but secretly, one suspects, he would have been overjoyed. There is no folly in recognising a man who has delighted and entertained so many people, and who through his film legacy will continue to do so for many years to come.

Filmography

Cast lists have been shortened.

The Riverside Murder (1935)

Fox British · b&w · 64m

Director:	Albert Parker
Screenplay:	Selwyn Jepson
(based on *Les Six Hommes Morts*)	
Cinematography:	Alex Bryce
Cast:	
Basil Sydney	Inspector Winton
Judy Gunn	Claire Harris
Zoe Davis	Mrs Harris
Alastair Sim	Sgt. McKay
Reginald Tate	Perrin
Tom Helmore	Jerome
Ian Fleming	Sanders
Martin Lewis	Gregg
Aubrey Mallalieu	Norman

The Private Secretary (1935)

Twickenham (Julius Hagen) · b&w · 70m

Director:	Henry Edwards
Screenplay:	A.Macrae, G.Broadhurst & H. Mear
(from the play by Sir Charles Hawtrey)	
Cinematography:	P. Strong, W. Luff

Cast:

Edward Everett Horton	Robert Spalding
Barry Mackay	Douglas Cattermole
Judy Gunn	Edith Marsland
Oscar Asche	Robert Cattermole
Sydney Fairbrother	Miss Ashford
Michael Shepley	Harry Marsland
Alastair Sim	Mr Nebulae

Late Extra (1935)

Fox British · b&w · 69m

Director:	Albert Parker
Producer:	Ernest Garside
Screenplay:	Fenn Sherie, Ingram d'Abbes
(based on a story by A. Richardson)	
Sound:	John Cox
Cinematography:	Alex Bryce

Cast:

Virginia Cherrill	Janet Graham
James Mason	Jim Martin
Alastair Sim	Mac
Ian Colin	Carson
Clifford McLaglen	Weinhardt
Cyril Chosack	Jules
David Horne	Editor
Antoinette Cellier	Sylvia
Donald Wolfit	Insp. Greville

A Fire has been Arranged (1935)

Twickenham (Julius Hagen · b&w · 70m

Director:	Leslie Hiscott
Screenplay:	H. Mear M. Barringer
(based on a story by H. Mear and J. Carter)	
Cinematography:	Sydney Blythe

Cast:

Bud Flanagan	Bud
Chesney Allen	Ches
Mary Lawson	Betty
Robb Wilton	Oswald
Harold French	Toby
C.D. Warren	Shuffle

Alastair Sim	Cutte
Hal Walters	Hal
The Buddy Bradley Girls	Shopgirls

The Case of Gabriel Perry (1935)

British Lion · b&w · 78m

Producer:	Herbert Smith
Director:	Albert de Courville
Screenplay:	James Dale, L. du Garde Peach

(from the play *Wild Justice* by J.Dale)

Cast:

Henry Oscar	Gabriel Perry
Olga Lindo	Mrs. Perry
Margaret Lockwood	Mildred Perry
Franklin Dyall	Prosecution
Raymond Lovell	Defence
John Wood	Godfrey Perry
Martitia Hunt	Mrs. Read
Alastair Sim	(uncredited)

Wedding Group (1936)

US title: *Wrath of Jealousy*

Fox British · b&w · 70m

Director:	A. Bryce, C. Gullan
Producer:	Leslie Landau
Screenplay:	S. Jepson H. Brooke

(based on the radio play by Philip Wade)

| Cinematography: | Roy Kellino |

Cast:

Fay Compton	Florence Nightingale
Patric Knowles	Robert Smith
Barbara Greene	Janet Graham
Alastair Sim	Angus Graham
Naomi Sim	Jessie
Bruce Seton	Dr Jock Carnegie
Ethel Glendinning	Margaret Graham

Troubled Waters (1936)

Fox British · b&w · 70m

| Director: | Albert Parker |

Producer: John Findlay
Screenplay: Gerard Fairlie
(based on a story by W. Lipscomb and R. Pound)
Cinematography: Roy Kellino
Cast:
Virginia Cherill   June Elkhardt
James Mason   John Merriman
Alastair Sim   Mac MacTavish
Raymond Lovell   Carter
Bellenden Powell   Dr. Garthwaite

The Man in the Mirror (1936)

J.H. Productions/Wardour (Julius Hagen) · b&w · 82m
Director: Maurice Elvey
Screenplay: F. Willis, Hugh Mills
(from the novel by William Garrett)
Cinematography: Curt Courant
Music: W.L. Trytel
Cast:
Edward Everett Horton   Jeremy Dilke
Genevieve Tobin   Helen
Garry Marsh   Tarkington
Ursula Jeans   Veronica
Alastair Sim   Interpreter
Aubrey Mather   The Bogus of Bokhara

Keep Your Seats Please (1936)

ATP · b&w · 82m
Producer: Basil Dean
Director: Monty Banks
Screenplay: T. Geraghty, A. Kimmins
(adapted from the novel by Ilf and Petrov)
Cinematography: John Boyle
Music: H. Parr-Davies, Gifford & Cliff
Cast:
Florence Desmond   Flo
George Formby   George
Maud Gill   Spinster
Gus McNaughton   Max
Margaret Moffatt   Landlady

| Alastair Sim | Drayton |
| Harry Tate | Auctioneer |

The Big Noise (1936)

Twentieth Century Fox · b&w · 65m

Producer:	John Findlay
Director:	Alex Bryce
Screenplay:	Gerard Fairlie
Cinematography:	Stanley Grant
Cast:	
Alastair Sim	Finny
Viola Compton	Mrs. Dayton
Howard Douglas	Gluckstein
Fred Duprez	Henry Hadley
Grizelda Harvey	Consuelo
Norah Howard	Mary Miller
Peter Popp	Jenkins
C. Dernier Warren	E. Pinkerton Gale

Strange Experiment (1937)

Fox British · b&w · 74m

| Director: | Albert Parker |
| Screenplay: | Edward Dryhurst |

(based on the play *Two Worlds* by H. Osborne)

Cast:	
Donald Gray	James Martin
Ann Wemyss	Joan
Mary Newcomb	Helen Rollins
Ronald Ward	Waring
Henri de Vries	Prof. Bauer
Alastair Sim	Lawler
James Carew	Dr. Rollins

Melody and Romance (1937)

British Lion · b&w · 71m

Producer:	Herbert Smith
Director:	Maurice Elvey
Screenplay:	L. du Garde Peach

(based on a story by Leslie Gordon, M. Elvey)

| Cinematography: | George Stretton |

Cast:

Hughie Green	Hughie Hawkins
Margaret Lockwood	Margaret Williams
Jane Carr	Kay Williams
Alastair Sim	Prof. Williams
Garry Marsh	Warwick Mortimer
C. Dernier Warren	Capt. Hawkins
Julien Vedey	Jacob
Margaret Scudamore	Mrs. Hawkins

Gangway (1937)

Gaumont · b&w · 90m

Producer:	Michael Balcon
Director:	Sonnie Hale
Screenplay:	L. Samuels, S. Hale

(based on a story by Dwight Taylor)

Cinematography:	Glen MacWilliams
Choreography:	Buddy Bradley

Cast:

Jessie Matthews	Pat Wayne
Barry Mackay	Insp. Bob Deering
Olive Blakeney	Nedda Beaumont
Liane Ordeyne	Greta Brand
Patrick Ludlow	Carl Freemason
Nat Pendleton	'Smiles' Hogan
Noel Madison	Mike Otterman
Alastair Sim	Taggett

Clothes and the Woman (1937)

JH · b&w · 70m

Producer:	Julius Hagen
Director:	Albert de Courville
Screenplay:	F. McGrew Willis

(based on a story by Franz Schulz)

Cast:

Rod La Rocque	Eric Thrale
Tucker McGuire	Joan Moore
Constance Collier	Eugenia
George E. Stone	Count Bernhardt
Dorothy Dare	Carol Dixon

Alastair Sim	Francois
Mona Goya	Cecilie
Mary Cole	Marie Thrale
Jim Gerald	Enrico Castigliani
Renee Gadd	Schoolmistress

A Romance in Flanders (1937)

London Film Production · b&w · 62m
Director:	Maurice Elvey
Screenplay:	M. Fort, H. Simpson
Cast:	

Paul Cavanagh	John Morley
Marcelle Chantal	Yvonne Berry
Gary Marsh	Rod Berry
Olga Lindo	Madame Vlandermaere
Alastair Sim	Colonel Wexton

The Squeaker (1937)

US title: Murder on Diamond Row
London Films Production · b&w · 77m
Producer:	Alexander Korda
Director:	William K. Howard
Screenplay:	E. Wallace & E. Berkman

(from the novel *The Squeaker* by E. Wallace)
Cinematography:	Georges Perinal
Music:	Miklos Rozsa
Cast:	

Edmund Lowe	Inspector Barrabal
Sebastian Shaw	Frank Sutton
Ann Todd	Carol Stedman
Tamara Desni	Tamara
Robert Newton	Larry Graeme

The Terror (1938)

Alliance · b&w · 63m
Producer:	Walter C. Mycroft
Director:	Richard Bird
Screenplay:	William Freshman

(from the play by Edgar Wallace)

Cinematography:	Walter Harvey
Cast:	
Wilfred Lawson	Mr. Goodman
Bernard Lee	Ferdie Fane
Arthur Wontner	Col. Redmayne
Linden Travers	Mary Redmayne
Henry Oscar	Connor
Alastair Sim	Soapy Marks
Iris Hoey	Mrs Elvery
Lesley Wareing	Veronica Elvery
Stanley Lathbury	Hawkins
John Turnbill	Inspector Hallick

Sailing Along (1938)

Gaumont · b&w · 80m

Director:	Sonnie Hale
Producer:	Michael Balcon
Screenplay:	L. Samuels, S. Hale
(Based on a story by Selwyn Jepson)	
Cinematography:	Glen MacWilliams
Cast:	
Jessie Matthews	Kay Martin
Barry Mackay	Steve Barnes
Jack Whiting	Dicky Randall
Roland Young	Anthony Gulliver
Noel Madison	Windy
Frank Pettingell	Skipper Barnes
Alastair Sim	Sylvester
Athene Seyler	Victoria Gulliver
Margaret Vyner	Stephanie
William Dewhurst	Winton

Alf's Button Afloat (1938)

Gainsborough · b&w · 89m

Producer:	Edward Black
Director:	Marcel Varnel
Screenplay:	Marriott Edgar, Val Guest, Ralph Smart
(from the play *Alf's Button* by W.A. Darlington)	
Cinematography:	Arthur Crabtree
Music:	Louis Levy

Cast:

Bud Flanagan	Alf Higgins
Chesney Allen	Ches
Jimmy Nervo	Cecil
Teddy Knox	Teddy
Charles Naughton	Charlie
Jimmy Gold	Jimmy
Alastair Sim	The Slave of the Button
Wally Patch	Sgt. Hawkins
Peter Gawthorne	Capt. Driscol
Glennis Lorimer	Frankie Driscol

This Man is News (1938)

Pinebrook · b&w · 77m

Producer:	A. Havelock-Allan
Director:	David MacDonald

Screenplay: A. Mackinnon, R. MacDougall, B. Dearden
(based on a story by R. MacDougall, A. Mackinnon)

Cinematography:	Henry Harris

Cast:

Barry K. Barnes	Simon Drake
Valerie Hobson	Pat Drake
Alastair Sim	Macgregor
Edward Lexy	Insp Hollis
Garry Marsh	Sgt. Bright
Kenneth Buckley	Ken Marquis
Philip Leaver	'Harelip' Murphy

Inspector Hornleigh (1938)

Twentieth Century Fox (Robert T. Kane) · b&w · 87m

Director:	Eugene Forde
Screenplay:	B. Wallace, G. Elliot

(based on the character 'Inspector Hornleigh' created by Hans Wolfgang
Priwin)

Cinematography:	D. Williams, P. Tannura
Music:	Bretton Byrd

Cast:

Gordon Harker	Inspector Hornleigh
Alastair Sim	Sergeant Bingham
Miki Hood	Ann Gordon
Hugh Williams	Bill Gordon

Steve Geray   Kavanos
Wally Patch   Sam Holt

This Man in Paris (1939)

Pinebrook · b&w · 86m
Producer: A. Havelock-Allan
Director: David MacDonald
Screenplay: A. Mackinnon, R. MacDougall
Cinematography: Henry Harris
Cast:
Barry K. Barnes   Simon Drake
Valerie Hobson   Pat Drake
Alastair Sim   Macgegor
Jacques Max Michel   Emile Beranger
Mona Goya   Torch Bernal
Edward Lexy   Holly
Garry Marsh   Sgt. Bright
Anthony Shaw   Gen. Craysham
Cyril Chamberlain   Swindon
Charles Oliver   Gaston

The Mysterious Mr. Davis (1939)

Oxford · b&w · 58m
Director/Producer: Claude Autant-Lara
Screenplay: Jacques Prevert
(from the book by Jenaro Prieto)
Cast:
Morris Harvey   Cecil Goldenburg
Kathleen Kelly   Audrey Roscoe
Henry Kendall   Julian Roscoe
Guy Middleton   Martin
Alastair Sim   Theodore Wilcox

Inspector Hornleigh on Holiday (1939)

Twentieth Century Fox (Edward Black) · b&w · 87m
Director: Walter Forde
Screenplay: Sidney Gilliat
(from the novel *Stolen Death* by Leo Grex)
Cinematography: John Cox
Music: Louis Levy

Cast:

Gordon Harker	Inspector Hornleigh
Alastair Sim	Sergeant Bingham
Linden Travers	Miss Meadows
Wally Patch	Police sergeant
Edward Chapman	Capt. Fraser
Philip Leaver	Bradfield
Kynaston Reeves	Dr. Manners

Climbing High (1939)

Gaumont British · b&w · 78m
Director: Carol Reed
Screenplay: Lesser Samuels
(based on an original story by Lesser Samuels and Marion Dix)
Cinematography: Mutz Greenbaum
Music: Louis Levy
Cast:

Jessie Matthews	Diana
Michael Redgrave	Nicky
Noel Madison	Gibson
Alastair Sim	Max
Margaret Vyner	Lady Constance
Mary Clare	Lady Emily

Law and Disorder (1940)

British Consolida · b&w · 74m
Producer: K.C. Alexander
Director: David MacDonald
Screenplay: Roger MacDonald
Cast:

Barry Barnes	Larry Preston
Edward Chapman	Inspector Bray
Diana Churchill	Janet Preston
Austin Trevor	Heinrichs
Alastair Sim	Samuel Blight

Inspector Hornleigh Goes To It (1940)

Twentieth Century Productions (Edward Black) · b&w · 87m
Director: Walter Forde
Screenplay: Frank Launder, Val Guest, J.O.C. Orton

Cinematography:	Jack Cox
Music:	Louis Levy
Cast:	
Gordon Harker	Inspector Hornleigh
Alastair Sim	Sergeant Bingham
Phyllis Calvert	Mrs Wilkinson
Edward Chapman	Mr Blenkinsop
Charles Oliver	Mr Wilkinson

Cottage To Let (1941)

US Title: Bombsight Stolen
Gainsborough · b&w · 90m

Producer	Edward Black
Director:	Anthony Asquith
Screenplay:	Anatole de Grunwald & J.O.C. Orton

(from the play by Geoffrey Kerr)

Cinematography:	Jack Cox
Music:	Louis Levy
Cast:	
Alastair Sim	Charles Dimble
Leslie Banks	John Barrington
John Mills	Flt Lt G. Perry
Jeanne de Casalis	Mrs Barrington
George Cole	Ronald
Carla Lehmann	Helen Barrington
Michael Wilding	Alan Trently

Let the People Sing (1942)

British National · b&w · 105m

Producer:	John Baxter
Director:	John Baxter
Screenplay:	J. Baxter, B. Emary & G. Orme

(based on the novel by J.B. Priestley)

Cinematography:	James Wilson
Music:	Kennedy Russell
Cast:	
Alastair Sim	The Professor
Fred Emney	Sir Denbury-Baxter
Edward Rigby	Timmy Tiverton

Oliver Wakefield	Sir R. Foxfield
Patricia Roc	Hope Ollerton
Annie Esmond	Lady Foxfield
Marian Spencer	Lady Shepshod

Waterloo Road (1944)

Gainsborough · b&w · 77m

Director and Screenplay:	Sidney Gilliat
Story:	Val Valentine, S Gilliat
Cinematography:	Arthur Crabtree
Music:	B. Busby
Cast:	
John Mills	Jim Colter
Stewart Granger	Ted Purvis
Alastair Sim	Dr. Montgomery
Joy Shelton	Tillie Colter

Green For Danger (1946)

Rank/Individual (Launder&Gilliat) · b&w · 93m

Director:	Sidney Gilliat
Screenplay:	S. Gilliat C. Guerney

(from the book by Christianna Brand)

Cinematography:	Wilkie Cooper
Music:	William Alwyn
Cast:	
Sally Gray	Nurse Linley
Rosamund John	Nurse Sanson
Trevor Howard	Dr Barnes
Leo Genn	Mr Eden
Megs Jenkins	Nurse Woods
Judy Campbell	Sister Bates
Alastair Sim	Inspector Cockrill
Moore Marriott	Joseph Higgins

Hue and Cry (1946)

Ealing · b&w · 82m

Director:	Charles Crichton
Screenplay:	T.E.B. Clarke
Cinematography:	Douglas Slocombe, John Seaholme
Music:	Georges Auric

Cast:

Alastair Sim	Felix Wilkinson
Jack Warner	Jim Nightingale
Harry Fowler	Joe Kirby
Valerie White	Rhona
Frederick Piper	Mr. Kirby

Captain Boycott (1947)

Individual · b&w · 93m

Producer:	Gilliat & Launder
Director:	Frank Launder
Screenplay:	Wolfgang Wilhelm & F. Launder

(from the novel by Philip Rooney)

Cinematography:	Wilkie Cooper
Music:	William Alwyn

Cast:

Stewart Granger	Hugh Davin
Kathleen Ryan	Anne Killain
Alastair Sim	Father McKeogh
Robert Donat	Charles Parnell
Cecil Parker	Captain Boycott
Mervyn Johns	Watty Connell
Noel Purcell	Daniel McGinty
Niall McGinnis	Mark Killain
Maureen Delaney	Mrs Davin

London Belongs to Me (1948)

US Title: Dulcimer Street

Rank/Individual (Launder & Gilliat) · b&w · 112m

Producer:	Launder & Gilliat
Director:	Sidney Gilliat
Screenplay:	S. Gilliat, J. Williams

(from the novel by Norman Collins)

Cinematography:	Wilkie Cooper
Music:	Benjamin Frankel

Cast:

Richard Attenborough	Percy Boon
Alastair Sim	Mr. Squales
Fay Compton	Mrs. Josser
Stephen Murray	Uncle Henry
Wylie Watson	Mr. Josser

Susan Shaw	Doris Josser
Ivy St. Helier	Connie Coke
Joyce Carey	Mrs Vizzard

The Happiest Days of your Life (1950)

London Films · b&w · 81m

| Director: | Frank Launder |
| Screenplay: | J. Dighton, F. Launder |

(from the play by John Dighton)

| Cinematography: | Stan Pavey |
| Music: | Mischa Spoliansky |

Cast:

Alastair Sim	Wetherby Pond
Margaret Rutherford	Muriel Whitchurch
John Turnball	Conrad Matthews
Richard Wattis	Arnold Billings
John Bentley	Richard Tassell
Guy Middleton	Victor Hyde-Brown
Percy Walsh	Monsieur Jove
Joyce Grenfell	Miss Gossage

Stage Fright (1950)

Warner/ABPC · b&w · 110m

Producer:	Alfred Hitchcock
Director:	Alfred Hitchcock
Screenplay:	Whitfield Cook

(from the novel *Man Running* by Selwyn Jepson)

Cinematography:	Wilkie Cooper
Art Director:	Terence Verity
Music:	Leighton Lucas

Cast:

Marlene Dietrich	Charlotte Inwood
Jane Wyman	Eve Gill
Richard Todd	Jonathan Cooper
Alastair Sim	Commodore Gill
Michael Wilding	Inspector Smith
Sybil Thorndike	Mrs Gill
Kay Walsh	Nellie Goode
Andre Morell	Inspector Byard
Ballard Berkeley	Sergeant Mellish

Scrooge (1951)

US Title: A Christmas Carol
Renown · b&w · 86m
Director: Brian Desmond Hurst
Screenplay: Noel Langley
(from the novel *A Christmas Carol* by Charles Dickens)
Cinematography: C. Pennington-Richards
Music: Richard Addinsell
Cast:
Alastair Sim   Ebenezer Scrooge
Mervyn Johns   Bob Cratchit
Kathleen Harrison   Mrs Dilber
Jack Warner   Mr Jorkins
Michael Hordern   Jacob Marley
Hermione Baddeley   Mrs Cratchit
George Cole   Scrooge (young man)
Miles Malleson   Old Joe

Laughter in Paradise (1951)

Associated British Picture Corporation · b&w · 93m
Producer: Mario Zampi
Director: Mario Zampi
Screenplay: Michael Pertwee & Jack Davies
Cinematography: William McLeod
Music: Stanley Black
Cast:
Alastair Sim   Deniston Russell
Fay Compton   Agnes Russell
Guy Middleton   Simon Russell
George Cole   Herbert Russell
Hugh Griffith   Henry Russell
Ernest Thesiger   Endicott
Beatrice Campbell   Lucille Grayston
Joyce Grenfell   Elizabeth Robson

Lady Godiva Rides Again (1951)

London Films · b&w · 90m
Producer: Gilliat & Launder
Director: Frank Launder
Screenplay: Val Valentine & F. Launder

Cinematography:	Wilkie Cooper
Music Composer:	William Alwyn
Cast:	
Pauline Stroud	Marjorie Clark
John McCallum	Larry Burns
Stanley Holloway	Mr Clark
Gladys Henson	Mrs Clark
Richard Wattis	Casting Director
Denis Price	Simon Abbott
Alastair Sim	Hawtrey Murington

Folly to be Wise (1952)

British Lion · b&w · 91m

Producer:	Sidney Gilliat
Director:	Frank Launder
Screenplay:	Frank Launder, John Dighton
(from the play *It Depends What You Mean* by J. Bridie)	
Cinematography:	Jack Hildyard
Music:	Temple Abady
Cast:	
Alastair Sim	Revd (Captain) William Paris
Roland Culver	George Prout
Elizabeth Allan	Angela Prout
Martita Hunt	Lady Dodds
Colin Gordon	Prof Mutch
Janet Brown	Jessie
Peter Martyn	Walter
Miles Malleson	Dr McAdam
Edward Chapman	Joseph Byres M.P.
George Cole	Soldier

Innocents in Paris (1953)

Romulus (Anatole de Grunwald) · b&w · 102m

Director:	Gordon Parry
Screenplay:	Anatole de Grunwald
Cinematography:	Gordon Lang
Music:	Joseph Kosma
Cast:	
Alastair Sim	Sir Norman Barker
Margaret Rutherford	Gladys Inglott
Jimmy Edwards	Capt Stilton

Claire Bloom   Susan Robbins
Ronald Shiner   Dicky Bird

An Inspector Calls (1954)

British Lion/Watergate · b&w · 79m
Producer: A.D. Peters
Director: Guy Hamilton
Screenplay: Desmond Davis
(from the play by J.B. Priestley)
Cinematography: Ted Scaife
Music: Francis Chagrin
Cast:
Alastair Sim   Inspector Poole
Jane Wenham   Eva Smith
Arthur Young   Arthur Birling
Olga Lindo   Sybil Birling
Brian Worth   Gerald Croft
Eileen Moore   Sheila Birling
Bryan Forbes   Eric Birling

The Belles of St Trinian's (1954)

British Lion/London Films/Launder and Gilliat · b&w · 87m
Director: Frank Launder
Screenplay: F. Launder, V. Valentine, S. Gilliat
Cinematography: Stanley Pavey
Music: Malcolm Arnold
Cast:
Alastair Sim   Miss Millicent Fritton
George Cole   Flash Harry
Joyce Grenfell   Ruby Gates
Hermione Baddeley   Miss Drownder
Betty Ann Davies   Miss Waters
Renee Houston   Miss Beimmer
Beryl Reid   Miss Witson
Irene Handl   Miss Gale
Lloyd Lamble   Superintendent Kemp Bird
Richard Wattis   Manton Bassett

Geordie (1955)

US Title: *Wee Geordie*
British Lion (S. Gilliat, F. Launder) · col · 99m

Director:	Frank Launder
Screenplay:	Sidney Gilliat, Frank Launder

(from the novel by David Walker)

Cinematography:	Wilkie Cooper
Music:	William Alwyn

Cast:

Bill Travers	Geordie
Alastair Sim	The Laird
Norah Gorsen	Jean Donaldson
Francis de Wolff	Henry Samson
Doris Goddard	Helga
Paul Young	Young Geordie

Escapade (1955)

Pinnacle (Daniel Angel) · b&w · 87m

Producer:	D. Angel, H. Weinstein
Director:	Philip Leacock
Screenplay:	G. Holland, D.O. Stewart

(from the play by Roger MacDougall)

Cinematography:	Eric Cross
Music:	Bruce Montgomery

Cast:

John Mills	John Hampden
Alastair Sim	Dr Skillingworth
Yvonne Mitchell	Stella Hampden
Colin Gordon	Deeson
Marie Lohr	Mrs Hampden
Peter Asher	Johnny Hampden
Andrew Ray	Max Hampden
Sean Barrett	Warren
Mark Dignam	Sykes
John Rae	Curly
Jeremy Spenser	Daventry

The Green Man (1956)

British Lion (Launder, Gilliat) · b&w · 80m

Director:	Robert Day
Screenplay:	Sidney Gilliat, Frank Launder

(from their play *Meet a Body*)

Cinematography:	Gerald Gibbs
Music:	Cedric Thorpe Davie

Cast:

Alastair Sim	Hawkins
George Cole	William Blake
Jill Adams	Ann Vincent
Terry-Thomas	Charles Boughtflower
Avril Angers	Marigold
John Chandos	McKechnie
Dora Bryan	Lily
Colin Gordon	Reginald Willoughby-Cruft
Raymond Huntley	Sir Gregory Upshott
Cyril Chamberlain	Sergeant Babbett

Blue Murder at St Trinian's (1958)

British Lion/John Marvel(Launder and Gillliat) · b&w · 83m

Director:	Frank Launder
Screenplay:	F. Launder V. Valentine S. Gilliat
Cinematography:	Gerald Gibbs
Music:	Malcolm Arnold

Cast:

Alastair Sim	Miss Amelia Fritton
Terry-Thomas	Romney
George Cole	Flash Harry
Joyce Grenfell	Ruby Gates
Judith Furse	Dame Maud Hacksaw
Sabrina	Virginia
Lionel Jeffries	Joe Mangan
Lloyd Lamble	Superintendent Kemp Bird
Eric Barker	Culpepper Brown
Richard Wattis	Manton Bassett

The Doctor's Dilemma (1959)

MGM/Anatole de Grunwald · Metrocolour · 99m

Director:	Anthony Asquith
Screenplay:	Anatole de Grunwald
(from the play by Bernard Shaw)	
Cinematography:	Robert Krasker
Music:	Joseph Kosma and Paul Sheriff

Cast:

Leslie Caron	Mrs Dubedat
Dirk Bogarde	Louis Dubedat
John Robinson	Sir Colenso Ridgeon
Alastair Sim	Cutler Walpole

Felix Aylmer	Sir Patrick Cullen
Robert Morley	Sir Ralph Bloomfield–Bonington
Michael Gwynn	Dr. Blenkinsop

Left, Right and Centre (1959)

British Lion/Launder and Gilliat · b&w · 95m

Director:	Sidney Gilliat
Screenplay:	Sidney Gilliat and Val Valentine
Cinematography:	Gerald Gibbs
Music:	Humphrey Searle
Cast:	
Ian Carmichael	Robert Wilcot
Alastair Sim	Lord Wilcot
Patricia Bredin	Stella Stoker
Richard Wattis	Harding–Pratt
Eric Barker	Bert Glimmer
Gordon Harker	Hardy

School for Scoundrels (1959)

ABP/Guardsman (Hal E. Chester) · b&w · 90m

| Director: | Robert Hamer |
| Screenplay: | Patricia Moyes, Hal E. Chester |

(from the books by Stephen Potter)

Cinematography:	Erwin Hillier
Music:	John Addison
Cast:	
Ian Carmichael	Henry Palfrey
Alastair Sim	Stephen Potter
Terry–Thomas	Raymond Delauney
Janette Scott	April Smith
Dennis Price	Dunstan

The Millionairess (1960)

Twentieth Century Fox/Dimitri de Grunwald (Pierre Rouve) · col · 90m

| Director: | Anthony Asquith |
| Screenplay: | Wolf Mankowitz |

(from the play by Bernard Shaw)

Cinematography:	Jack Hildyard
Music:	Georges Van Parys
Cast:	
Sophia Loren	Epifanie

Peter Sellers	Doctor Kabir
Alastair Sim	Sagamore
Vittorio de Sica	Joe
Dennis Price	Adrian

The Anatomist (1961)

Towers of London Production · b&w · 82m

Producer/Director:	Dennis Vance
Screenplay:	Adapted for television by Denis Webb from the play by James Bridie
Cinematography:	Lionel Banes
Cast:	
Alastair Sim	Dr Knox
Jill Bennett	Mary Belle Dishart
George Cole	Walter Anderson
Adrienne Corri	Mary Paterson
Michael Ripper	William Hare
Diarmuid Kelly	William Burke
Margaret Gordon	Amelia Dishart

Misleading Cases (1967) (TV)

BBC	32 episodes x 30 mins
Producer:	Series 1 Michael Mills
	Series 2–3 John Howard Davies
Writers:	Series 1–2 A. Melville H. Cecil
	Series 3 M. Gilbert C. Bond

Cast: Alastair Sim, Roy Dotrice, Thorley Walters, Avice Landon.
(Guest star for each episode given in brackets)

Series 1:
The Negotiable Cow [20 June 1967]
Is a Golfer a Gentleman? [27 June 1967]
Port to Port [4 July 1967]
The Last Glass [11 July 1967]
The Whale Case [18 July 1967]
Is Britain a Free Country? [25 July 1967]

Series 2:
Over My Shoulder Goes One Case (Peter Bayliss) [18 September 1968]
Skirting the Issue (B. Berkeley, E. Burnham) [25 September 1968]
The Major and the Mynah (W. Kendall) [2 October 1968]
Right of Way (P. Whitsun-Jones) [9 October 1968]
Ill Met by Sunlight (Geoffrey Sunner) [16 October 1968]
The Tax on Virtue (A. Melville) [23 October 1968]
Who Giveth This Woman (E. Summerfield) [30 October 1968]

Series 3:
The Usual Channel [30 July 1971]
What is a Snail? [6 August 1971]
The Sitting Bird [20 August 1971]
A Tiger in your Bank [27 August 1971]
How Free is a Freeman [3 September 1971]
Regina versus Sagittarius [10 September 1971]

Cold Comfort Farm (1971) (TV)

Director:	Peter Hammond
Producer:	David Conrov
Screenplay:	S. Gibbons D. Turner

(from the novel by S. Gibbons)
Cast:

Sarah Badel	Flora Poste
Brian Blessed	Reuben Starkadder
Fay Compton	Ada Doom
Rosalie Crutchley	Judith Starkadder
Peter Egan	Seth Starkadder
Fionnula Flanagan	Mary Smiling
Sheila Grant	Rennett Starkadder
Freddie Jones	Urk Starkadder
Alastair Sim	Amos Starkadder

The Ruling Class (1972)

Keep Films/Avco Embassy Pics Corp. · col · 151m

Producer:	Jules Buck & Jack Hawkins
Director:	Peter Medak
Screenplay:	Peter Barnes

(from his play *The Ruling Class*)

Cinematography:	Ken Hodges
Music:	John Cameron
Cast:	
Peter O'Toole	Jack Gurney
Alastair Sim	Bishop Lampton
Arthur Lowe	Tucker
Harry Andrews	13th Earl of Gurney
Coral Browne	Lady Claire Gurney
Michael Bryant	Dr Herder
Nigel Green	McKyle
William Mervyn	Sir Charles Gurney
Carolyn Seymour	Grace Shelley
James Villiers	Dinsdale

The General's Day (1972) (TV)

(from the TV series *Play for Today*) · 50m

Director:	John Gorrie
Screenplay:	William Trevor
Cast:	
Alastair Sim	General Suffolk
Dandy Nichols	Mrs Hinch
Annette Crosbie	Elsie Lorrimer
Nan Munro	Mrs Consitine
Julia Goodman	Muriel

A Christmas Carol (1972)

Richard Williams Productions · col · 24m

Director:	Richard Williams
Executive Producer:	Chuck Jones
Music:	Tristram Cary

(from the short story by Charles Dickens)

Cast:	
Alastair Sim (voice)	Ebenezer Scrooge
Michael Redgrave (voice)	Narrator
Michael Hordern (voice)	Marley's Ghost
Melvyn Hayes (voice)	Bob Cratchit
Joan Sims (voice)	Mrs Cratchit

The Prodigal Daughter (1975) (TV)

Director: Alastair Reid
Screenplay: David Turner
Cast:
Alastair Sim   Father Perfect
Carolyn Seymour   Christine Smith
Charles Kay   Father Veron
Tiffany Kinney   Mary Fallon
Karl Howman   Patrick O'Donnell

Royal Flash (1975)

Twentieth Century Fox · col · 102m
Director: Richard Lester
Screenplay: George MacDonald Fraser
(from the novel by George MacDonald Fraser)
Cinematography: Geoffrey Unsworth
Music: Ken Thorne
Cast:
Malcolm McDowell   Cap. H. Flashman
Alan Bates   Rudi Von Sternberg
Florinda Bolkan   Lola Montez
Oliver Reed   Otto Von Bismarck
Tom Bell   De Gautet
Joss Ackland   Sapten
Christopher Cazenove   Eric Hansen
Henry Cooper   John Gully MP
Lionel Jeffries   Krafstein
Alastair Sim   Mr. Greig

Rogue Male (1976) (TV)

BBC · col · 103m
Producer: Mark Shivas
Director: Clive Donner
Screenplay: G. Household, F. Raphael
(from novel by G. Household)
Cast:
Peter O'Toole   Capt. Thorndyke
John Standing   Major Quive-Smith
Alastair Sim   The Earl

The Littlest Horse Thieves (1977)

Walt Disney Pictures · col · 104m

Producer:	H. Attwooll, R. Miller
Director:	Charles Jarrott
Screenplay:	B. Kennedy R. Sisson
Cinematography:	Paul Beeson
Music:	Ron Goodwin
Cast:	
Alastair Sim	Lord Harrogate
Peter Barkworth	Richard Sandman
Maurice Colbourne	Luke Armstrong
Susan Tebbs	Violet Armstrong
Andrew Harrison	Dave Sadler
Chloe Franks	Alice Sandman

Play Chronology

As a professional actor.

Role	Play	Date
Messenger	*Othello*	1930 May
(various)	*Caviare*	1930 Dec
Vasiliy	*Betrayal*	1931 Jan
Cardinal Medici	*The Venetian*	1931 Feb
Trebonuis, Lucilius	*Julius Caesar*	1932 Jan
John Wilkes Booth	*Lincoln*	1932 Feb
Duke of Venice	*Othello*	1932 Mar
Antonio	*Twelfth Night*	1932 Mar
Claudius	*Hamlet*	1932 Apr
Pothinus	*Caesar & Cleopatra*	1932 Sep
Cymbeline	*Cymbeline*	1932 Oct
Duke Senior	*As You Like It*	1932 Oct
Banquo	*Macbeth*	1932 Nov
Polixenes	*The Winter's Tale*	1933 Jan
Cetewayo	*The Admirable Bashville Or, Constancy Rewarded*	1933 Feb
Sir Thomas Randolph	*Mary Stuart*	1933 Feb
Apothecary	*Romeo and Juliet*	1933 Mar
Crabtree	*The School For Scandal*	1933 Mar
Antonio	*The Tempest*	1933 Apr
Carl Salter	*As You Desire Me*	1933 Sep
Sir Thomas Audley	*The Rose Without a Thorn*	1933 Nov
Donald Geddes	*The Man Who Was Fed Up*	1933 Nov
Dominican Friar	*The Devil's in the News*	1934 Jun

(not known, 1 performance)	*Volpone*	1934 Oct
Don Giorgio	*The Life That I Gave Him*	1934 Oct
The Judge	*Murder Trial*	1934 Oct
Ponsonby	*Youth at the Helm*	1934 Nov
General Wei	*Lady Precious Stream*	1934 Nov
Mad Hatter	*Alice in Wonderland*	1934 Dec
Ponsonby	*Youth at the Helm*	1935 Feb
Collie	*The Squeaker*	1937 Mar
Peter Bogle	*The Gusher*	1937 Jul
(producer)	*Consultation*	1938 Feb
Professor Hayman	*What Say They*	1939 (Malvern Festival)
Vane Barra	*Old Master*	1939 (Malvern Festival)
Portwine	*You of all People*	1939 Nov
Professor Hayman	*What Say They*	1940 Mar
Charles Dimble	*Cottage To Let*	1940 Jul
Charles Dimble	*Cottage To Let*	1941 May
(director only)	*Holy Isle*	1941 Dec
Capt Hook & Mr Darling	*Peter Pan*	1941 Dec
Capt Hook & Mr Darling	*Peter Pan*	1942 Dec
Mr McCrimmon	*Mr Bolfry*	1943 Aug
Reverend William Paris	*It Depends What You Mean*	1944 Oct
Old MacAlpin	*The Forrigan Reel*	1945 Oct
Wouterson	*Death of a Rat*	1946 Jan
Capt Hook	*Peter Pan*	1946 Dec
Dr Angelus	*Dr Angelus*	1947 Jul
Dr Knox	*The Anatomist*	1948 Nov
Mr Gillie	*Mr Gillie*	1950 Mar
(director only)	*Misery Me!*	1955 Apr
Mr Bolfry	*Mr Bolfry*	1956 Aug
Emperor	*The Brass Butterfly*	1958 Apr
(director only)	*A Clean Kill*	1959 Dec
George Selwyn	*The Bargain*	1961 Jan
Prospero	*The Tempest*	1962 May
Alexander Lindsay	*Windfall*	1963 Jul
Capt Hook	*Peter Pan*	1963 Dec
Shylock	*The Merchant of Venice*	1964
Capt Hook	*Peter Pan*	1964 Dec
Freer	*The Elephant's Foot*	1965 Apr
Colonel Tallboys	*Too True To Be Good*	1965 Sep

Lord Ogleby	*The Clandestine Marriage*	1966 Summer (Chichester Festival)
Prime Minister	*Number Ten*	1967 Aug
Captain Hook	*Peter Pan*	1968 Dec
Mr Poskitt	*The Magistrate*	1968 Summer (Chichester Festival)
Mr Poskitt	*The Magistrate*	1969 Sep
Marquis	*The Jockey Club Stakes*	1970 Oct
Willy	*Siege*	1972 Feb
Mervyn Dakyns	*A Private Matter*	1973 Jan
Dean	*Dandy Dick*	1973 Summer (Chichester Festival)
Dean	*Dandy Dick*	1973 Oct
Lord Ogleby	*The Clandestine Marriage*	1975 Apr

Endnotes

Preface

1. *Picturegoer*, 2 December 1950.
2. Kenneth Tynan, *Observer*, June 1962. Tynan was referring to Alastair's portrayal of Prospero in the 1962 production of *The Tempest* at the Old Vic.
3. Ronald Mavor, *Dr Mavor and Mr Bridie*, 1988, p. 125.
4. Sidney Gilliat (1980).
5. Peter Copley (2003).
6. Christopher Fry (2004).
7. *The Cinema Studio*, August, 1951.
8. *Picturegoer*, 2 December 1950.
9. *Picture Show*, 26 January 1952, p. 12
10. *Dance and Skylark*, Naomi Sim, p. 81
11. *Dance and Skylark*, Naomi Sim, p. 72.
12. John Howard Davies (2003).
13. George Cole (*Heroes of Comedy*).
14. David Ambrose (2004).
15. David Ambrose (2004).

1 From Birth to the Fulton Lectureship

1. *Picturegoer*, 2 December 1950
2. *Dance and Skylark*, Naomi Sim.
3. *Dance and Skylark*, Naomi Sim.
4. *Dance and Skylark*, Naomi Sim.
5. *Dance and Skylark*, Naomi Sim.

6   Margaret Whitaker (2004) - whose Father's cousin, Margaret Colquhoun Montgomerie Bell (1885–1957) taught Alastair at James Gillespie's School.

7   Ronnie Corbett (2004).

8   As recalled by Alasdair Alpin MacGregor in *The Turbulent Years*.

9   The Certificate identifies five subjects at which he achieved a standard of proficiency to warrant their endorsement. These subjects were: English, Mathematics, French, Science and Drawing.

10 'The Rectorial Address', *The Student*, 1948–49, p. 504.

11 'The Rectorial Address', *The Student*, 1948–49, p. 504.

12 *Dr Mavor and Mr Bridie*, Ronald Mavor.

13 *Theatre World*, April 1935.

14 Essay about Alastair Sim, James Bridie, 1951. Glasgow University, Special Collections.

15 'The Rectorial Address', *The Student*, 1948–49, p. 504.

16 *Picturegoer*, 2 December, 1950.

17 'Highbrow Turned Lowbrow', John Newnham, *Film Weekly*, 15 January 1938, p. 29.

18 Letter from Mrs Tobias Matthay, F.R.A.M., Professor of Diction and Elocution, Royal Academy of Music, dated 23 April 1925.

19 Letter from Mrs Tobias Matthay, F.R.A.M., Professor of Diction and Elocution, Royal Academy of Music, dated 23 April 1925.

20 'The Rectorial Address', *The Student*, 1948–49, p. 503.

21 From a letter signed by John Stewart, Executive Officer, at the Education Offices in Edinburgh, dated 7 April 1925.

22 A letter of Testimony written by George Murray, Head Teacher at Dalry, dated 6 April 1925.

23 A letter of Testimony written by George Murray, Head Teacher at Dalry, dated 6 April 1925.

24 A letter of Testimony written by George Murray, Head Teacher at Dalry, dated 6 April 1925.

25 A letter of Testimony written by Daniel S. Calderwood, Principal Master of Method, Moray House, dated 1 April 1925.

26 This reference is not repeated here since it can be found almost in its entirety in *Dance and Skylark* by Naomi Sim.

27 'The Rectorial Address', *The Student*, 1948–49, p. 504.

28 *Woman's Journal*, 1950, p. 125.

29 'The Rectorial Address', *The Student*, 1948–49, p. 505.

30 'The Rectorial Address', *The Student*, 1948–49, p. 505.

31 'The Rectorial Address', *The Student*, 1948–49, p. 505.

32 'The Rectorial Address', *The Student*, 1948–49, p. 505–6.

2 Naomi

[1]   *Dance and Skylark*, Naomi Sim, inside dust cover.
[2]   'How I Met Alastair', Naomi Sim, *The Oldie*, July 1995, Vol 76.
[3]   'How I Met Alastair', Naomi Sim, *The Oldie*, July 1995, Vol 76.
[4]   'How I Met Alastair', Naomi Sim, *The Oldie*, July 1995, Vol 76.
[5]   'Still Life with Tractor', Naomi Sim, *The Oldie*, 18 February 1994.
[6]   'How I Met Alastair', Naomi Sim, *The Oldie*, July 1995, Vol 76.
[7]   'How I Met Alastair', Naomi Sim, *The Oldie*, July 1995, Vol 76.
[8]   'How I Met Alastair', Naomi Sim, *The Oldie*, July 1995, Vol 76.
[9]   Letter from Gordon Bottomley to Alastair Sim, dated 3 September 1928.
[10]   John Masefield insisted that all the cast, including the chorus, had to consist of students who had previously won honours in the Oxford competition during the past six years. Alastair was a past winner.
[11]   Letter from Gordon Bottomley to Alastair Sim, dated 3 September 1928.
[12]   *Dance and Skylark*, Naomi Sim p.70.
[13]   *Dance and Skylark*, Naomi Sim, p. 72.
[14]   *Dance and Skylark*, Naomi Sim, p. 72.

3 The Professional Stage Actor

[1]   'Highbrow Turned Lowbrow' John Newnham, *Film Weekly*, 15 January 1938, p. 29.
[2]   Letter from John Drinkwater to Alastair Sim, dated 10 February 1930.
[3]   As Alastair's fame grew, and he had a say in such matters, he would take a very relaxed view on casting, much to the vexation of producers such as Frank Launder and Sidney Gilliat. Margaret Wedlake, who appeared in *Windfall* (1963), remembers that 'John Gale... asked me to come for an audition for Alastair, who said after a brief appraisal, "Well, if the management says you're all right, I don't think we need see any others"— Bliss for a young actress only too accustomed to "Next please!".'
[4]   Essay about Alastair Sim, James Bridie, 1951. Glasgow University, Special Collections.
[5]   Letter from Hugh Watt to Alastair Sim, dated 1 October 1930.
[6]   *Dance and Skylark*, Naomi Sim, p. 81.
[7]   Essay about Alastair Sim, James Bridie, 1951. Glasgow University, Special Collections.
[8]   *Dance and Skylark*, Naomi Sim, p. 74. Riposte by Lilian Bayliss.
[9]   Peter Copley (2003)
[10]   *The Times*, September 1933.
[11]   *The Times*, September 1933.
[12]   *The Stage*, 9 October 1933.
[13]   Essay about Alastair Sim, James Bridie, 1951. Glasgow University, Special Collections.

14 Letter from Clifford Bax to Alastair Sim, undated.
15 Letter from Clifford Bax to Alastair Sim, undated.
16 Peter Copley (2003).
17 'The Rectorial Address', *The Student*, 1948–49, p. 506.
18 Peter Copley (2003).
19 *The Times*, 28 November 1933.
20 Ivor Brown, *The Times*, 7 October 1934.
21 *The Times*, 5 October 1934.
22 *The Times*, 6 November 1934.
23 Vernon Woodhouse, *The Bystander*, 11 December 1934.
24 Vernon Woodhouse, *The Bystander*, 11 December 1934.
25 *The Times*, 21 February 1935.
26 'Highbrow Turned Lowbrow', John Newnham, *Film Weekly*, 15 January 1938, p. 29.
27 *Theatre World*, April 1935.

4 'Quota Quickies' and the Early Film Years

1 'Highbrow Turned Lowbrow', John Newnham, *Film Weekly*, 15 January 1938, p. 29.
2 *Dance and Skylark*, Naomi Sim, p. 94.
3 Geoffrey Jowitt (2003).
4 Valerie Grove interviewing Naomi Sim, *The Sunday Times*, 4 October 1987.
5 *Dance and Skylark*, Naomi Sim, p. 87–8.
6 Playwright and son of James Bridie.
7 *Dr Mavor and Mr Bridie*, Ronald Mavor, p. 115.
8 Peter Copley (2003).
9 Margaret Wedlake (2003).
10 Richard Owens (2003).
11 John Howard Davies (2003).
12 John Howard Davies (2003).
13 Essay about Alastair Sim, James Bridie, 1951. Glasgow University, Special Collections.
14 *Daily Mail*, 13 March 1937.
15 *Daily Mail*, 13 March 1937.
16 *The Tatler*, 31 March 1937.
17 *Woman's Journal*, 1950, p. 125.
18 *The Times*, 2 August 1937.
19 Clive Macmanus, *Daily Mail*, 2 August 1937.
20 *Theatre World*, September 1937.
21 'Highbrow Turned Lowbrow', John Newnham, *Film Weekly*, 15 January 1938, p. 29.

22 'Highbrow Turned Lowbrow', John Newnham, *Film Weekly*, 15 January 1938, p. 29.

23 'Highbrow Turned Lowbrow', John Newnham, *Film Weekly*, 15 January 1938, p. 29.

24 *Picturegoer*, 15 October 1938.

25 This may also have had something to do with the fact that following the outbreak of war, the government requisitioned the British film studios in order to control film production and inject Allied propaganda into the scripts whenever possible. Equally it could be argued that the Americans had already monopolised the comedy thriller genre – and in fact, could do it better.

26 *Inspector Hornleigh on Holiday* (1939) was scripted by a writing partnership – Launder and Gilliat – that would later provide Alastair with some of his most memorable film roles.

27 Sidney Gilliat (1980).

28 'Highbrow Turned Lowbrow', John Newnham, *Film Weekly*, 15 January 1938, p. 29.

29 *James Bridie and his Theatre*, Winifred Bannister, p. 146.

30 *Glasgow Herald*, 1939.

31 *Dance and Skylark*, Naomi Sim, p. 100.

32 'Highbrow Turned Lowbrow', John Newnham, *Film Weekly*, 15 January 1938, p. 29.

33 'Highbrow Turned Lowbrow', John Newnham, *Film Weekly*, 15 January 1938, p. 29.

5 Cottage to Let

1 Valerie Grove interviewing Naomi Sim, *The Sunday Times*, 4 October 1987.

2 *Picture Show*, 6 July, 1940.

3 *Picture Show*, 6 July, 1940.

4 George did not keep to the promise in his telegram. George Cole senior died from his debilitating illness the year after George left home. Florence stayed temporarily with George at Egypt Cottage during the war (when George Cole was effectively a child evacuee) but returned to London and slowly drifted into obscurity.

5 *Cottage to Let* transferred to Wyndham's Theatre on 31 July 1940 and then toured the country before returning to Wyndham's for a second spell in May 1941.

6 *The Tatler & Bystander*, 7 August 1940.

7 Those people familiar with the film will notice from this quote an immediate plot difference between the stage and screen version.

8 From the theatre programme *Cottage to Let*.

9 'A Daley Special Wit', Alan Franks, *The Times*, 29 November 1997.

10 Valerie Grove interviewing Naomi Sim, *The Sunday Times*, 4 October 1987.

11 Naomi Sim (*Heroes of Comedy*).

12 *The Times*, 11 August 1941.

13 Larry Barnes (2003).

14 Larry Barnes (2003).

15 Geoffrey Jowitt (2003).

16 Cecil King also directed these two productions of Peter Pan.

17 Geoffrey Jowitt (2003).

18 Essay about Alastair Sim, James Bridie, 1951. Glasgow University, Special Collections.

6 Alastair Sim and James Bridie

1 *Dr Mavor and Mr Bridie*, Ronald Mavor, p. 114.

2 *Doctors Devils Saints and Sinners*, John Thomas Low, p. 152.

3 *Tedious and Brief*, James Bridie, p. 93.

4 *The Tatler & Bystander*, Anthony Cookman, 29 March 1950.

5 *Glasgow Herald*, 1942.

6 *James Bridie and his Theatre*, Winifred Bannister, p. 26.

7 *Tedious and Brief*, James Bridie, p. 14.

8 Essay about Alastair Sim, James Bridie, 1951. Glasgow University, Special Collections.

9 *James Bridie and his Theatre*, Winifred Bannister, p. 190.

10 *James Bridie and his Theatre*, Winifred Bannister, p. 194.

11 Council for the Encouragement of Music and the Arts – later, the Arts Council.

12 *James Bridie and his Theatre*, Winifred Bannister, p. 206.

13 After two years, the Glasgow Citizens' Theatre was relocated to the reno-vated Princess's theatre, which was some forty years ahead of its time by operating a 'no smoking' policy.

14 *James Bridie and his Theatre*, Winifred Bannister, p. 211.

15 *James Bridie and his Theatre*, Winifred Bannister p. 148.

16 *Glasgow Herald*, 1942.

17 *James Bridie and his Theatre*, Winifred Bannister, p. 149.

18 *James Bridie and his Theatre*, Winifred Bannister, p. 151.

19 *James Bridie and his Theatre*, Winifred Bannister, p. 154.

20 *James Bridie and his Theatre*, Winifred Bannister, p. 154.

21 *Doctors Devils Saints and Sinners*, John Low, p. 73.

22 *Mr Bolfry*, James Bridie, p. 53.

23 James Agate, *The Times*, 8 August 1943.

24 *Theatre World*, November 1943.

25 James Agate, *The Times*, 8 August 1943.

26 unsigned, *The Times*, 4 August 1943.

[27] unsigned, *The Times*, 4 August 1943.

[28] Sidney Gilliat (1980)

[29] Essay about Alastair Sim, James Bridie, 1951. Glasgow University, Special Collections.

[30] *The Times*, 13 October 1944.

[31] *Daily Mail*, 13 October 1944.

[32] Ivor Brown, *The Observer*, 28 October 1945.

[33] Ivor Brown, *The Observer*, 28 October 1945.

[34] A letter from James Bridie to Alastair Sim, dated 4 July 1945. Glasgow University, Special Collections.

[35] Ivor Brown, *The Observer*, 28 October 1945.

[36] *The Sunday Times*, 28 October 1945.

[37] Although when the British Board of Film Censors (BBFC) learnt of the nature of the film, they were reluctant to allow filming to continue. Their concern was that the British public might lose confidence in the medical profession when they saw doctors and nurses acting in such a neurotic fashion. It took a meeting between Sidney Gilliat and the Censor, which involved a lot of reassurances, before the BBFC backed down.

[38] Sidney Gilliat (1980).

7 Green for Danger

[1] Sidney Gilliat (1980).

[2] *Trevor Howard, A Personal Biography*, Terence Pettigrew, p. 81.

[3] *Green For Danger*, Christianna Brand (1997 ed.) p. 57.

[4] Sidney Gilliat (1980).

[5] The success of the film also meant that it was broadcast on the radio from the great concert hall in Broadcasting house as part of the live BBC Picture Parade broadcast.

[6] Sidney Gilliat (1980).

[7] *The Times*, 10 February 1947.

[8] I am grateful to Louise for responding to my enquiries regarding her grandfather and providing me with this excellent anecdote.

[9] Judy Campbell (1999).

[10] *Picture Show*, 14 June, 1947.

[11] 'Just an Idea', T.E.B. Clarke from *The Cinema,* 1951, p. 150.

[12] *Picturegoer*, 7 June 1947.

[13] Filming for *Captain Boycott* took place on location at Mullingar in Co. West Meath. The locals were invited to appear in the film as extras with the promise of extra money if they provided their own costumes. 1,094 locals applied to appear in the film, of which more than two-thirds turned up in period costume. Alastair, on reading the script, was under the impression that *Captain Boycott* would be his first opportunity to go on location. However, this was not to be as, all his scenes were shot on soundstages.

14   Sidney Gilliat (1980).

15   'Wild Thing', Naomi Sim, *The Oldie*, January 1995.

16   'Wild Thing', Naomi Sim, *The Oldie*, January 1995.

17   There was a reconciliation when Norah was old and became ill with terminal bronchitis.

18   *Theatre World*, October, 1947.

19   *James Bridie and his Theatre*, Winifred Bannister, p. 165.

20   Pritchard's infamous claim to fame was to be the last man to have a public hanging on Glasgow Green.

21   Some reports concerning Dr. Pritchard's crime remark that the motive for the murders was simply to prove that he had the will to commit such a deed. Bridie introduced the insurance scam in order to provide more plausibility for his actions.

22   Probably loosely based on Dr. Paterson who was allegedly aware of Dr Pritchard's activities but refused to become involved in the matter because of professional etiquette.

23   *Stage*, 3 August, 1947.

24   *James Bridie and his Theatre*, Winifred Bannister, p. 165.

25   Richard Clowes, *The Sunday Times*, 3 August 1947.

26   Richard Clowes, *The Sunday Times*, 3 August 1947.

27   Richard Clowes, *The Sunday Times*, 3 August 1947.

28   Writer and original source unknown.

29   Writer and original source unknown.

30   Larry Barnes (1926–) appeared with Alastair in *Peter Pan* (1941–1942 season).

31   *Picturegoer*, 3 January 1948.

32   *Picturegoer*, 11 September 1948.

33   Sidney Gilliat (1980).

34   Sidney Gilliat (1980).

35   *Alec Guinness, Master of Disguise*, Garry O'Connor, p. 149.

36   *Alec Guinness, Master of Disguise*, Garry O'Connor, p. 149.

37   *The Anatomist* was Bridie's fourth play, written in 1930, and forms one of a trio of doctor morality plays, the others being *Dr Angelus* (1947) and *The Switchback* (1929).

38   Burke and Hare took to murdering their lodgers and prostitutes in order to supply fresh bodies to Knox. When eventually captured, Hare turned King's evidence and Burke was hanged.

39   *Woman's Journal*, 1950, p. 125.

40   From the programme notes to the 1930 production of *The Anatomist*.

41   *Doctors Devils Saints and Sinners*, John Low, p. 19.

42   Both quotes from *The Times*, 3 November 1948.

43   As commented in *Doctors Devils Saints and Sinners*, John Low, p. 18.

44   Review written by Leonard Mosley and referenced 'D.E.', 3 November 1948.

45 *The Anatomist*, James Bridie, Act II Scene II.
46 *The Sunday Times*, 7 November 1948.
47 *The Anatomist*, James Bridie, Act II Scene II.
48 *Evening Standard*, 5 November, 1948.
49 From the notes in *The Anatomist*, James Bridie.
50 *Tedious and Brief*, James Bridie, 1944.
51 *Evening Standard*, 5 November, 1948.
52 *The Times*, 3 November 1948.
53 *Dance and Skylark*, Naomi Sim, p. 129.
54 Alastair polled 2078 votes to Harold Macmillan's 802 votes. Previously
    appointed Lord Rector's included Churchill, Gladstone, Carlyle and Lloyd
    George.
55 'The Rectorial Address', *The Student*, 1948–49, p. 503.
56 'The Rectorial Address', *The Student*, 1948–49, p. 503.
57 'The Rectorial Address', *The Student*, 1948–49, p. 503.
58 'The Rectorial Address', *The Student*, 1948–49, p. 507.
59 'The Rectorial Address', *The Student*, 1948–49, p. 509.
60 'The Rectorial Address', *The Student*, 1948–49, p. 506.
61 Alastair Sim's speech. (*Heroes of Comedy*).
62 Stephen Fry, (*Heroes of Comedy)*.
63 Valerie Grove interviewing Naomi Sim, *The Sunday Times*, 4 October
    1987
64 Alastair Sim was in turn succeeded by Dame Flora Robson.
65 Sidney Gilliat (1980).
66 *Picturegoer*, 14 February 1948.

8 The Happiest Days of your Life

1   Sidney Gilliat (1980)
2   'The origin of *The Happiest Days of Your Life*. . . is a mystery even to
    Dighton himself. '"It simply occurred to me!' he'll tell you." *Picturegoer* 17
    March 1951. In fact, by 1950, John Dighton was an established screenwriter
    having spent the previous nineteen years working in film studios produc-
    ing something in the region of 35–40 screenplays. His output included
    Kind Hearts and Coronets (1949) and *The Man in the White Suit* (1951).
3   In the play, the boy's school was referred to as Hilary School, but this was
    changed to Nutbourne College for the film version.
4   *Picturegoer*, 2 December, 1950.
5   *Dance and Skylark*, Naomi Sim, p. 132.
6   *Dance and Skylark*, Naomi Sim, p. 132.
7   *Picturegoer*, 22 December, 1951.
8   *In Pleasant Places*, Joyce Grenfell, p. 118.

⁹ *Joyce, by Herself and her friends*, edited by Reggie Grenfell and Richard Garnett.

¹⁰ *Joyce, by Herself and her friends*, edited by Reggie Grenfell and Richard Garnett.

¹¹ Played on stage by Jeremy Brett.

¹² *The Monthly Film Bulletin*, March–April, 1950.

¹³ *The Times*, 13 March 1950.

¹⁴ *Picturegoer*, 2 December 1950.

¹⁵ *Picture Show*, 26 January 1952, p. 12.

¹⁶ *The Cinema Studio*, August 1951.

¹⁷ *Picturegoer*, 2 December 1950. In fact, a whole page article manages only two quotes from Alastair Sim.

¹⁸ Geoffrey Jowitt (2003).

¹⁹ Peter Cellier (1999).

²⁰ Dora Bryan (1999).

²¹ Avril Angers (1999).

²² *Dr Mavor and Mr Bridie*, Ronald Mavor, 1988, p. 124.

²³ Ronnie Corbett (2004).

²⁴ John Howard Davies (2003).

²⁵ Peter Cellier (1999).

²⁶ John Howard Davies (2003).

²⁷ Ian Carmichael (1999).

²⁸ Dora Bryan (1999).

²⁹ Avril Angers (1999).

³⁰ *Robert, My Father*, Sheridan Morley, p. 193.

³¹ Christopher Fry (2004).

³² *Dance and Skylark*, Naomi Sim, p. 94.

³³ *Picturegoer*, 7 January 1950.

³⁴ *The Monthly Film Bulletin*, June 1950.

³⁵ *The Times,* 29 May 1950.

³⁶ *The Times,* 29 May 1950.

³⁷ *The Films of Alfred Hitchcock*, Neil Sinyard, p. 73.

³⁸ *Doctors Devils Saints and Sinners*, John Low, p. 77.

³⁹ *Theatre World*, June 1950.

⁴⁰ *The Times*, 11 March 1950.

⁴¹ *The Tatler & Bystander*, Anthony Cookman, 29 March 1950.

⁴² *James Bridie and his Theatre*, Winifred Bannister, 1955, p. 181.

⁴³ *Dance and Skylark*, Naomi Sim, p. 130.

⁴⁴ *The Tatler & Bystander*, Anthony Cookman, 29 March 1950.

⁴⁵ Sidney Gilliat (1980).

⁴⁶ 'The Bridie I knew', *The Prompter,* Alastair Sim.

⁴⁷ 'The Bridie I knew', *The Prompter*, Alastair Sim.

⁴⁸ 'The Bridie I knew', *The Prompter*, Alastair Sim.

49 Sidney Gilliat (1980).

50 Sidney Gilliat (1980).

51 *Tedious and Brief*, James Bridie, 1944, Preface.

52 The most successful of the writers that Alastair turned to was Michael
    Gilbert who wrote three plays for him: *A Clean Kill* (1959), *The Bargain*
    (1961) and *Windfall* (1963). Other notable authors whose plays he appeared
    in were William Golding who wrote *The Brass Butterfly* for him, and
    William Trevor who wrote *The Elephant's Foot* – although this latter play
    never succeeded past the pre-tour.

53 *Picture Show*, 6 October 1951.

54 *Picturegoer*, Duncan Blair, 6 October 1951.

55 *The Times*, 4 June 1951.

56 *Picture Show Annual*, 1952.

57 Aubrey Hepburn had been initially offered the part played by Beatrice
    Campbell, but turned it down in order to prepare a new cabaret act with
    Marcel le Bon. This fell through and so Audrey returned to Mario Zampi,
    the director, and requested a second chance. Her enigmatic appearance
    on screen in three short scenes attracted the attention of several producers
    and directors.

58 *Picturegoer*, 18 November 1950.

59 Letter quoted in *Dr Mavor and Mr Bridie*, Ronald Mavor, p. 137.

60 *Picturegoer*, 30 June 1951 (interview with Hugh Samson).

61 Stephen Fry (*Heroes of Comedy*).

62 *Picturegoer*, 24 November 1951.

63 *The Monthly Film Bulletin*, November 1951.

64 Margaret Hinxman, *Picturegoer*, 22 December 1951.

65 *Picturegoer*, 25 August 1951.

66 *Picturegoer*, 25 August 1951.

67 *Picturegoer*, 24 November 1951.

68 *The Times*, 23 November 1951.

69 *Picture Show*, 22 Dec 1951.

70 *The Cinema Studio*, August 1951.

71 *The Cinema Studio*, August 1951.

72 *The Cinema Studio*, August 1951.

73 *The Cinema Studio*, August 1951.

74 All quotes in this section from *Picturegoer*, 30 June 1951.

75 The 1951 Oscar for best actor went to Humphrey Bogart and the 1952
    Oscar went to Gary Cooper for *High Noon*.

76 *Picturegoer*, 8 March 1952.

77 *The Times*, 1951.

78 Sidney Gilliat (1980).

79 *The Times*, 1951.

80 *The Monthly Film Bulletin*, January 1953.

81 Janet Brown (1999).

82 Sidney Gilliat (1980).

83 One of the stories features Margaret Rutherford as an amateur artist, Gladys Inglott, who finds companionship with the Mona Lisa fixated Arbuthnot (Stringer Davis). The other romances in the film involve Andy MacGregor (James Copeland) and Josette (Gaby Bruyere) in some truly cringe worthy scenes that would have been better dispensed with on the cutting room floor. Susan Robbins (Claire Bloom) and Max de Lonne (Claude Dauphin) appear in a much more subtle and pleasing vignette and the final story tells of Captain George Stilton (Jimmy Edwards) – an anglophile abroad, who savours the local culture in a British bar.

84 *Kenneth Williams Diaries* (edited by Russell Davies) Tuesday 16 September 1952.

85 *Picturegoer*, 4 October, 1952.

9 Miss Fritton and The Belles of St Trinians

1 Searle and his wife played two visiting parents in the film.

2 *Picture Show*, 20 November 1954.

3 Lloyd Lamble, who played Superintendent Kemp-Bird said, '[Alastair] had a clear idea of the character from the word 'go' but was quite amenable to the director's suggestion'. Lloyd Lamble (1999).

4 Vivienne Martin was nineteen years old and acting in her first film. She described the experience as one of 'fear', though remembers Alastair as being 'sweet and gentle'. Vivienne Martin (1999).

5 The racehorse Arab Boy was 'played' by Windsor Cottage – a racehorse owned by the keen race-goer Frank Launder. Windsor Cottage won several races in England and Ireland.

6 *Dance and Skylark*, Naomi Sim.

7 3 June 1993 Centipede column.

8 The battered black felt hat worn by George Cole as Flash Harry was provided by Alastair.

9 From the screenplay of *The Belles of St Trinian's* (1954).

10 Stephen Fry, (*Heroes of Comedy*).

11 From the screenplay of *The Belles of St. Trinian's* (1954).

12 *The Belles of St Trinian's* (1954) was banned from being seen by schoolchildren in South Africa.

13 John Howard Davies (2003).

14 David Ambrose (2004).

15 David Ambrose (2004).

16 Sir Ian McKellen, (*Heroes of Comedy*).

17 Avril Angers (1999).

18 Sidney Gilliat (1980).

19 *The Cinema Studio*, August, 1951.

20   Essay about Alastair Sim, James Bridie, 1951. Glasgow University, Special Collections.
21   Sir Ian Mckellen, *The Times*, 10 May 1975.
22   Derek Fowlds (1999).
23   *Dr Mavor and Mr Bridie*, Ronald Mavor, p. 136.
24   *Woman's Journal*, 1950, p. 125.
25   *Picturegoer*, 6 October, 1951.
26   Freddie Jones (2004).
27   Maurice Denham (1999).
28   Letter quoted in *Dr Mavor and Mr Bridie*, Ronald Mavor, p. 136.
29   *Picturegoer,* 19 September 1953, p. 11.
30   *Picturegoer,* 19 September 1953, p. 17.
31   *Picturegoer,* 19 September 1953, p. 17.
32   Pressbook – *An Inspector Calls*.
33   Pressbook – *An Inspector Calls*.
34   *The Monthly Film Bulletin*, September 1955.
35   The stage version of *Escapade* ran for 14 months at the Strand Theatre.
36   Pressbook –*Escapade*.
37   *The Monthly Film Bulletin*, September 1955.
38   Pressbook –*Escapade*.
39   *The Monthly Film Bulletin*, September 1955.
40   Andrew Ray (1999).
41   Andrew Ray (1999).
42   'Obituary of Naomi Sim', Faith Evans, *The Guardian*, 7 August 1999.
43   Andrew Ray (1999).
44   Quote attributable to Jeremy Brett – from an interview with John Howard Davies (2004).
45   John Howard Davies (2004).
46   *Dance and Skylark*, Naomi Sim.
47   Christopher Fry (1907–2007). Playwright responsible for a resurgence in English verse drama with his four seasonal plays; *The Lady's Not for Burning*, *Venus Observed*, *The Dark is Light Enough* and *A Yard of Sun*.
48   The meeting almost took place several years earlier when James Bridie insisted Alastair went to see Christopher Fry's big success *The Lady's Not For Burning*. Although Alastair saw the play, he did not make contact with Christopher Fry at that time.
49   Christopher Fry (2004).
50   Christopher Fry (2004).
51   Sarah Badel (1999).
52   Sidney Gilliat (1980).
53   John Howard Davies (2003).
54   David Ambrose (2004).
55   Peter Copley (2003).
56   Faith Evans, *The Guardian*, 7 August 1999.

57 John Howard Davies (2003).

58 John Howard Davies (2003).

59 Margaret Wedlake (2003).

60 Essay about Alastair Sim, James Bridie, 1951. Glasgow University, Special Collections.

61 Letter from Alastair Sim to Patrick Armstrong, dated 29 August 1951.

62 Private letters written by Alastair to James Bridie and Gordon Bottomley show him to have a natural written way with words. It is quite perplexing therefore as to why he chose at times to write some letters with language so baffling that it made it difficult for the reader to make any sense of what he was saying.

63 This movement had been set up in Chicago in 1937 by Lola Lloyd and Rosika Shwimmer and it is suggested that Henry Usborne founded his group (APPGWG) around similar ideals. This would seem reasonable given that Usborne was in regular correspondence with the Crusade for World Government.

64 Letter from Alastair Sim to John Fitzgerald, dated 20 March 1952.

65 John Howard Davies (2003).

66 John Howard Davies (2003).

67 Peter Copley (2003).

68 *Dr Mavor and Mr Bridie*, Ronald Mavor, p. 124.

69 Lucinda Gane (2003).

70 Sidney Gilliat (1980).

71 Peter Copley (2003).

72 Margaret Wedlake (2003).

73 David Ambrose (2004).

74 David Ambrose (2004).

75 *Radio Times*, 22 June 1967.

76 Richard Owens (2003).

77 J.W. Lambert, *The Times*, 22 August 1976.

78 Sir Ian McKellen, *The Times*, 10 May 1975.

79 *Dr Mavor and Mr Bridie*, Ronald Mavor, 1988, p. 124.

80 Sidney Gilliat (1980).

81 *Theatre World*, February 1955.

82 *Illustrated London News* (undated).

83 *Misery Me!* was jointly presented by E.P. Clift and Daniel M. Angel.

84 *Daily Mail*, 19 March 1955.

85 One assumes a typing error lead to the character of 'Jean' being renamed 'Joan' in the theatre programme for the 1956 production.

86 *Dance and Skylark*, Naomi Sim, p. 133–4.

87 *The Complete Terry-Thomas*, Robert Ross, p. 94.

88 *Picturegoer*, 20 October 1956.

89 Avril Angers (1999).

90 Sidney Gilliat (1980).

[91]   Copy on the US quad advertising posters.
[92]   From the US pressbook for *The Green Man*.

10 Sim v Heinz: The Faltering Years

[1]   Cecil Wilson, *Daily Mail*, 18 April 1958.
[2]   Anthony Cookman, *The Tatler & Bystander*, 30 April 1958.
[3]   The Brass Butterfly is the name given to the safety catch on a bomb.
[4]   George Cole's wife.
[5]   *The Times*, 15 April 1958.
[6]   Cecil Wilson, *Daily Mail*, 18 April 1958.
[7]   *Picture Show*, 26 January 1952, p. 12.
[8]   Notice that Miss Fritton's first name had changed from Millicent Fritton in *The Belles of St Trinian's* (1954) to Amelia Fritton in *Blue Murder at St Trinian's* (1958).
[9]   *Picturegoer*, 22 March 1958.
[10] *Picturegoer*, 25 June 1955.
[11] Of course exceptions existed but these were few and far between. *Those Magnificent Men in their Flying Machines* (1965) and *The Italian Job* (1969) were beautifully created British films that combined style with enormous international appeal, but perhaps these could be considered as a backlash to the dour realism of the previous years.
[12] *Will the Real Ian Carmichael. . .* , Ian Carmichael, p. 365. Although, Ian Carmichael goes on to blame his over-exposure in the preceding years as the root cause.
[13] Incident recalled in the court case summaries presented in *The Times*.
[14] *The Times*, 19 December, 1958.
[15] i.e. 'passing off' one's services as those of another thus by misrepresentation causing damage to the original's 'goodwill' – or reputation.
[16] *The Times*, 19 December 1958.
[17] *The Times*, 19 December 1958.
[18] *The Times*, 6 February 1959.
[19] The more recent Copyright Designs and Patents Act 1988 gives a right to performers whereby their performance cannot be exploited without their permission.
[20] *The Times*, 6 February 1959.
[21] *The Times*, 6 February 1959.
[22] *The Times*, 6 February 1959.
[23] *The Times*, 6 February 1959.
[24] *The Times*, 6 February 1959.
[25] *The Times*, 7 February 1959.
[26] *The Times*, 7 February 1959.
[27] *The Times*, 7 February 1959.
[28] *Picture Show*, 3 October 1959.

29 *Picture Show*, 3 October 1959.
30 *Picture Show*, 3 October 1959.
31 Ian Carmichael (1999).
32 Sidney Gilliat (1980).
33 Sidney Gilliat (1980).
34 Sidney Gilliat (1980).
35 Larry Barnes (2003).
36 Janet Brown (1999).
37 Sidney Gilliat (1980).
38 Sidney Gilliat (1980).
39 Sidney Gilliat (1980).
40 *The Doctor's Dilemma* was put into production partly as a result of the huge
    success of the 1956 screen adaptation of Shaw's Pygmalion – otherwise
    known as *My Fair Lady* (1956)
41 *Picture Show*, 30 May 1959.
42 *Picturegoer*, 2 May 1959.
43 Ian Carmichael (1999).
44 *Picture Show*, 12 November, 1960.
45 The three sets are the Drawing Room, the Three Tuns Tavern and the
    Lobby at Surgeon's Square. Although at the beginning of the film we see
    a close shot of Dr Knox lecturing to his students which sets the scene,
    and the title sequence has Burke and Hare up to no good in a graveyard.
46 When Merlith finished school at 17 she became an unpaid student at
    the Liverpool Playhouse where she learnt the skills of stage manage-
    ment. After her apprenticeship she was offered the job of Assistant Stage
    Manager.
47 Peter Copley (2003).
48 Peter Copley (2003).
49 Peter Copley (2003).
50 Sidney Gilliat (1980).
51 Alastair's Obituary, *The Times*, 21 August 1976.
52 Take a simple sentence: It was a cold, foggy day. Now try repeating it with
    heavy emphasis on 'a' and a slight pause immediately thereafter. The sen-
    tence still makes sense although one might expect the emphasis to appear
    on the words 'cold' or 'foggy' or 'day'. Is there supposed to be something
    special about the fact that it was a singular day?
53 Peter Copley (2003).
54 Kenneth Tynan, *Observer*, June 1962
55 Margaret Wedlake (2003).
56 Margaret Wedlake (2003).
57 Margaret Wedlake (2003).
58 Naomi Sim was a distant cousin of John Standing.
59 John Standing (1999).
60 *The Times*, 14 December 1963.

[61] J.W. Lambert, *The Times*, 22 August 1976.
[62] This was released as a 3 record set and the cast included: Brenda de Banzie, Alan Howard, Tony Tanner and Claire Bloom.
[63] *The Times*, 7 September 1965.
[64] Dora Bryan (1999).
[65] Dora Bryan (1999).
[66] *The Times*, 23 September 1965.

11 The Chichester Festival Years

[1] John Clements's contribution to the theatre had been immense over the previous thirty-five years and in respect of this, he had received the CBE in the 1956 Birthday Honours.
[2] *The Times*, 2 June 1966.
[3] Sarah Badel (1999).
[4] Sarah Badel (1999).
[5] Sarah Badel (1999).
[6] Sarah Badel (1999).
[7] *The Times*, 2 June 1966.
[8] John Howard Davies (2003).
[9] My thanks to Gwen Lord of the Official Roy Dotrice Fan Association for providing me with this cutting and quote although the original source is unknown.
[10] *The Times*, 26 July 1967.
[11] John Cleese (2003).
[12] John Howard Davies (2003).
[13] John Howard Davies (2003).
[14] John Howard Davies (2003).
[15] Michael Billington, *The Times*, 16 November 1967.
[16] David Ambrose, amongst others, heard Alastair use this line when he was trying to startle people into a reaction.
[17] Freddie Jones (2004).
[18] *The Times*, 8 November 1968.
[19] Renee Asherson (1999).
[20] Peter Lewis interview with Patricia Routledge from *The Times*, 5 May 1994.
[21] Peter Copley (2003).
[22] *The Times*, 19 September 1969.
[23] Hugh Leonard, *Plays and Players*, July 1969, p. 22.
[24] Hugh Leonard, *Plays and Players*, July 1969, p. 22.
[25] Sidney Gilliat (1980).
[26] Sidney Gilliat (1980).
[27] Michael Billington, *The Times*, 1 October 1970.
[28] Michael Billington, *The Times*, 1 October 1970.

29 Alastair's Obituary, *The Times*, 21 August 1976.
30 Charles Lewsen, *The Times*, 16 February 1972.
31 Charles Lewsen, *The Times*, 16 February 1972.
32 David Ambrose (2004).
33 David Ambrose (2004).
34 Charles Lewsen, *The Times*, 16 February 1972.
35 When asked to comment on her experience of working with Alastair, Annette replied, 'I found Alastair intimidating and unapproachable – but I was so in awe that it's a subjective and probably totally wrong impression'. Annette Crosbie (2003).
36 Leonard Buckley, *The Times*, 22 November 1972.
37 Leonard Buckley, *The Times*, 22 November 1972.
38 Pressbook –*The Ruling Class*.
39 Peter Ackroyd, *The Times*, 12 Jan 1983.
40 Sir Ian McKellen (2003).
41 Sir Ian McKellen (2003).
42 Peter Cellier (1999).
43 Peter Cellier (1999).
44 Derek Fowlds (1999).
45 Derek Fowlds (1999).
46 Charles Lewsen, *The Times*, 22 February 1973.
47 *Dr Mavor and Mr Bridie*, Ronald Mavor, p. 125.
48 Charles Lewsen, *The Times*, 22 February 1973.
49 Both quotes by Harold Hobson, *The Times*, 4 March 1973.
50 Patricia Routledge was again in the cast.
51 Harold Hobson, *The Times*, 29 July 1973.
52 Irving Wardle, *The Times*, 26 July 1973.
53 Lucinda Gane (2003).
54 Richard Owens (2003).
55 *Dr Mavor and Mr Bridie*, Ronald Mavor, 1988, p. 125.
56 *The Times*, 21 August 1976.
57 *The Cinema Studio*, August 1951.

12 The Escape to the Dark: The Last Years

1 *Dance and Skylark*, Naomi Sim, p. 147.
2 'Still Life with Tractor', Naomi Sim, *The Oldie*, 18 February 1994.
3 John Gibbons (2004).
4 Sir Ian McKellen, *The Times*, 10 May 1975.
5 e.g. J.W. Lambert article in *The Times* 22 August 1976.
6 Harold Hobson, *The Times*, 4 May 1975.
7 Irving Wardle, *The Times*, 30 April 1975.
8 David Ambrose (2004).
9 Sir Ian Mckellen (2003).

[10] Peter Dunn, *The Sunday Times*, 26 September 1976.

[11] Michael Ratcliffe, *The Times*, 23 September 1976.

[12] The location for filming was Thorpe-Hesley colliery near Sheffield.

[13] Pressbook – *The Littlest Horse Thieves*.

[14] *The Times*, 21 August 1976.

[15] Derek Fowlds (1999).

[16] Lloyd Lamble (1999).

[17] John Standing (1999).

[18] Peter Copley (2003).

[19] Peter Cellier (1999).

[20] Larry Barnes (2003).

[21] Geoffrey Jowitt (2003).

[22] Richard Owens (2003).

[23] George Cole (*Heroes of Comedy*).

[24] Alastair plays the hero in the film version and the villain in the stage play.

[25] J.W. Lambert, *The Sunday Times*, 22 August 1976.

[26] Sir Ian McKellen (2003) explains: 'Alastair Sim's fans in his native city invited me to unveil the plaque. I wish it were lower down the wall so it could be more easily read. I thought it a good thing to do because I like informative plaques on buildings.'

Bibliography

Ackroyd, Peter, *The Times*, 12 Jan 1983

Agate, James, *The Times*, 8 August 1943

Ambrose, David (2004), Interview with the author

Angers, Avril (1999), Letter to the author

Asherson, Renee (1999), Letter to the author

Badel, Sarah (1999), Letter to the author

Bannister, Winifred, *James Bridie and his Theatre*, Rockiff, 1955

Barnes, Larry (2003), Interview with the author

Barr, Charles, *Ealing Studios*, University of California Press, 1999

Billington, Michael, *The Times*, 16 November 1967, 1 October 1970

Blair, Duncan, *Picturegoer*, 6 October 1951 p. 15

Brand, Christianna, *Green For Danger*, Pan Macmillan, 1997

Bridie, James, *A Sleeping Clergyman*, Constable, 1946

Bridie, James, *Plays for Plain People*, Constable, 1944

Bridie, James, *Tedious and Brief*, Constable, 1944

Britton, Eric, *Hue and Cry* – Book of the Film – World Film Publications Ltd, 1947

Brown, Ivor, *The Times*, 7 October 1934, 3 August 1943

Brown, Ivor, *The Observer*, 4 August 1940, 28 October 1945

Brown, Janet (1999), Letter to the author

Bryan, Dora (1999), Letter to the author

Buckley, Leonard, *The Times*, 22 November 1972

Campbell, Judy (1999), Letter to the author

Centipede column, 3 June 1993

Clarke, T.E.B., 'Just an Idea', from *The Cinema*, A Pelican Book, Penguin, 1951, p. 150

Clowes, Richard, *Sunday Times*, 3 August 1947

Cole, George, *Heroes of Comedy*, Thames Television

Cole, George, 'Alastair Sim: A Qualified Fool', BBC programme

Carmichael, Ian (1999), Letter to the author

Carmichael, Ian, *Will the Real Ian Carmichael. . .*, Futura, 1980

Cellier, Peter (1999), Letter to the author

Chrisafis, Angelique, '£50m facelift for girls at St Trinian's', *The Guardian*, 28 August, 2002

Cleese, John (2003), Letter to the author

Clements, John, Letter written to Margaret Rutherford, dated 28 December 1965 quoted in full in *The Times*, 2 June 1966

Cookman, Anthony, *The Tatler & Bystander*, 29 March 1950, 30 April 1958

Copley, Peter (2003), Letter to the author

Corbett, Ronnie, *High Hopes, My Autobiography*, Ebury Press, Random House, 2000

Corbett, Ronnie (2004), Letter to the author

Crosbie, Annette (2003), Letter to the author

Daily Mail, 13 March 1937, 13 October 1944, 19 March 1955

Davies, John Howard (2003), Interview with the author

Davies, Russell, *The Kenneth Williams Diaries*, Harper Collins, 1993

Denham, Maurice (1999), Letter to the author

Dunn, Peter, *The Sunday Times*, 26 September 1976

Evans, Faith, *The Guardian*, 7 August 1999

Evening News, 7 December 1945

Foale, Alan, 'The St Trinian's Cycle and British Comedy', from *The Electronic Journal of British Cinema*, (undated)

Fowlds, Derek (1999), Letter to the author

Franks, Alan, 'A Daley Special Wit' from *The Times* 29 November 1997

Fry, Christopher (2004), Interview with the author

Fry, Stephen, *Heroes of Comedy*, Thames Television

Gane, Lucinda (2003), Letter to the author

Gaye, Freda, *Who's Who in the Theatre*, Fourteenth Edition, Pitman, 1967

Gibbons, John (2004), Interview with the author

Gilliat, Sidney (1980), Letter written to Dan Kowalewski

Grenfell, Joyce, *In Pleasant Places*, Macdonald Futura Publishers, 1979

Grenfell, Joyce, *Requests the Pleasure*, MacMillan London, 1976

Grenfell, R. & Garnett, R., *Joyce, by Herself and her Friends*, MacMillan London, 1980

Griffiths, T. & Woddis, C., *Bloomsbury Theatre Guide*, Bloomsbury Publishing, 1988

Grove, Valerie, *Sunday Times*, 4 October 1987

The Guardian, 14 October 1993

Halliwell, Leslie, *Halliwell's Film Guide*, Paladin Grafton Books, Fifth Edition, 1986

Hampton, Janie, *Joyce Grenfell*, John Murray Publishers, 2002

Hinxman, Margaret, *Picturegoer*, 22 December 1951

Hobson, Harold, *The Times*, 4 March 1973

Hobson, Harold, *The Times*, 4 May 1975

Illustrated London News, undated references

Independent Weekend Landscapes, 21 December 1991

Jones, Freddie (2004), Letter to the author

Jongh, N., *The Guardian*, 21 August 1976

Jowitt, Geofrey (2003), Interview with the author

Lambert, J.W., *The Sunday Times*, 22 August 1976

Lamble, Lloyd (1999), Letter to the author

Leish, Kenneth, *Cinema*, Newsweek Books, 1974

Leonard, Hugh, *Plays and Players*, July 1969, p. 22

Lewis, Peter, Interview with Patricia Routledge, *The Times,* 5 May 1994

Lewis, Roger, *The Life and Death of Peter Sellers*, Century, Random House, 1994

Lewisohn, Mark, *Radio Times' Guide to TV Comedy*, BBC Books, 2003

Lewsen, Charles, *The Times*, 16 February 1972, 22 February 1973

Low, J.T., *Doctors Devils Saints and Sinners*, Ramsey Head Press, 1980

Luyben, H., *James Bridie: Clown and Philosopher*, Pan, 1999

Lumley, F, *New Trends in Twentieth Century Drama*, Barrie & Rockliff, 1967

MacGregor, Alasdair, *The Turbulent Years*, Methuen & Co Ltd, 1945

Macmanus, Clive, *Daily Mail*, 2 August 1937

Malcolm, David, *The Guardian*, 22 August 2002

Mannon, Warwick, *Captain Boycott* – Book of the Film – World Film Publications Ltd, 1947

Manvell, Roger, *The Cinema 1951*, A Pelican Book, Penguin, 1951

Martin, Vivienne (1999), Letter to the author

Mavor, Ronald, *Dr Mavor and Mr Bridie*, Canongate Books Ltd, 1988

McKellen, Ian, *Heroes of Comedy*, Thames Television

McKellen, Ian, *The Times*, 10 May 1997

McKellen, Ian (2003), Letter to the author

Morley, Sheridan, *Dirk Bogarde, Rank Outsider*, Bloomsbury Publishing PLC, 1999

Morley, Sheridan, *Robert, My Father*, Weidenfeld and Nicolson, London 1993

Newnham, John, 'Highbrow Turned Lowbrow', *Film Weekly*, 15 January 1938 p. 29

O'Connor, Gary, *Alec Guinness, Master of Disguise*, Hodder & Stoughton, 1994

Osborne, Charles, *The Life and Crimes of Agatha Christie*, Michael O'Mara Books Limited, 1990

Observer, 7 November 1948

Owens, Richard (2003), Letter to the author

Parker, Alan, 'A Turnip-Head's Guide to British Cinema', Documentary, 1984

Pettigrew, Terence, *Trevor Howard, A Personal Biography*, Peter Owen Publishers, 2001

Picturegoer, 7 June 1947, 15 October 1938, 14 February 1948, 11 September 1948, 7 January 1950, 18 November 1950, 2 December 1950, 17 March 1951, 30 June 1951, 25 August 1951, 24 November 1951, 22 December 1951, 8 March 1952, 4 October 1952, 19 September 1953, 25 June 1955, 20 October 1956, 22 March 1958, 2 May 1959

Picture Show, 14 June 1947, 22 December 1951, 26 January 1952, 20 November 1954, 30 May 1959, 3 October 1959, 12 November 1960.

Picture Show Annual, 1952

Pressbook: E*scapade, Inspector Hornleigh, An Inspector Calls, The Doctor's Dilemma, The Ruling Class, The Littlest Horse Thieves*

Radio Times, 22 June 1967

Ratcliffe, Michael, *The Times*, 23 September 1976

Ray, Andrew (1999), Letter to the author

Redgrave, Michael, *In My Mind's Eye*, Weidenfeld & Nicolson, 1983

Ross, Robert, *The Complete Terry-Thomas*, Reynolds & Hearn Ltd, 2002

Samson, Hugh, *Picturegoer*, 30 June 1951

Scott, Richard, *The Times*, 7 January 1995

Searle, Ronald, *The Female Approach*, Alfred A.Knopf, New York, 1954

Searle, Ronald, *The St Trinian's Story*, Penguin, 1959

Sellar, Maurice, *Best of British*, Sphere, 1987

Sinyard, Neil, *The Films of Alfred Hitchcock*, Admiral (Multimedia Publications Co Ltd), 1986

Sim, Naomi, *Dance and Skylark*, Bloomsbury Publishing Ltd, 1987

Sim, Naomi, 'How I Met Alastair', from *The Oldie*, July 1995, Vol 76

Sim, Naomi, 'Life With Still Tractor', from *The Oldie*, 18 February 1994

Sim, Naomi, 'Wild Thing', from *The Oldie*, January 1995, No.70

Sim, Naomi, 'Alastair Sim: A Qualified Fool', BBC programme

Simmons, Dawn Langley, *Margaret Rutherford – A Blithe Spirit*, Sphere Books, 1983

Stage, 9 October 1933, 3 August 1947

Standing, John (1999), Letter to the author

Sunday Times, 28 October 1945, 7 November 1948, 4 October 1987

Thomson, P. & Salgado, G., *The Everyman Companion to the Theatre*, Weidenfeld & Nicholson, 1987

Theatre World, April 1935, September 1936, September 1937, August 1940, November 1943, October 1947, June 1950, February 1955, December 1955

The Monthly Film Bulletin March–April, 1950, June 1951, November 1951, January 1953, September 1955

The Prompter, 'The Bridie I Knew', Issue 70, September 1952

The Student, 'The Rectorial Address' by Alastair Sim, Vol. XLV, 1948–49

The Tatler & Bystander, 31 March 1937, 7 August 1940, 29 March 1950

The Times, 19 September 1933, 28 November 1933, 5 October 1934, 6 November 1934, 21 February 1935, 2 August 1937, 11 August 1941, 4 August 1943, 13 October 1944, 10 February 1947, 3 November 1948, 3 November 1948, 13 March 1950, 29 May 1950, 11 March 1950, 4 June 1951, 23 November 1951, 15 April 1958, 6 February 1959, 7 February 1959, 14 December 1963, 7 September 1965, 23 September 1965, 2 June 1966, 26 July 1967, 8 November 1968, 19 September 1969, 21 August 1976 (Obituary), 12 January 1983, 17 April 1993

Tynan, Kenneth, *Observer*, 20 April 1958

Wardle, Irving, *The Times*, 26 July 1973, 30 April 1975

Webb, Kaye, *The St Trinian's Story*, London House, 1959

Wedlake, Margaret (2003), Letter to the author

Whitaker, Margaret (2004), Letter to the author

Wilson, Cecil, *Daily Mail*, 18 April 1958

Woman's Journal, 1950, p. 125

Woodhouse, Vernon, *The Bystander*, 11 December 1934

Acknowledgements

This project has spanned nine years and could not have been completed without the help of a great many people, some of whom offered their time freely and others who required a degree of cajoling. Nevertheless I am indebted to them all and would like to take this opportunity to mention some names.

I should like to begin by thanking Ian Carmichael who was the first to respond in a very helpful way to my vague enquiries on the subject of Alastair Sim in 1999. I also offer sincere thanks to the following for taking the time to contribute to the text: David Ambrose, Avril Angers, Renee Asherson, Sarah Badel, Larry Barnes, Janet Brown, Dora Bryan, Judy Campbell, Ian Carmichael, Peter Cellier, John Cleese, Peter Copley, Annette Crosbie, John Howard Davies, Maurice Denham, Derek Fowlds, Christopher Fry, Lucinda Gane, John Gibbons, Freddie Jones, Geoffrey Jowitt, Lloyd Lamble, Vivienne Martin, Sir Ian McKellen, Richard Owens, Andrew Ray, John Standing and Margaret Wedlake. I also thank Merlith McKendrick (Alastair and Naomi's daughter) for correcting an error in the text; George Cole for allowing me to quote him in this biography; Thames Television and John Fisher who graciously allowed me to quote from the *Heroes of Comedy* television programme on Alastair Sim; and Stephen Fry for allowing me to quote him from *Heroes of Comedy*.

I am indebted for the help and assistance of the Theatre Museum Archives, the National Library of Scotland, Edinburgh University Library and the Special Collections Library at Glasgow University. Special thanks go to Dan Kowalewski who kindly provided for this book a detailed letter written by Sidney Gilliat about his association with Alastair. Thanks also to Margaret Whitaker for the school photograph and Anne Inglis at James Gillespie's High School for trusting me with their only copy of the 1912 edition of the school magazine.

I am grateful to my father and John Doherty for their immense support with this project and Stewart Newman, Chris Quinton, Clare McGovern and Jon Davies for their help in reviewing the progress of this text. I offer heartfelt thanks to David Peacock, Andrew Rawlinson, Stuart Sim, Mike Mac Hale, Hazel Bent, Ian Brown, Brian, Elizabeth, and Eleanor Quinton, Mair and Andy Johns, Sally Riddette and Zuzana Galova for their friendship and support during the past twenty years or so and Sarah Flight for having faith in the book. Also I would like to thank the Chadwick Players and Associates: Doug, Marisa, Alex, Emma, Jenny, Mike, Colin, Charles, Tim, Heather, Sophia, David and Richard. Thanks also to Gary, Lucy and Siubhan of The History Press. And last, but not least, Alys, Camilla, Benny and Oliver.

The Author makes grateful acknowledgement for the use of quotations in the text from the following works:

Quotations by Kenneth Williams from *The Kenneth Williams Diaries* (Copyright © The Estate of Kenneth Williams 1994) is reproduced by permission of PFD (www.pfd.co.uk) on behalf of The Estate of Kenneth Williams.

Quotations from *James Bridie and his Theatre* by Winifred Bannister, published by Rockliff. Reprinted by permission of The Random House Group Ltd.

Quotations from the *Glasgow Herald* are reproduced with the permission of The Herald, Glasgow © 2007 Herald & Times Group.

Quotations from Naomi's articles in the *Oldie Magazine* are reproduced with permission from Nick Parker of the *Oldie Magazine*.

Quotations from *Dance and Skylark* by Naomi Sim are reproduced with the permission of Bloomsbury Publishing PLC.

Permission has been granted by Canongate to use quotations from *Dr Mavor and Mr Bridie*, by Ronald Mavor, first published in Great Britain by Canongate Books Ltd, 14 High Street, Edinburgh EH1 1TE.

Trustees of the National Library of Scotland as owner of a variety of documents used as source material for this book.

Quotations from various *Monthly Film Bulletins* are reproduced with the permission of the The British Film Institute.

Quotations from *Heroes of Comedy* are reproduced with the permission of John Fisher, Executive Producer, Thames Television.

Quotations from *The Complete Terry-Thomas* by Robert Ross are reproduced with the permission of Marcus Hearn.

Quotations from the *Illustrated London News* are reproduced with the permission of The Illustrated London News Picture Library.

Green for Danger by Christianna Brand (Copyright © Christianna Brand) Reprinted by permission of A.M. Heath & Co Ltd.

Permission to quote from Alastair's Rectorial Address from *The Student*, has been granted by Edinburgh University.

Permission to quote from *The Times* and *The Sunday Times* has been granted through license by NI Syndication Ltd.

Permission to quote from Naomi Sim's Obituary in *The Guardian*, 7 August 1999, has been granted by Faith Evans.

Permission to quote from the *Observer* has been granted through license by Guardian News and Media Limited. Copyright Guardian News & Media Ltd 1940 and 1958.

Permission to quote from the *Daily Mail* and *Evening Standard* has been granted through license by SOLO syndication.

Permission to quote from *Picturegoer*, *Picture Show*, *Film Weekly* and *Woman's Journal* has been granted through license by © IPC+ Syndication.

Quotations from the *Radio Times* 1967 are reproduced with the permission of the BBC.

Quotations from *Robert, My Father* by Sheridan Morley are reproduced with the permission of the Orion Publishing Group.

Quotations from *TEDIOUS AND BRIEF*, Reproduced by permission of The Agency (London) Ltd, © James Bridie 1944.

Quotations from *PLAYS FOR PLAIN PEOPLE*, Reproduced by permission of The Agency (London) Ltd, © James Bridie 1944.

Quotations from *A SLEEPING CLERGYMAN*, Reproduced by permission of The Agency (London) Ltd, © James Bridie 1934.

For the above three James Bridie titles, all rights reserved and enquiries to The Agency (London) Ltd, 24 Pottery Lane, London W11 4LZ info@theagency.co.uk.

The Author gratefully acknowledges the following for supplying and/or allowing the reproduction of images for this book:

Brian Quinton for his illustrations and producing the map of Edinburgh.

Henry Levy, Mrs N. Campbell-Vickers and the John Vickers Theatre Collection for Alastair Sim as Mr Bolfry.

Anne Inglis, James Gillespie's High School, for the photograph of the Sim's shop, printed in their school magazine of 1912.

Margaret Whitaker, for the school photograph of Alastair Sim.

© IPC+ Syndication for the licence to use the front covers of *Picture Show* and *Picturegoer*.

Canal+ Image UK Limited for various film stills (credited on the page).

Gettyimages for the front illustration.

BBC for reproduction of the front cover of the *Radio Times*, June 12–18, 1960.

Every effort has been made to contact copyright holders. The History Press apologises for any unintentional omissions, and would be pleased, if any case should arise, to add an appropriate acknowledgement in future editions.

Index

Alf's Button Afloat, 56, 63, 192
Alice in Wonderland, 44
Ambrose, David, 134, 178–9, 188,
The Anatomist (film), 161
The Anatomist (play), 58, 64, 92–5, 111,
161–2
Angers, Avril, 11, 104–5, 127, 141–2
Asherson, Renee, 175
As You Desire Me, 41–2

Badel, Sarah, 169–71
Baked Beans (Court Case), 150–5,
172
Banks, Leslie, 58–9
The Bargain, 162–3
Barnes, Larry, 66–7, 88, 157, 184, 191
Bax, Clifford, 42
The Belles of St Trinian's, 121–5, 146–7
160–1
Betrayal, 40
The Big Noise, 53
Blue Murder at St Trinian's, 52, 147–8
Mr Bolfry, 72–4, 111, 140–1
Bottomley, Gordon, 33, 43
The Brass Butterfly, 145–6
Bride, James,
    The Anatomist, 92–5, 161
    Bridie's death, 110–11, 120, 158
    Bridie on Alastair's highland roaming,
    20

Bridie on Alastair's stage personality,
    68, 128–9
Bridie on Alastair typecast as a villain,
    40, 42
    describing Alastair, 71, 75
    Dr Angelus, 86–8
    Forrigan Reel, 76–7
    Holy Isle, 71–2
    It Depends What You Mean, 75–6, 118
    meeting Alastair for the first time, 69
    Mr Bolfry, 72–4, 111, 140–1
    Mr Gillie, 108–9
    roles written for Alastair, 70, 146
    Scottish Theatre, 71
    staying with the Sims, 65, 133
    structure of the play, 70–1, 73
    What Say They, 58
Brown, Janet, 119, 158
Browne, Maurice, 37–8
Bryan, Dora, 104–5, 167

Captain Boycott, 84
Carmichael, Ian, 105, 149, 156–7, 159–60
The Case of Gabriel Perry, 49
Caviare, 40, 170
Cellier, Peter, 104–5, 181–2, 191
A Christmas Carol, 216
The Clandestine Marriage, 101, 169–71,
187–9
A Clean Kill, 162

Cleese, John, 173
Clements, John, 170–1
Climbing High, 59–60
Cold Comfort Farm, 174
Cole, George, 56, 62–7, 86, 92, 123, 140–2, 145, 161, 191
Copley, Peter, 42, 51, 137–8, 162–4, 175, 191
Cottage to Let (film), 65–6, 68, 192
Cottage to Let (play), 62–4, 192
Corbett, Ronnie, 17, 104
Crosbie, Annette, 180

Dandy Dick, 51, 139, 183–4
Davies, John Howard, 51, 105, 173
Denham, Maurice, 130
Denison, Michael, 174
The Doctor's Dilemma, 159
Dotrice, Roy, 172
Dr Angelus, 86–8
Drinkwater, John, 37–8

The Elephant's Foot, 167
Escapade, 132

A Fire Has Been Arranged, 49
Flanagan and Allen, 49, 56
Folly to be Wise, 119–20
Formby, George, 52, 60
The Forrigan Reel, 76–77
Fowlds, Derek, 129, 181–2, 191
Fry, Christopher, 106, 133–4
Fry, Stephen, 97, 114, 124

Gane, Lucinda, 138, 184
Gangway, 55, 60
The Garrick Club, 139, 170
The General's Day, 180
Geordie, 131–2
Gilliat, Sidney,
    Alastair's speed of delivery, 74, 157
    describes the *Hornleigh* films, 57
    falling out with Alastair, 119–20, 157

The Belles of St Trinian's, 121–2, 124
Folly to be Wise, 118–19
Green For Danger, 78, 79–81
The Green Man, 141, 143–4
The Happiest Days of Your Life, 100
Lady Godiva Rides Again, 118
Left Right and Centre, 156–8
London Belongs to Me, 89–91, 177
Waterloo Road, 74
    meets Alastair for the last time, 176–7
    on James Bridie, 111
    on Alastair Sim, 128, 138
    staying at Forrigan, 134
Mr Gillie, 108–10
Glasgow Citizen's Theatre, 71, 111
Green For Danger, 78, –83, 98, 174
The Green Man, 141–4
Grenfell, Joyce, 102 112, 122, 148
Guinness, Alec, 91–2, 142
The Gusher, 54
Guthrie, Sir Tyrone, 169

Hall, Edward, 46
Hagen, Julius, 49, 52
The Happiest Days of Your Life, 98–103, 125, 160
Hepburn, Audrey, 114
Herbert, A.P., 172–3
Hitchcock, Alfred, 107–8
Holy Isle, 71–2
Howard, Trevor, 80
Hue and Cry, 83–4, 98

Innocents in Paris, 101, 119–20
An Inspector Calls, 130–1
Inspector Hornleigh series, 57–9
It Depends What You Mean, 75–6, 118

The Jockey Club Stakes, 178
Jones, Freddie, 130, 174
Jowitt, Geoffrey, 50, 67–8, 104, 191

Keep Your Seats Please, 52

Kidd, Robert, 178–9

Lady Godiva Rides Again, 117–18, 129–30, 157
The Ladykillers, 91–2
Lady Precious Stream, 44
Lamble, Lloyd, 191
Land of Heart's Desire, 29–32
Late Extra, 49
Laughter in Paradise, 112–15
Launder, Frank, 100
Law and Disorder, 62
Left Right and Centre,, 156–9
The Life That I Gave Him 43
A Life of the General, 181
Littlest Horse Thieves, 190
London Belongs to Me, 89–92, 129, 176–7

The Magistrate, 175–7
Malvern Festival, 58, 69
The Man in the Mirror, 51–2
This Man series, 57
The Man Who Was Fed Up, 43
Marsden, Betty, 88
Masefield, John, 33
Mason, James, 49
Mavor, Ronald, 51, 104, 138, 181, 183, 188
McKellen, Sir Ian, 129, 182, 187–8, 192
Melody and Romance, 54
The Millionairess ,161
Misleading Cases, 43, 172–3
Misery Me!, 111, 140
Morley, Sheridan, 106
Moody, Ron, 151, 187
Murder Trial, 43
The Mysterious Mr. Davis, 59

Number 10, 173–4

Old Master, 58
Old Vic/Sadler's Wells, 40–1, 53, 76, 163

Olivier, Laurence, 170
Orton, Joe, 177
Othello, 38–40
O'Toole, Peter, 180–1, 189
Owens, Richard, 51, 139, 184, 191

Peter Pan, 66–8, 98, 166–7
Priestley, J.B., 130
A Private Matter, 181–3
The Private Secretary, 49
The Prodigal Daughter, 189

Quota Quickies, 47–9, 52–4, 62, 113

Ray, Andrew, 132–3
The Riverside Murder, 46, 48–9
Rogue Male, 189–90
The Rose Without a Thorn, 41–2
Routledge, Patricia, 175
Royal Flash, 189
The Ruling Class, 164, 180–1, 185
Rutherford, Margaret, 99–103, 122, 170

Sailing Along, 56, 60
School for Scoundrels, 160–1
Scrooge, 114–17, 129
Searle, Ronald, 121, 125
Sellers, Peter, 161
She Stoops To Conquer 167
Siege, 178–80
Sim, Alexander, 14–17, 26, 110
Sim, Alastair,
   approach to directing, 119, 162–3, 165
   auditions for *Othello,* 38
   attitude towards his Father, 15, 17
   attitude towards film stardom, 127–8
   back problems, 45–6
   Bridie's death, 110–11
   casting decisions, 119, 173
   CBE, 120, 131
   collaborating with Bridie 73
   Egypt Cottage, 65
   Forrigan, 85–6, 133–6
   faith in the young, 64, 94, 139

falling out with Launder and
   Gilliat, 143–4, 157–8
friendship with Bridie, 69, 110–11
frugal, 85, 139
games, 134–5
Garrick Club, 139, 170
hair loss, 20
kindness to young cast of *Peter
   Pan*, 67–8
meeting Naomi, 30
OTC, 18–19
Oxford Recitations, 33–4
phonetic skills, 24, 52, 164, 181
politics and World Government,
   136–7
Rector of Edinburgh University, 94–7
religious beliefs, 138
reluctance to be interviewed, 35,
   104–5, 117
refusing to sign autographs, 105–6
roaming the highlands, 19–20
school days, 16–17
School of Drama and Speech Traning,
   25–7, 33–4, 38
Sim v H.J. Heinz Co Ltd, 150–6
smoking cigars, 139, 185
support from Naomi, 50–51, 179
teaching, 21–5, 63
tops the film polls, 103
views on play structure, 70–1
Sim, Isabella (McIntyre), 14–16, 45
Sim, Naomi,
   acting with Alastair, 49–50
   applies to RADA, 39
   breeding cats, 138–9
   describing Alexander Sim, 16
   invitations/hosting, 64–5, 135
   life after Alastair, 187
   meeting Alastair, 30
   supporting Alastair, 50–1, 179
The Squeaker (play), 53
The Squeaker (film), 53
Stage Fright, 107–8
Standing, John, 191
Strange Experiment, 54
St Trinian's, 125–6

The Tempest, 163–4
Terry-Thomas, 142, 160
Too True to be Good, 167–8
Troubled Waters, 51

Volkenburg, Ellen Van, 38, 40
The Venetian, 40, 170

Waterloo Road, 74–5
Wedding Group, 49–50
Wedlake, Margaret, 51, 138, 165
What Say They, 58
What the Butler Saw, 177
Williams, Harcourt, 42
Williams, Kenneth, 119–20
Windfall, 165

Youth at the Helm, 43–5
You of All People, 58